This volume is the first comprehensive account in the English language that addresses the genesis, organization and operations of Italian forces that fought alongside the Germans and other contingents allied with them in Russia beginning with Operation Barbarossa in June 1941 until the defeat of the Italian forces there in early 1943.

In accordance with his anti-Bolshevik ideology, Mussolini felt obligated to join with Germany's attack against the Soviet Union. Italy thus formed the CSIR (Corpo di Spedizione in Russia – Italian Expeditionary Corps in Russia), consisting of some 62,000 men in three divisions (two infantry and one cavalry, plus a Blackshirt legion) which was sent to participate in the Axis attack against the Soviet Union in June 1941. In July 1942 the CSIR was upgraded to the ARMIR (Armata Italiana in Russia – Italian Army in Russia, also known as the Italian 8th Army), consisting of seven additional divisions (four infantry and three mountain or alpini). By late 1942 the size of the ARMIR had grown to some 235,000 men. However, both the CSIR and the ARMIR suffered from organizational shortcomings as well as lack of proper equipment and clothing to cope with the operational environment in Russia. Throughout 1941, along with the Germans, the CSIR conducted a number of successful operations. With the advent of the ARMIR, initial actions were also favourable for the Italians, but by December 1942 the Italians, who were deployed along the Don River, were subjected to a massive Soviet operation, Little Uranus, which forced the Italians to withdraw under unimaginably harsh conditions. The Italians were unprepared for the brutal Russian weather as well as for the overwhelming Soviet superiority in men and equipment that they had to face. Nevertheless, the Italians fought well, especially the troops of the Italian alpine corps, but ultimately they were defeated, the survivors returning to Italy.

Ralph Riccio is a retired US Army officer who has had a life-long interest in military history, with a focus on Italian military history. He has authored or co-authored numerous books and magazine articles dealing with Italian as well as Irish military subjects. A native Italian speaker, he is actively involved in translating texts by various Italian authors from Italian to English. In 1981 he was awarded an honorary Italian knighthood. Born in Connecticut, he has travelled extensively throughout Europe and Southeast Asia while in the army and while later working for the Department of Defense and now resides in rural Pennsylvania.

Massimiliano Afiero was born in Afragola (Naples) in 1964. He is an information technology teacher and programmer, but above all is a passionate student of the Second World War, having written many articles in major history journals in Italy and abroad. He is among the few Italian historical researchers to have interviewed numerous veterans of Axis units, in particular of the Waffen SS, publishing their previously unpublished stories. He has attended numerous conferences relating to the presence of foreign volunteers in the German armed forces during the Second World War. He has written an impressive number of books, and since 2004 he has been editor of several periodicals, both in Italian and English, mainly dedicated to Axis formations of the Second World War.

Snow, Ice and Sacrifice

The Italian Army in Russia 1941-1943

Ralph Riccio & Massimilano Afiero

Helion & Company Limited

Helion & Company Limited
Unit 8 Amherst Business Centre
Budbrooke Road
Warwick
CV34 5WE
England
Tel. 01926 499 619
Email: info@helion.co.uk
Website: www.helion.co.uk
Twitter: @helionbooks
Visit our blog at blog.helion.co.uk

Published by Helion & Company 2022
Designed and typeset by Mach 3 Solutions (www.mach3solutions.co.uk)
Cover designed by Paul Hewitt, Battlefield Design (www.battlefield-design.co.uk)

Text © Massimilano Afiero & Ralph Riccio 2022
Photographs © as individually credited
AFV and Equipment colour plates © David Bocquelet 2022
Uniform colour plates by Anderson Subtil © Helion & Company Ltd 2022
Maps drawn by George Anderson © Helion & Company Ltd 2022

ISBN 978-1-915070-86-9

British Library Cataloguing-in-Publication Data.
A catalogue record for this book is available from the British Library.

For details of other military history titles published by Helion & Company Limited contact the above address or visit our website: http://www.helion.co.uk.

We always welcome receipt of book proposals from prospective authors.

Contents

List of Maps

List of Colour AFV and Equipment Plates

List of Colour Uniform Plates

Introduction

In the summer of 1941, on 22 June 1941, German military forces invaded the Soviet Union, giving rise to one of the greatest military campaigns of the Second World War. It was a premeditated action that had been long in the planning, but which caught European and world-wide diplomacy by surprise, considering that in August 1939 Stalin and Hitler had concluded an agreement, the so-called Ribbentrop-Molotov Pact, which defined their respective spheres of influence on the European continent. Participating in the invasion of Soviet territory alongside the Germans were numerous foreign contingents from countries allied with Germany, such as Finland, Hungary, Romania, Slovakia and, later, Italy and Spain, not forgetting the numerous foreign volunteer formations organized by the Germans in the occupied counties: France, Denmark, Norway, Holland and Belgium. German propaganda was adept a transforming the military invasion as a proper 'Crusade against Bolshevism' against the Stalin regime, which was accused of itself wanting to invade the European continent. This explains how so many volunteers coming from all corners of Europe went to fight on the Eastern Front to destroy Stalin's communist regime. Since the October 1917 revolution, a tyrannical state had arisen which from its earliest days adopted a policy of terror and violence to impose its false socialist creed. The birth of fascist movements throughout Europe was due precisely to this desire to put the brakes on the Bolsheviks in their attempt to expand the Red terror over all of the European continent, from the end of the Great War until the beginning of the Second World War. Thanks to his alliance with Hitler, Stalin was able to take the opportunity to invade Poland, Finland, the Baltic republics, the Romanian regions of Bukovina and Bessarabia and was not about to stop. Hitler forestalled any further moves, invading Soviet Russia and renouncing the pact that he had agreed to with the communist dictator. When Stalin was able to obtain alliances with and massive amounts of military aid from the Americans and British, all of Eastern Europe fell under domination of the Soviet communist dictatorship. The western democracies, France and England at first and later the United States, chose to defeat Hitler by allying themselves directly with Stalin. The Italians, initially with an expeditionary corps in Russia and later with an entire army, took part in the crusade against Bolshevism, carrying on the ideological conflict that began in 1922 with the March on Rome and then continuing with participation in the Spanish Civil War. There were naturally also reasons of national prestige, to keep Italy in step with German territorial conquests, but the march on Moscow was a natural progression of the March on Rome. The expedition began well in 1941 and went even better in the summer of 1942, but then unfortunately turned into a disastrous military defeat, caused by the collapse of the Axis forces at Stalingrad but above all due to the lack of proper weapons and equipment capable of sustaining combat in such a hostile environment. Italian soldiers, sent to fight with inadequate weapons and equipment, nevertheless wrote pages of high military valor, distinguishing themselves by courage and determination, despite the fact that both official Italian and foreign historiography continue to denigrate their combat effectiveness. It is our intention with this book to recount the history of Italian units on the Eastern Front between 1941 and 1943, using facts and witness accounts to describe the battles, major offensive and defensive actions and, in particular, the great tragedy of the retreat from the Don front in the winter of 1942-1943, during which Italian soldiers continued to fight in order to open a road to safety but who often sacrificed themselves to cover the retreat of their comrades. This book above all represents a remembrance of the many Italians who fell in combat in Russia between 1941 and 1943, or later in Soviet prison camps.

Massimiliano Afiero & Ralph Riccio

1

Operation Barbarossa

In 1940, following urgent Soviet requests to obtain the Romanian regions of Bukovina and Bessarabia, Hitler decided that the time had come to put a halt to the territorial ambitions of the Soviet dictator, as Mussolini wrote in a letter to Hitler: 'Your lebensraum is in Russia and not elsewhere. It is foreign to Europe. Germany's task is this: Defend Europe from Asia'. And thus, in September 1940, German armed forces entered Romania to protect that country from further Soviet advances. The Soviets protested in vain and from that moment on the flow of German troops to the Eastern Front knew no respite. In November 1940, Romania joined the Tripartite Pact, thus becoming an Axis satellite. German influence also extended to other countries in the Balkan-Danube area, such as Hungary, Bulgaria and Yugoslavia.

On the day that Operation Barbarossa opened (22 June 1941), Hitler sent a letter to Mussolini in which he said: 'I write you this letter at a time in which, finally, after months of worry, reflection and continuous wait which has worn down my nerves, I was able to make the most serious decision of my life … Let me say something once again, Duce: After having wrestled to reach this decision, I feel myself spiritually liberated once again. Having allied myself with the Soviet Union, despite the absolute sincerity of our efforts to reach a lasting conciliation, it was very difficult for me because one way or another it seemed to be at odds with all of my earlier behavior, with my concepts and with my previous positions. Now I am very happy to have freed myself from this spiritual discomfort'.

From a note from the German Foreign Ministry to the Soviet Government on 21 June 1941: 'In the future strife the German people know that it fights not only to protect its homeland, but that it is called to save the entire cultural world from the deadly danger of Bolshevism, and to free the way for a true social rebirth of Europe'.

The Duce, Benito Mussolini. (Period postcard, Massimiliano Afiero collection)

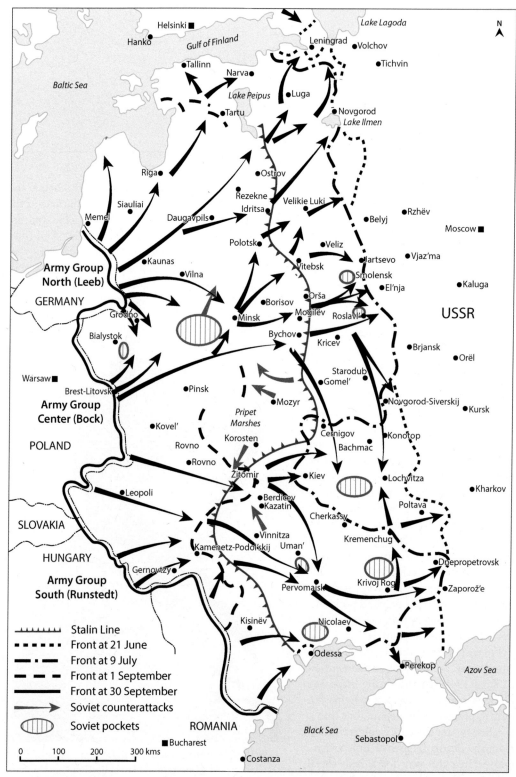

Map of Operation Barbarossa depicting movement of various units in the early months of the invasion.

The defense of Europe

Hitler had expressed the idea of invading the Soviet Union many years earlier, in the lines of his notorious autobiography *Mein Kampf*: 'We National Socialists again take up the moves from where we stopped centuries ago: we wish to stop the continuous movement of Germans towards the south and west of Europe and turn our eyes to the east…When today we speak of a new territory in Europe, we have to think first of Russia and its neighboring satellite countries. If we had the Urals at our disposal with their incalculable riches of primary materials and the forests of Siberia, if the endless grain fields of the Ukraine belonged to Germany, our people would be bathed in opulence'.

This was the theory of Lebensraum, or of vital space. Perhaps Stalin had read Mein Kampf, and thus was preparing to fend off the attack. But the Soviet regime was not acting in the interests of Europe, but rather in the interests of one man only, who had preceded Hitler in the creation of concentration camps (called Gulags) and had exterminated entire populations. When Stalin's heel began to fall on Europe, Hitler dusted off his old plan and on 18 December 1940 signed Directive 21, Operation Barbarossa, fixing its date as 15 May 1941. The worsening situation in the Balkans caused the date of the beginning of the operation to slip by four weeks, during which Stalin, deaf to the warnings of the Allied intelligence services, did not worry at all about preparing himself for the worst.

The great invasion begins

At dawn on Sunday, 22 June 1941, the armies of the Third Reich attacked the Soviet Union; along a front that ran from the Baltic Sea to the Black Sea, millions of German soldiers burst into Soviet territory, overwhelming everyone and everything. The greatest military invasion in history had begun. The news spread throughout the world, and all of Germany's allies hastened to declare war against the USSR in order to take part in the crusade against Bolshevism. German propaganda did its utmost to transform the invasion into a crusade which pitted European civilization against Soviet barbarity. The war that had broken out in the east involved not only National Socialist Germany but would soon involve the whole of the European continent.

The German invasion plan developed in three directions: in the north, the army group under Marshal von Leeb (29 divisions, of which three were armoured) was to move from East Prussia, pass through the Baltic states and aim at Leningrad. In the center, the army group under von Bock (50 divisions, of which nine were armoured), jumping off from Poland, was to skirt north of the Pripet Marshes and aim at Minsk and then at Moscow. In the south the army group under von Rundstedt (40 divisions, of which five were armoured) was to invade the Ukraine and the Donets basin, and then the Caucasus with its oil fields. The final objective called for the conquest of all of European Russia from Arkhangelsk on the White Sea to Astrakhan on the Caspian.

Satellite forces

The satellite forces were on the two wings of the attack front: in the extreme north of Finland, in Karelia were 16 Finnish divisions under the command of Marshal Mannerheim, reinforced by five German divisions. At the extreme south of the front were the Romanian, Hungarian, Slovak and Italian forces. Romania participated with the Third and Fourth Armies under Antonescu, for a total of twelve infantry divisions and ten mountain, cavalry and tank brigades. Hungary fielded the Carpathian Group, led by Marshal Ferenc Szombathely, consisting of the VIII Army Corps and the Mobile Corps with a total force of some 44,500 men. The CSIR (Corpo di Spedizione in

A French poster praising the crusade against Bolshevism and calling for participation by all of Europe.
(Authors' collection)

Russia – Italian Expeditionary Corps in Russia) under General Giovanni Messe, consisted of the 'Pasubio' and 'Torino' infantry divisions, the 'Principe Amedeo d'Aosta' fast (cavalry) division and the 'Tagliamento' Blackshirt Legion, for a total of about 62,000 men. The Slovak government sent its own expeditionary force to Russia, forming the Slovak Army Group, under Minister of Defense Ferdinand Catlos; owing to a lack of motorized vehicles the unit was later transformed into a formation designated the Pilfousek Brigade, taking its name from its commander Rudolf Pilfousek, subordinated to the German 17th Army. The Croats formed two volunteer legions subordinated to the Italian and German commands. Francisco Franco's Spain, although remaining neutral, sent an expeditionary corps to Russia, which also included about a hundred Portuguese volunteers.

All of Europe had valid reasons to join the fight against Stalin. The Finns wanted to regain territory they had lost in 1940 after the Soviet invasion. The Romanians wanted to reclaim the regions of Bessarabia and Bukovina that had been taken from them by the USSR in June 1940. The Hungarians desired to expand to the east at the expense of the Russians. Italy participated in the Russian campaign for reasons of prestige and to reciprocate for Germany's military aid in the Balkans and North Africa. The Slovaks and Croats fought to maintain their own national independence, which only a victory by the Axis forces in Europe could guarantee. The Spaniards went to Russia in exchange for the 'visit' made by the Soviets during their civil war.

2

Italian Expeditionary Corps

Since May 1941, upon completion of the intervention of the Axis forces in the Balkans and as news regarding the imminent German-Soviet conflict intensified, The Duce, Benito Mussolini had called upon his chief of general staff, General Ugo Cavallero, to tell him that in case of war between Germany and the USSR, Italy would have to ready a corps consisting of a motorized division, an armoured division and a grenadier division to be used on the Eastern Front. When war seemed now inevitable, Mussolini hastened to add that Italy could not remain out of the fight because this was a fight against communism. In reality, according to German strategic plans, Italian participation had not been foreseen, considering instead participation by only Finland and Romania, countries who had territorial claims against the USSR.

On the morning of 22 June, with the beginning of German operations against the Soviet Union, Mussolini immediately ordered Cavallero to hasten preparations for organizing the expeditionary corps and ordered the Minister of Foreign Affairs, Galeazzo Ciano, to deliver via diplomatic channels the declaration of war to Soviet ambassador Nikolai Vasil'evič Gorelkin. On 23 June the Duce wrote to Hitler to inform him of his intention to send an expeditionary corps to the Eastern Front. This was done not only for reasons of national prestige, but mainly to continue military collaboration on all fronts following German intervention in North Africa and the Balkans. There was also the ideological aspect: it was necessary to continue the fight against Bolshevism. For his part, Hitler tried to dissuade Mussolini, asking instead for a greater Italian military effort in North Africa. But in the end, despite his misgivings, he had to accept the offer of Italian troops on the Russian front.[1] Hitler's response arrived on 30 June … I accept with gratitude your generous offer, Duce, to send an Italian corps and Italian fighter aircraft to the Eastern Front'.

---

1   According to historian Renzo De Felice, the main reason that prompted Mussolini to participate in the Russian campaign was the fear that, following a German victory, a disproportionate participation in the conflict would have prejudiced the Italian position with respect Germany's other allies; this fear hid the main reason for Italy's military adventure against the Soviet Union, in which Mussolini hoped to renew his image as a champion in the fight against Bolshevism which would have allowed him to exert his influence at the time of redefining a new international equilibrium.

Formation of the Corps

Even before Berlin's official response, the units of the Italian expeditionary corps in Russia (CSIR – Corpo di Spedizione Italiano in Russia) had been assembled in Cremona, beginning with the Corpo d'Armata Autotrasportabile,[2] commanded by General Francesco Zingales,[3] consisting of a "fast" (mobile cavalry) division and two partially motorized divisions: the 3rd 'Principe Amadeo duca d'Aosta' fast division commanded by General Mario Marazzani,[4] the 9th "Pasubio" infantry division led by General Vittorio Giovanelli and the 52nd "Torino" infantry division commanded by General Luigi Manzi. The 'Pasubio' and 'Torino' divisions were designated as 'transportable' in the sense that they could be moved by truck, but if trucks were not available, they had to march on foot.[5]

---

2   Initially organized in Cremona on 1 June 1939 as the Autotransportable Corps Headquarters, with the transportable infantry divisions 'Pasubio' and 'Piave', in 1940 it was moved to a reserve status in the areas of Verona, Padova, Reggio nell'Emilia and Cremona. In July, the 'Torino' division was also subordinated to it, and on 6 April the 'Littorio' armoured division was also added. At the beginning of hostilities with Yugoslavia, its units were deployed along the border between Opicina and San Pietro del Carso, in reserve for 2nd Army. On 10 April, it went on the attack, eliminating the resistance of enemy covering units and entered into Yugoslav territory through the Planina Gap. Once it had passed through Susssak and Karlovac, on 12 April it occupied Segna, Otocac, Gospić and on 14 April Gracac. On 15 April it reached Sebenico and Spalato, Mostar and Vergoraz on the 16th, and Ragusa and Trebinje on the 17th. There its units joined with the troops of XVII Army Corps coming from Albania. In early May it returned again to Italy and Cremona.

3   Francesco Zingales was born in Longi, in the province of Messina, on 10 January 1884. After having attended the Royal Military Academy of Modena, from which he graduated as a second lieutenant, he took part in the Italo-Turkish war where he was awarded a Silver Medal and a Bronze Medal for Military Valor. During the First World War, he distinguished himself in the Oslavia area and was wounded in action on 27 September 1915. He then took part in the conquest of Gorizia in August 1916 and in the battle of Vittorio Veneto (October-November 1918) as a general staff officer in the 48th Division. At the end of the war, he was awarded another two Silver Medals and a Bronze Medal for Military Valor and promoted to major. In 1925 he was promoted to colonel and became commander of the 23rd Infantry Regiment. In 1936 he was promoted to brigadier general and commanded the Infantry and Cavalry Academy and later of the Application School in Parma. In 1939 he was promoted to major general and commanded the 10th 'Piave' Infantry Division. In 1941, as a lieutenant general, he assumed command of the Corpo d'Armata Autotrasportabile (Autotransportable Army Corps). On 13 April 1941 he took part in the invasion of Yugoslavia and was awarded the Knight's Cross of the Military Order of Savoy and in June of that same year assumed command of the newly constituted Corpo di Spedizione in Russia (CSIR).

4   Mario Marazzani was born in Vercelli on 28 July 1887. He attended the Modena Military Academy, graduating as a cavalry second lieutenant in the 'Lancieri di Novara' in 1908. He participated in the First World War, distinguishing himself in risky missions along the Pasubio. In the post-war years he attended the War College and from 1928 to 1932 was a staff officer and teacher at the War College. Between 1933 and 1937 he was a military attaché to Poland and later to Latvia, Estonia and Finland. In 1937, upon returning to Italy, he assumed command of the 'Piemonte Reale Cavalleria'. He was then promoted to brigadier general, as deputy commander and then commander of the 3rd Fast Division 'Principe Amadeo Duca d'Aosta' beginning in September 1939. With the beginning of the war, still in command of the Fast Division, he took part in the Balkan campaign.

5   The CSIR had only one autoraggruppamento, organized into two motor groups: one was assigned to the expeditionary corps' logistic services, and the other for transportation of a single division. The Supreme Headquarters had in fact planned that the autotransportable divisions could be transported one at a time with vehicles that would then return after having completed the move of the first division. Naturally, in the field this hypothetical system never worked at all and operational needs dictated that the trucks available to one division would continue to operate with that division; this worked to the detriment of the 'Torino' division, which found itself marching on foot for thousands of kilometers.

Soldiers of the Celere and Pasubio divisions parading before Mussolini prior to their departure.
(Authors' collection)

In addition to these three divisions, representing the Fascist national party and to mark the ideological aspect of the expedition, a Blackshirt legion was also attached; subordinate to it were the 63rd CC.NN. (Blackshirt) Assault Legion 'Tagliamento', consisting of about 2,000 men under the command of Consul Niccolò Nicchiarelli.[6]

---

6   Niccolò Nicchiarelli was born in Castiglione del Lago in the province of Perugia in 1898.He partici-pated in the First World War joining as a volunteer at 16 years of age, serving in the 1st Regiment 'Granatieri di Sardegna' in which he had his baptism of fire on the Sabotino. Following an officers' course, he was posted to the 37th Regiment of the 'Ravenna' brigade. He was seriously wounded during an attack against Monte Seluggio in July 1916. The following year, he was assigned as a reserve lieutenant to the 261st Infantry Regiment of the 'Elba' brigade, in which he fought valorously on the Bainsizza Plateau. On 27 October, during the battle of Caporetto, he was captured along with his men while he was fighting in a trench near San Pietro al Natisone. He was imprisoned with several hundred other officers and men and was sent to various prison camps, first at Grahovo, then to Rastatt and finally in the Celle Gefangenenlager, near Hannover, where he remained until December 1918. Once repatriated, he volunteered for service in Libya as part of the 241st Infantry Regiment of the 'Teramo' Brigade, fighting against local insurgents who had rebelled against Italian rule. An ardent nationalist before the war, he quickly joined the nascent Fascist movement. He obtained a law degree and participated in the March on Rome. In 1923 he joined the newly created Milizia Volontaria per la Sicurezza Nazionale (M.V.S.N., or Volunteer Militia for National Security), initially commanding the 'Cacciatori del Tevere' Legion, and later an independent unit on the border with Lipari. Assigned again to Libya in 1935, he commanded the 3rd Libyan Legion and was president of a special tribunal for Cyrenaica. With the beginning of the war, he took part in military operations at Buq Buq and Sidi el Barrani until January 1941 leading the 23rd CC.NN. Legion, as part of the 1st CC.NN. Division '23 marzo'. He was the Federal Administrator of Benghazi, and in this role, in July 1941 was placed in command of the 63rd CC.NN. Assault Legion 'Tagliamento'.

The structure of the 'Pasubio', 'Torino' and 'Celere'[7] divisions, inasmuch as they were special divisions, did not include units of the M.V.S.N. as did other infantry divisions. Assignment of the 'Tagliamento' was dictated in part by the need to provide the corps headquarters with a unit that could intervene directly in the fighting. The Legion was reinforced by a support weapons battalion (81mmm mortar company and a 47/32 gun company), which was not part of the normal establishment of the divisional militia legions.

Despite the straits in which Italian military industry found itself at the time, with forces engaged in North Africa, efforts were made to equip and arm the expeditionary corps with the best material available. After the bitter experiences in Africa and Greece, Mussolini asked General Ugo Cavallero, Chief of the General Staff, to do everything possible to render the Italian expeditionary corps highly operational and able to fight.

In late June, the Autotransportable Army Corps was declared operational and ready to be sent to the front. It consisted of a total of 17 rifle battalions (12 infantry, 3 bersaglieri motorcycle, 2 Blackshirt), 7 battalions of support weapons (heavy weapons), one sapper battalion, 14 independent companies, 10 cavalry squadrons (the 'Savoia Cavalleria' Regiment (3rd) and the 'Lancieri di Novara' Regiment (5th); 4 CV33 light tank squadrons, 24 artillery groups, 10 engineer battalions, one chemical battalion and 12 Carabinieri sections.

The corps was rounded out by a Regia Aeronautica contingent (55 fighters, 22 reconnaissance aircraft, 10 Savoia-Marchetti SM-81 tri-motor transport planes). The overall strength of the corps consisted of about 58,000 men, 2,900 officers, 4,600 mules, 220 artillery pieces and 5,500 motor vehicles.

On 9 July 1941, the corps was officially designated as the Corpo di Spedizione Italiano in Russia, by following order of the Supreme Command: 'All of the forces, ground and air, designated to operate on the Russian front will constitute the Corpo di Spedizione Italiano in Russia (C.S.I.R.). Consequently, as of 10 July 1941 the Comando di Corpo d'Armata Autotrasportabile will assume the designation of Comando del Corpo di Spedizione in Russia [Headquarters Italian Expeditionary Command in Russia].' The Italian expeditionary corps was to be sent to Army Group South in southern Ukraine.

Weapons and Equipment

Despite General Cavallero's efforts, the lack of the Regio Esercito's adequate equipment, vehicles and weapons was quite evident in Russia. The Italian soldier's personal armament continued to be based on the old but robust Carcano Model 1891 rifle, the Breda Model 37 heavy machine gun and the 81mm Model 35 mortar. These were complemented by the Breda Model 30 and Breda Model 5C light machine guns which jammed easily, the 45mm Brixia Model 35 mortar which fired a round that was too light, and hand grenades with fuses that were ineffective in the snow and mud. A serious shortcoming was the lack of an individual small arm comparable to the Soviet PPSh 41 or the German MP40; although the excellent Beretta MAB 38A submachine gun was issued to Italian troops in Russia, the numbers available were pathetically small. The infantry also lacked any effective antitank guns and the Model 1935 47/32 gun, a support weapon pressed into the role of

---

7   The 3rd Cavalry Division 'Principe Amadeo Duca d'Aosta' (PADA) was commonly referred to as the 'Celere' Division. The 'Celere' (literally, 'fast') division was a hybrid division with two traditional horse-mounted cavalry regiments, a horse-drawn artillery regiment, a bersaglieri regiment, a light tank battalion and other smaller units. In March 1942 the division was restructured as a light mechanized division.

Spring 1941, Italian soldiers in combat on the Balkan front, with hand grenades and Carcano Model 38 rifles. (Authors' collection)

A Blackshirt in action in Montenegro, armed with a Breda Model 30 light machine gun. (Authors' collection)

an antitank gun, was essentially worthless against the Soviet T-34 tanks.[8] Artillery holdings ran the gamut from extremely effective Breda 20mm light automatic cannon to the equally capable 210/22 howitzer, but by and large, the bulk of Italian artillery in Russia consisted of dated pieces, many of which were Austro-Hungarian war booty; although Italian gunners generally performed well, numbers of guns themselves were essentially insufficient to provide the supported needed by Italian forces. With respect to armour, the Italians were able to send only a miniscule number of pathetically under-armoured and under-gunned light tanks, self-propelled guns and armoured cars to Russia.

8   The Italian 47/32 antitank gun fired a shell capable of penetrating a 43mm steel plate at a distance of 500 meters with a normal impact, that is, at a 90-degree angle of incidence, or a 32mm steel plate with an impact at 60 degrees. The Soviet T-34 tank weighed 26 tons and was armed with a 76mm gun and two machine guns, and had 45mm thick turret and hull armour in the areas most exposed to enemy fire.

3

Transfer to Russia

The move of Italian units to the Eastern Front began in phases on 10 July 1941, at first by train from Rome ('Torino' division), from Verona ('Pasubio' and 'Celere' divisions) and from Cremona (Headquarters CSIR) as far as the areas where they detrained in eastern Hungary, between the towns of Marmaros Sziget, Borsa and Felsővisó. From there, the units were to move to the assembly area in Romania, in the areas of Gura Hormolui, Falticeni and Suceava for the divisions, and Botosani for the CSIR headquarters and the service units. The transfer operations lasted 27 days, using 216 trains moving in five phases and concluded on 5 August.

During the movement, on 13 July the corps commander, General Zingales, was hit by a serious bout of influenza along with pulmonary congestion and fever and had to be sent to a clinic in Vienna on an urgent basis. General Giovanni Messe[1] was called upon to replace Zingales as corps commander, joining the Italian formations at Marmaros Sziget.

---

[1] Giovanni Messe was born in Mesagne (Brindisi) on 10 December 1883. He entered service as a volunteer cadet sergeant in 1901. On 30 June 1903 he was given the rank of sergeant and was sent to China where he stayed until 1905. On 31 October 1908 he was admitted to the Modena Military Academy and on 10 September 1910 was promoted to second lieutenant. Sent to Libya during the Italo-Turkish war, he participated in various actions in the Tripoli area where he earned his first awards in the field but was sent back to Italy in September 1912 for reasons of health. Having regained health and promoted to first lieutenant, in 1913 he was assigned to the III Battalion of the 84th Infantry Regiment stationed in Libya. Promoted to captain on 17 November 1915, Messe was repatriated in late 1916 to participate on the Italian front during the First World War. He fought with the 57th Battalion 'Abruzzi' and with various arditi (elite assault) units, among which was the IX Assault Unit which he commanded on Monte Grappa, distinguishing himself during the conquest of Col Moschin and being wounded twice. He was proposed for the Gold Medal for Military Valor, later downgraded to a third Silver Medal for Military Valor for the action on Monte Asolone, and he received two promotions (to major and lieutenant colonel) for 'wartime merit'. When the war ended, in June 1919 he was assigned to a depot in Padova which he left to participate in operations in Albania in 1920, when that nation sought to become independent of the Italian protectorate of Albania. Returning to Italy in 1923, he was nominated as aide-de-camp of King Victor Emanuel III; after four years he was promoted to colonel and assigned as honorary aide-de-camp. He then took command of the 9th Bersaglieri Regiment until 16 September 1935, when he was designated commander of the Brigata 'Celere' of Verona. After being promoted to brigadier general, he took command the 'Celere' brigade and was subsequently named as deputy commander of the 'Cosseria' Division with which he participated in the last phases of the campaign in East Africa during the conquest of Ethiopia. He returned to Italy on 28 September 1936 and, after having held the post of inspector of the 'Celere' (fast cavalry) troops, he was promoted to major general and commander of the 3rd 'Principe Amadeo Duca d'Aosta' Division. In March 1939 Messe was nominated as deputy commander of the expeditionary corps in Albania and in that role participated in operations for the conquest of that country, leading the column that landed in Durazzo in the period immediately preceding the outbreak of the Second World War. Returning to Italy, he reassumed command of the 'Celere' Division until he definitively left it following the outbreak of the Greek-Albanian campaign where on 19 December 1940, as commander of the Special Army Corps, he was able to contain the enemy advance directed against Valona. After the failed offensive

The first Italian unit to arrive in Borsa on 13 July was the 79th Infantry Regiment of the 'Pasubio' division, followed by hundreds of trains, one after another, until the end of the month. A logistic center had been set up in Borsaso so that the units could move quickly towards Botosani, which was 250 kilometers further to the east, beyond the Carpathians. The locale was not connected to a railway line and this forced the CSIR units to move with their own transport or on foot! Despite the presence of only a single road, the limited availability of trucks and the mountainous nature of the region, within a few days the move of the two divisions and the non-motorized corps service units was able to be completed. Only the horse-mounted units of the cavalry division took a longer time to reach the assembly area in Romania.

Once the units had been assembled, the CSIR consisted of the following units:

General Giovanni Messe, commander of the Italian Expeditionary Corps in Russia. (USSME)

Headquarters Autotransportable Army Corps with the following units directly subordinate: one machine gun battalion; one antitank gun battalion; one company of Bersaglieri motorcyclists; one motorized artillery regiment with three groups; two antiaircraft artillery groups; four engineer battalions, two of which bridging, one pioneer and one signals, one air force aerial observation group of three squadrons; one Blackshirt legion of three battalions;

Two autotransportable divisions: the 9th 'Pasubio' with the 79th and 80th 'Roma' infantry regiments and the 8th divisional artillery regiment; the 52nd 'Torino' with the 81st and 82nd 'Torino' infantry regiments and the 52nd divisional artillery regiment'

A 'Celere' (fast cavalry) division, the 3rd 'Principe Amadeo Duca d'Aosta' (PADA), with the 3rd Bersaglieri Regiment, the 'Savoia Cavalleria' and 'Lancieri di Novara' cavalry regiments, a group of L3/33 tanks and the horse-drawn artillery regiment;

Nine autoreparti (transportation units) parceled out among all of the CSIR units

A Special Quartermaster East consisting of the following logistic services: medical, commissariat, administration, artillery, engineer, chemical, horse and veterinary, transportation

of March 1941, the troops under his command participated in the final phase of the campaign and, following the April armistice with Greece, were stationed in the Athens area. The excellent results achieved in the period December 1940 to April 1941 earned him a promotion for wartime merit as lieutenant general. Returning to Italy in June, on 14 July 1941 Messe was given command of the Italian expeditionary corps in Russia, replacing the designated commander, General Francesco Zingales, who was ill in Vienna.

Italian soldiers in a Hungarian railway station, summer 1941. (USSME)

Trucks and cars on a train convoy during the move to Russia. In the foreground is a small Fiat 508 truck and in the background is a Bianchi Miles medium truck. (USSME)

(1 transportation group for a total of 12 transportation companies), vehicle, postal and telegraph;
Twelve Carabinieri sections.

Total complement was as follows:

62,000 men
17 rifle battalions
7 support weapons battalions
1 sapper battalion
14 independent companies (2 motorcycle, 4 81mm mortar, 8 47/32 AT gun)
10 cavalry squadrons (8 horse squadrons and 2 machine gun squadrons)
4 light tank squadrons
14 artillery groups (3 105/32, for 9 batteries with 36 guns; 2 100/27, for 6 batteries with 24 guns; 7 75/27, for 18 batteries with 72 guns; 2 75/46 antiaircraft, for 8 batteries with 32 guns)
10 independent batteries (2 65/17 for 8 guns and 8 20mm antiaircraft, for 64 guns)
4 engineer battalions (1 pioneer, 1 signals, 2 bridging)
6 independent engineer companies (3 pioneer and 3 signals)
1 chemical battalion[2]

Early employment

Once its deployment had been completed, the CSIR was initially subordinated to the 11.Armee under Generaloberst Eugen Ritter von Schobert, which was in turn subordinate to Heeresgruppe Süd. At the beginning of Operation Barbarossa, 11.Armee had been deployed along the Soviet-Romanian border along the Prut River, between the Romanian 3rd Army under General Petre Dumitrescu in the north and the Romanian 4th Army led by General Nicolae Ciupercă in the south; formally the three units formed an army group commanded by Romanian General Ion Antonescu, but in fact were all subordinate to Heeresgruppe Süd under Field Marshal Gerd von Rundstedt. Von Schobert's forces initially maintained a strictly defensive posture, but after having created a bridgehead across the Prut on 30 June near Iasi they went on the offensive on 2 July during the course of the so-called Operation München; the German-Romanian forces forced the line of the Prut but the Soviet forces of the Southern Front under General Ivan Vladimirovič Tyulenev put up stiff resistance, withdrawing slowly towards the banks of the Dniester River and not hesitating to mount counterattacks.

In late July 1941, the commander of 11.Armee asked to have at least one Italian division made immediately available, considering that at that moment the CSIR units had had yet completed their assembly. The German army was deployed along the course of the Dniester, between 17.Armee and the Romanian 4th Army. Von Schobert's forces had forced the river in several points and were attempting to strike in depth to trap the Soviet forces in a pocket and to annihilate them. The aim of the German commander was to make an enveloping move between the Dniester and the Bug. Nonetheless, the lack of armoured units prevented von Schobert from being able to surround the withdrawing Soviet units and several key points that had been taken were lost due to ferocious counterattacks by the enemy. The 11.Armee also had no reserves,

---

2   AA.VV.: *Le Operazioni delle Unità Italiane al Fronte russo (1941-1943)*, page 81.

except for the CSIR, which, however, as previously mentioned was not in the best of conditions for immediate employment.

On 21 July 1941, by order n.3409/41, army headquarters ordered the concentration of the CSIR in the vicinity of the Dniester River in the Yampol area, as a reserve unit. However, this concentration could not be effected because of the rapid movement of the German units. Therefore, the CSIR headquarters established a new concentration area along the Isvorj-Yampol road, with the aim of deploying at least one division on the left of the Dniester. The move of the units was to be carried out by successive truck moves, carried out by the XXIX Transportation Group alone, as the II Transportation Group was engaged in moving the logistic services. Thus, by operations order Number 1 dated 26 July 1941, General Messe ordered the move of the 'Pasubio' to the operational area by truck, reinforced by a motorcycle company. The movement of the units, which began on 30 July, was hampered by bad weather conditions. The heavy rain transformed the only Botosani-Belzy-Isvory road into a bog, forcing the columns to stop continually.

In the meantime, in an attempt to have the expeditionary corps assembled and ready for operational employment as quickly as possible, Messe also ordered the 'Torino' units to move to the Stefanesti-Sagajacani area, marching on foot. Between 3 July and 1 August, another two requests were made by 11.Armee headquarters: employment of two Italian artillery groups to support the attack of its XXX.Armee-Korps (Generaloberst Hans von Salmuth) and a request that the advance of the CSIR to the Goraba-Plot-Piskarevka-Sudenoye area be hastened, in order to sweep the area between the LIV and XXX.Armee-Korps and to reestablish contact between the two corps.

With this order, however, the Italian units ran the risk of being employed separately, which was contrary to the CSIR's operational concept, contained in the directives of the Italian Supreme Command which had been imparted to General Messe. The CSIR commander then decided to adhere to the 11.Armee order, only after having had grouped at least the 'Pasubio' and 'Torino' divisions and all of their artillery in the deployment area specified by the German headquarters.

Accordingly, a new operations order (Number 4, dated 2 August 1941) was issued, according to which the 'Pasubio' was to forego its truck transport and proceed on foot as far as Olschanka, while the 'Torino' was to be loaded aboard trucks made available by the 'Pasubio' in the Scholkani area, while the 'Celere' division, still en route, was to continue to march as far as Soroky.

At the same time, Messe informed the army headquarters the uselessness of using the CSIR in sweep operations and to consider a more profitable use of its units.

On 6 August, despite the bad weather that had transformed the Ukrainian plains into immense bogs, aboard their Lancia 3Ro trucks the infantrymen of the 'Pasubio' reached Yampol. On 7 August, the CSIR tactical headquarters moved from Botosani to Olshanka.

Meanwhile, the situation of 11.Armee and of the other units operating on its flanks improved considerably and at least three groups of forces became available to be used in eliminating the enemy between the Dniester and the Bug. In particular, von Kleist's panzer group had reached Pervomaysk after a rapid advance, 17.Armee had made contact with the left wing of 11.Armee at Gaivoron and 11.Armee had been able to force the Dniester in several places. The German headquarters then decided to exploit the advantage gained by its left wing, ordering a conversion to the south and southeast to annihilate the Soviet forces between the two rivers. To do that, it was necessary to have forces capable of moving rapidly to prevent the enemy from withdrawing and at that moment the German army could count only on the 'Pasubio' division. To that end, General Messe issued operations order Number 8 to hasten the move of the Italian units across the Dniester, with the 'Pasubio' already attacking the bridges over the Bug, near Voznessensk. The 'Celere' division had moved ahead of the 'Torino' in the Botosani area, which was marching on foot and had to cede its vehicles to the 'Pasubio'.

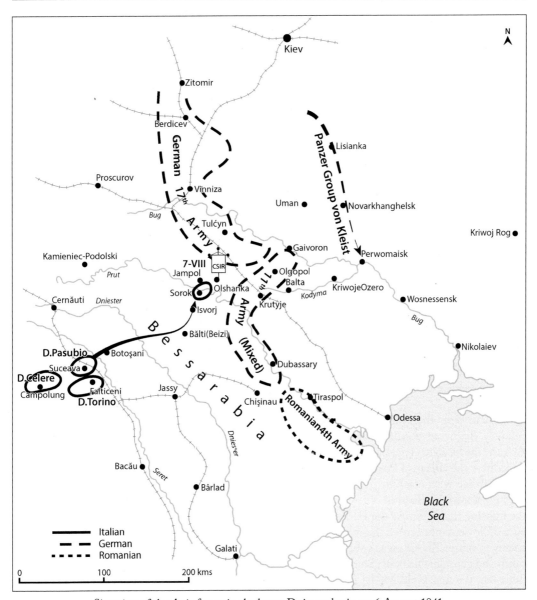

Situation of the Axis forces in the lower Dniester basin on 6 August 1941.

Battle between two rivers

In order to eliminate the Soviet forces between the Dniester and the Bug, the 'Pasubio', reinforced with the 30th Artillery Group and by the 1st Motorcycle Company, had been ordered to quickly reach the Bug north of Voznessensk and to continue along the right bank as far as Nikolayev in order to complete the encirclement of the enemy and to eliminate the Soviet bridgehead in that area.

Marching on roads that had been transformed into morasses and overcoming many roadblocks set up by the retreating Soviets, on 10 August the 'Pasubio' reached Voznessensk. The following morning the march to the south resumed, but an unexpected and violent storm blocked any further

An Italian truck convoy moving past the Russian border in the summer of 1941. (USSME)

movement. Only the vanguard,[3] led by Colonel Epifanio Chairamónti,[4] commander of the 80th Infantry Regiment 'Roma', managed to push on for another 30 kilometers and at 13:00 on 11 August, the forward elements of the 1st Bersaglieri Motorcycle Company made contact with Soviet forces near the village of Pokrovskoye. The enemy sought to hit the Italian columns first with artillery and then with machine gun fire. Colonel Chiaramonti quickly sent the 3rd Artillery Group ahead under Major Rossi in order to reply to enemy fire and to support the attack of his infantry. In the fighting that followed the III Battalion of the 80th Regiment was heavily engaged. The presence of Soviet tanks caused the worst to be feared, but quick response by Italian artillery forced the enemy to retire. The area was swept with the arrival of other units, during which 38 prisoners were taken and considerable booty was seized. The Italians suffered two killed and three wounded. That same day the first Gold Medal for Military Valor was awarded, for bersagliere Santino Alfredo Lutri, who fell in combat at the age of 23.

---

3   Consisting of the 80th Infantry Regiment 'Roma', the II Gruppo of the 8th Artillery Regiment 'Pasubio', the 1st Bersaglieri Motorcycle Company, the 141st 47/32 Antitank Company, the 1st 81mm Mortar Company of the IX divisional mortar battalion, the 3rd 81mm Mortar Company of the V Mortar Battalion, a section of the 20mm divisional battery, a divisional engineer platoon and two radio stations for a total of 4,500 men.

4   Colonel Epifanio Chiarimonti. A combat officer in the First World War, during the Second he was assigned to the 80th Regiment 'Roma' of the 'Pasubio' Division, around which he organized the Colonna Chiarimonti within the CSIR, a sort of forward assault unit. Badly wounded in one eye he was repatriated in 1942 and put in command of the Milan Officer Candidate School which was, however, located in Cremona. On 8 September 1943 he fought against the Germans and was able to save his men from being executed but was imprisoned for two years in Poland and Germany. He returned to Italy after the war.

Torino division troops marching on foot with mules following carrying equipment, summer 1941. (USSME)

Following is the text of his commendation: 'A motorcyclist in advanced reconnaissance, targeted by intense enemy fire from ambush positions, he persisted in his reconnaissance mission, until he was seriously wounded along with his motorcycle companion. With supreme effort he resumed driving his motorcycle in order to report the results of his reconnaissance to his commander and to bring his companion to safety. He died shortly afterwards but was concerned only about the wounds of his companion who he wanted to be tended to before himself A magnificent example of dedication to duty, of military spirit and of comradeship until the ultimate sacrifice. – Pokrovskoye (Russian Front), 11 August 1941 – XIX'

Battle for Yasnaya Polyana

The next day, 12 August, the vanguard of the 'Pasubio' continued its march to the south. The motorcycle recon troops intercepted enemy units near the village of Yasnaya Polyana; this time the I Battalion of the 80th Regiment, commanded by Major Moscardini, was heavily engaged in the fighting. The battle lasted several hours, from 15:00 to 19:30; after a violent exchange of artillery and mortar fire, with the Soviet units threatened on their flanks and to their rear, they decided once again to withdraw, leaving hundreds of dead on the field as well as hundreds of prisoners. Through interrogation of prisoners, it was learned that the enemy forces belonged to the Soviet 469th Infantry Regiment, reinforced by numerous mortars and three horse-drawn batteries. At nightfall, the Soviet forces abandoned the Nikolayev bridgehead.

The following is an extract from a report written by Colonel Chiarimonti about this fighting:

For 14 days we had been sent on a desperate race across the Dniester towards the Bug in order to find an enemy that we could never catch. Therefore, to let them get away now after having made contact with them and having driven them off, the only chance to fight them after so much effort and so much worry, because the German units would surely have encountered them before we did...I did not know who I would come up against, and my forces were not excessive...I thus decided on my own initiative to take the crossroads immediately to the west of Korvalevka...Having quickly called the commanders of the battalions, the group and the independent units, I gave orders for an immediate departure, having however replaced the III Battalion by the I Battalion, both because it had been engaged the day before, but mainly because I wanted to put on point the battalion that had one rifle company less, and which was therefore leaner, while I kept III Battalion, which was stronger, in the second echelon ...

And thus around 13:30 I began the movement very quickly, cutting away from the large German cavalry formations that barely two kilometers from me had already reached the road coming from the west and were heading towards the Bug...

At 15:00, after about 10 km, the commander of the bersaglieri company reported to me that he had run into, slightly north of Yasnaya Polyana, and past the village of Pokrovskoye, about 5 km from it, strong enemy resistance, having had one officer already killed, and asking me to send him a company to reinforce him as soon as possible. At that time, finding myself in the lead with the group commander and with my adjutant major, I ordered Lieutenant Rota, the commander of the point company, to get the men off the trucks immediately, to get the unit in order and to advance until he reached the tail end of the motorcyclists, while I called for Major Moscardini, the battalion commander, to give him orders...Meanwhile enemy artillery salvos began to fall on the column.

Rota's 2nd Company, having reached the motorcyclists, was ordered by the motorcycle commander to move to the left of the road towards a cornfield from which rifle and machine gun fire had come. A violent fight then broke out during which numerous 81mm mortars began to fire and the artillery fire became more intense. In the meantime, while Major Moscardini saw to getting the entire battalion off the trucks...and getting it in action, he pointed out to the artillery group commander the area where he should deploy his battery...The fighting thus heated up with only the leading elements engaged; the only important element was that we were facing a beaten enemy that was retreating...I ordered Major Moscardini to go personally to the left, where the fire was most intense...After a few moments, I saw major Moscardini advance from the line, held up by two men, because he had been badly wounded in his right arm by an explosive round...The major, having reached me, with admirable calm and stoicism, filled me in on the situation: the enemy, in his judgement two companies strong, was deployed in a very favorable area straddling a large haystack which was about 150 meters from our leading elements...The company had already taken heavy losses...After that I had him go to the aid station, as he was bleeding heavily. There were no captains in the battalion to replace him, and I took the lead. Having called Lieutenant Genovesi, commander of the battalion's 4th AA Company...I ordered him to go with all his available men, drivers included, to reinforce the 2nd Company and to assume command; I ordered the 3rd Company, Lieutenant Mori, to move ahead on the right side of the road...Meanwhile, while I ordered Major Minchiotti to close up with his battalion [III Battalion, author's note] and with his 75/27 battery, I ordered the group commander, Major Rossi, to open fire by the 9th against the haystack...The battery accomplished its mission brilliantly ... With this happy result, with our mortars intensifying their fire and above all because of the really heroic and enthusiastic advance by Lieutenant Mori and his glorious 3rd Company, which in Garibaldi fashion cleared every obstacle, the enemy began to give way. Meanwhile, however, Lieutenant Genovesi, who had done wonders, and Lieutenant Rota, commander of the 2nd Company, had been wounded...I then ordered

Lieutenant Carbonati to move to the left with all of his men, the last of the battalion...and Major Minchiotti to join me with his battalion, ready to be thrown to the left or to the right, depending on where the enemy was giving way. Mori's company meanwhile had advanced more than a kilometer, pushing out anything he came up against, and beating off repeated incursions by armoured cars...

It was by now around 19:00 and we had been fighting for quite a few hours...The first shadows of night began to fall, while the enemy continued to pull back under our pressure. I did not feel it was any longer the case to commit any other elements, because I would have only caused a useless waste of human lives, and at 19:30 the fighting ceased...All of the numerous prisoners captured declared that they were from the 469th Infantry Regiment, which had been deployed facing us, reinforced by many mortars and three horse-drawn batteries, covering the units that were crossing the Bug. The fight thus had been between unequal forces and weapons: a battalion, a battery and an 81mm mortar company against a regiment, three batteries and who knows how many mortars. The enemy had fought stubbornly, as shown by their losses. But the infantry grunts of the 'Pasubio' never bothered to count the enemy, faithful to the commandment they had been given; ahead at all costs, 'in the name of Rome', the proud motto of my 80th.[5]

The losses reported on the morning of 13 August were as follows: 2 officers killed, 13 NCOs and soldiers killed, 8 officers wounded, 74 NCOs and soldiers wounded.

General von Schobert, 11.Armee commander, sent General Messe a message in which he wrote that the 'Pasubio' had contributed greatly to his army's victorious action: 'The rapid march made by the 'Pasubio' Division, despite the difficulties of the environment, contributed greatly to the victorious action of 11.Armee.'

In the meantime, the 'Celere' division had reached Petshanka, south of Oligopol, with its own transport, while the 'Torino' division had continued to march on foot towards the Dniester. The CSIR tactical command moved from Olshanka to Oligopol.

Dnieper Front

While fighting was still going on between the Dniester and the Bug, headquarters of Heeresgruppe Süd decided to transfer the CSIR to the direct subordination of von Kleist's panzer group, beginning on 14 August. On 13 August the units of the CSIR were deployed as follows: headquarters at Oligopol, the 'Pasubio' division from the Prokovskoye area continued over the Bug towards Bratskoye while awaiting orders for the concentration of all of the CSIR units on the Dnieper. The 'Celere' division was in the Oligopol-Petshanka area and was moving towards Pervomaysk. The 'Torino' division was in the Sagajacani area and was moving towards Oligopol. The corps' service units were located in the Botosani-Olshanka-Oligopol area.

Subordinate to von Kleist's panzer group, the CSIR was to initially carry out a defensive action protecting the left flank of the German corps in its march to the Dniester and subsequently was to conduct offensive actions in depth across that river. These new missions called for rapid mobility of the units and as early as 11 August Messe had requested at least two transportation units from the Supreme Command and had telegraphed the following message to Rome: 'It is indispensable that all of the units sent to this front be exclusively truck borne stop. In a contrary case it is preferable to

---

5   AA.VV.: *Le operazioni delle Unità Italiane al Fronte Russo (1941-1943)*, pages 548-558.

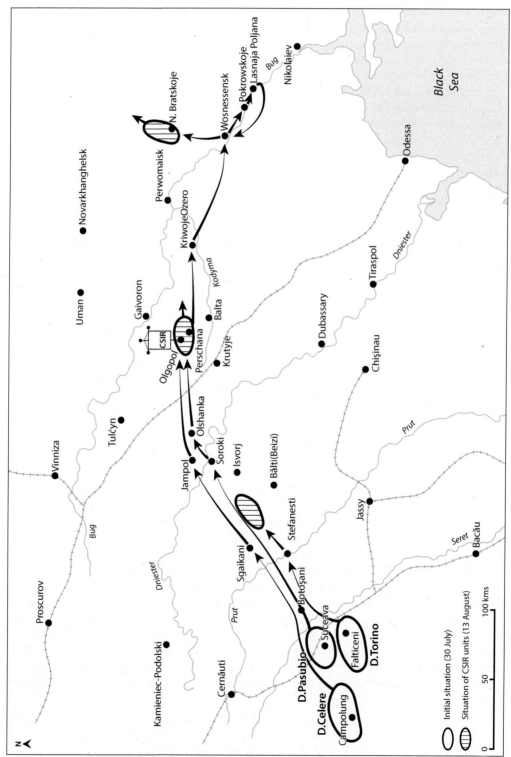

CSIR dispositions at the beginning and end of the Battle of the Two Rivers (30 July–13 August 1941)

A tractor being used to pull a truck that has been bogged down in the mud, summer 1941.
(Authors' collection)

Celere division cavalrymen on the march on the Ukrainian steppe summer 1941. (Vincenzo de Gaetano
collection)

Left: Italian cavalrymen parading past General Giovanni Messe and other officers in the summer of 1941. (USSME)
Below: Italian soldiers attacking a Russian village, August 1941. The soldier on the left is manning a Breda Model 30 light machine gun. (USSME)

Italian soldiers attacking a Russian village, August 1941 (USSME)

Italian soldiers attacking a Russian village, August 1941. Note the fixed bayonets. (USSME)

Italian soldiers with captured prisoners in a Russian village, summer 1941. (USSME)

Celere motorized units on the move, August 1941. Three-wheeled motorcycles were widely used by the
Regio Esercito. (Vincenzo de Gaetano collection)

Celere recon motorcyclists on a Russian road, August 1941. (Vincenzo de Gaetano collection)

forego any further forces because they would inevitably remain hundreds of kilometers to the rear stop'.[6] There was no response from Rome.

On 14 August, Messe issued new orders to the units: the 'Pasubio' was to concentrate in the Annovka, Bratskoye area and then continue along the Kirovo-Kremenchug route. The 'Torino' was to continue to march on foot as far as the Dniester, then to be ferried by truck once the 'Pasubio' had reached the Dnieper. The 'Celere' division was to concentrate at the Bug, in the Pervomaysk-Lissaya Gora area and then to continue on towards the Dnieper. The CSIR air element was to displace to the field at Kirovo beginning on 22 August because the field at Tudora was too far from the new operational sector.

Meantime, von Kleist's panzer group was busy seizing the bridges at Dniepropetrovsk and Zaporozhe over the Dnieper in order to cut off the retreating enemy forces and to establish two bridgeheads for the new offensive to the east. To protect his left flank, on 15 August the 'Pasubio' division was subordinated to III.Armee-Korps (Generaloberst Eberhard von Mackensen) and quickly sent to the Tschigirin area in order to be deployed on the right bank of the Dnieper, between Topilovka and Kryukov, to replace the SS-Division 'Wiking' which was to be employed further to the south.

The march of the 'Pasubio' units to the Dnieper was carried out amongst a thousand difficulties and under constant bombardment by Soviet aircraft. In any case, two days later the Italian division

6   AA.VV.: *Le operazioni delle Unità Italiane al Fronte Russo (1941-1943)*, p. 91, n.

Soldiers pushing a bogged-down SPA 38R truck in Russia in August 1941. (USSME)

reached the river, relieved the 'Wiking' and on 18 August assumed control of the new defensive sector.

On 21 August, after having been relieved by elements of three German divisions, the 'Pasubio' was trucked further south, taking up positions between Koluskino and Verhniednieprovsk, relieving the 'Wiking' units once again as well as other German III.Armee-Korps forces engaged in combat for the Dniepropetrovsk bridgehead. In the order of the day for 21 August 1941, General von Mackensen wished to cite the Italian units:'...the premise for the rapid advance of the 13th Panzer Division was created by the SS Wiking Division and by the Italian 'Pasubio' division, which despite the unfavorable conditions of exercise of command and in part also due to the unfavorable fuel situation, with truly encouraging speed overcame al of the difficulties they faced. These two divisions contributed equally to the success of the corps.'

In the meantime, because of the action by the 'Pasubio' and the lack of a transportation group, the 'Torino' had reached the Dniester on foot in the Soroki area. From 11.Armee headquarters the request was made to have all of the CSIR units on the Dnieper as soon as possible. But, considering the lack of trucks and in an attempt to have at least two divisions deployed along the river, Messe decided to move all of the motorized units of the 'Celere' towards the Dnieper, as well as the 'Torino''s artillery regiment and the corps truck-borne units. The horse-mounted units would join them later.

Von Kleist's panzer group headquarters, however, was not able to resupply the Italian units with fuel in time, forcing those units to remain halted for several days, unable to make up for the time lost by the 'Torino'. With respect to the other units of the corps, because the field at Kirovo was not ready, the air element reached Krivoy Rog on 21 August, from where they began their sorties to protect the bridges for the units deployed along the Dnieper. At the request of the German headquarters, two Italian engineer bridging units were sent to Dniepropetrovsk to be used in building

A bersaglieri squad marching on foot along a Ukrainian road, August 1941. (USSME)

Italian soldiers with a 75mm Model 1911 75/27 gun. (USSME)

An Italian motorized column passing over a bridge built by Italian engineers across the Dnieper, August 1941. The truck in the foreground is a SPA CL 35 light truck. (Authors' collection)

defenses and crossing in the bridgehead. The CSIR tactical headquarters moved to Pervomaysk on the Bug River.

Fuel supplies did not arrive until 28 August, when units were able to resume their march, reaching the Dnieper on 3 September. On that date, units of the 'Pasubio', of the 'Celere' and some of the corps units had reached the river. Units of the 'Torino' were also slowly approaching the river, while many corps logistic train units were still scattered to the rear, due to the chronic lack of trucks.

The Duce visits

In late August Mussolini made an official visit to the Eastern Front. After having reached the Wolfschanze (the Wolf's Lair) by train in the forests of East Prussia where Hitler had moved his headquarters in order to be able to follow operations in Soviet territory from a close vantage point, on 26 August the two dictators left by air for Brest-Litovsk, where the Soviets had held out until just a few days earlier. The following day, by train, the Duce and the Führer reached the headquarters of Army Group South at Strykov, in southern Ukraine. On 29 August, Hitler and Mussolini moved by air to Uman in the Ukraine, greeted by the local populace in a festive manner, happy to have been liberated from the communist dictatorship. Along the way, the column ran across a unit of bersaglieri motorcyclists. Initially, the soldiers drew up in parade formation, but in their enthusiasm to see the Duce close-up, broke ranks and clustered around Mussolini's car, who then got out of the car and exchanged salutes and shook hands. Later, the two dictators passed a German unit in review and the scene was naturally quite different. At Tekusha, the Duce met with General Messe and reviewed all of the CSIR units. During the meeting with Mussolini, Messe spoke of the excellent behavior of the troops, but pointed out the poor armament, the lack of trucks

Adolf Hitler and Benito Mussolini during their visit to the Eastern Front. Behind them is General Giovanni Messe, August 1941. (Authors' collection)

Benito Mussolini and Adolf Hitler being briefed on the military situation by General Keitel. To the right of Mussolini is General Ugo Cavallero. Uman airfield, August 1941. (USSME)

and the inadequate winter gear. The Duce promised to do whatever was possible and above all promised to pressure the German headquarters to respect their agreements: the Wehrmacht had in fact agreed to provide the necessary logistic support to the CSIR, all of the fuel it needed, as well as medical supplies, food and equipment. However, until the battle between the two rivers these agreements had been honored, but during the march to the Dnieper the resupply of fuel had been significantly reduced. Little convinced of the Duce's assurances, mindful of the thousands of cases of frostbite that Italian troops had sustained in Albania and Greece which he had seen first-hand and expecting little assistance from the German ally to deal with the Russian winter, Messe paid Romanian traffickers, made use of NCOs who were commissary experts and, paying in cash with funds from his own headquarters, bought horses, carts, sleds, fur coats and a few trucks on the Romanian black market.

On the Dnieper River

On the morning of 8 September, the CSIR assumed control of its stretch of the front, deployed in a sector covering about 100 kilometers, between the Vorskla River and Dniepropetrovsk with the 'Pasubio' and 'Celere' divisions on the front line, reinforced respectively by the 1st Motorcycle Company and by the II Antitank Battalion (minus one company). Artillery assets were a group in the 'Pasubio' sector and two in the 'Celere' sector. In the second echelon there was the other company of the antitank battalion and, later, the 'Torino' division and the 'Tagliamento' Blackshirt Legion. Profiting from several days without any fighting, the trucks made available by the 'Pasubio' were used to move the men of the 'Torino'. From von Kleist's panzer group headquarters came the request to be able to use the 'Torino' in defense of the area south of Dniepropetrovsk. To that end, Messe ordered the 'Torino' to hasten its move. Thus, on 13 September, the 81st Infantry Regiment, reinforced by the 52nd Artillery, assumed the defense of the new sector which, by the 15th, was garrisoned by the entire 'Torino' division.

The actions of the Italian units in this period were part of the great German maneuver, begun on 14 August and which ended on 19 September in Kiev: two panzer groups, Guderian in the north and von Kleist in the south, were to encircle the Soviet positions on the Dnieper in the Kiev sector, then to join in the rear of the enemy units drawn up in defense of that area, trapping them in a huge pocket. At the same time, the infantry units deployed along the river were to attack the Soviet forces and break through their defenses and isolate them in other smaller pockets. Initially, the mission of the CSIR was to ensure the defense of the Dnieper line, between the 17.Armee and III.Armee-Korps, a sector of about a hundred kilometers, which with the arrival of the 'Torino' was extended another 50 kilometers as far as Augustinovka. The III.Armee-Korps forces had not however been able to break the strong resistance put up by the Soviets and to move from the bridge-head at Dniepropetrovsk, which led von Kleist's panzer group to cross the river at Kremenchug on 12 September, leaving the defense of the river to other German forces and to the CSIR.

The actions carried out by Italian units between 5 and 18 September 1941 on the Dnieper front were characterized mainly by patrol activity, raids and intense artillery activity. Of particular note was the fire support provided by two 105/32 groups of the 30th Regiment and by a 100/17 group of the 'Torino' to the operations to enlarge the bridgehead towards Kamenka, northwest of Dniepropetrovsk and the defensive fighting by the 81st Infantry Regiment in repelling continuous Soviet attempts to set foot on the right bank of the river, particularly in the stretch of the front where there were numerous small islands near the confluence of the Samara into the Dnieper.

An Italian lieutenant using binoculars to observe enemy movements on the Dnieper front, August 1941.
(USSME)

4

The Petrikovka Maneuver

The Italian action at Petrikovka entered into the overall scheme of the great battle of the Dnieper, during which the retreating Soviet forces tried to halt the advance of the Axis forces at the river and was also the first major operation that the CSIR conducted independently, with only its own forces and its own assets. On 15 September 1941 the German headquarters requested the commander of the CSIR to have the 'Pasubio' division cross the Dnieper on 18 September to protect the right flank of 17.Armee, which was engaged in attacking towards Kobelyaki and Poltava. All of this was because around mid-September, after the difficulties encountered by III. Armee-Korps in crossing the Dnieper from the bridgehead at Dniepropetrovsk, General von Kleist had with part of his forces, in particular the XIV.Armee-Korps, reached the right bank of the river and had crossed the Dnieper at Kremenchug, which had been taken on 10 September. From there, the German units had continued on to the north, and along with the 2nd Panzer Group, had surrounded a great number of Soviet forces. At the same time, the road towards Poltava was open to the advance of 17.Armee, whose right flank was to be protected by the 'Pasubio'.

Italian motorized units on the march on the Dnieper front, September 1941. Several of the trucks are towing trailers; note the chains on the rear wheels of the Fiat 508 CM staff car in the foreground. (Authors' collection)

A column of Fiat 626 trucks of the Tagliamento Blackshirt Legion, September 1941
(Authors' collection)

Autumn 1941, the Pasubio division crossing the Dnieper on a pontoon bridge built by the Germans. A
20mm Breda Model 35 antiaircraft gun is in the foreground. (USSME)

On 16 September, General Messe issued operations order Number 16, with which he ordered that the sector previously occupied by units of the 'Pasubio' should pass under control of elements of the 'Celere'. The 'Pasubio', transferred to subordination of 17.Armee, crossed the Dnieper at Deriyevka on 18 September, taking up positions on the Oril, in the stretch between its confluence with the Dnieper and Voinovka.

Four days later the rest of the CSIR, along with the III. Armee-Korps, constituted the Gruppe Mackensen, engaged in ensuring the defense of the Dnieper between the mouth of the Oril and that of the Mokraya Sura, but at the same time was to prepare to exploit the success of the large, armoured forces. To that end, the 'Torino' division, reinforced by 63rd 'Tagliamento' Blackshirt Legion and by II Antitank Battalion, was transferred to the Dniepropetrovsk bridgehead and on 21 September began to cross the river. Thus, when the 'Pasubio' crossed the river at Deriyevka, the 'Celere' remained to defend the Dnieper and the 'Torino' moved to the left bank of the river, the conditions were created for the forces of the CSIR to be employed in a cohesive manner, to engage the enemy forces in the great bend of the Dnieper between Oril and Dniepropetrovsk, to surround them and prevent any chance of escape.

The 'Pasubio' in action

In the night of 22 September, units of the 'Pasubio', reinforced by the 1st Motorcycle Company, by a squadron of light tanks from the 'Celere' and by the German Gruppe Abraham (consisting of 231st Infantry Regiment of the 76.Inf.Div , and artillery assets) commanded by Oberst Erich Abraham and subordinated to the Italian regiment, deployed between Voinovka and the confluence of the Oril and the Dnieper, with the aim of establishing a bridgehead at Zaritchanka to allow German armoured units to cross. The action began at 5:00 on 23 September and was carried out by the 79th Infantry Regiment 'Roma', supported by two groups from the 8th Artillery and by the Gruppe Abraham. Despite strong Soviet resistance, including intense artillery fire and air attacks, the bridgehead was established and strongly defended by Italian and German units. However, the Soviets did not give up and for three more days, between 24 and 26 September, counterattacked continually, sparking furious close-quarter fighting, from which the Axis forces always emerged as the victors. The bridgehead was thus further consolidated, allowing the armoured units to cross the Oril.

At the same time, further to the north, troops of the 80th Infantry Regiment 'Roma', with a surprise attack, were able to reestablish the bridgehead at Voinovka, holding it and fending off enemy counterattacks until the arrival of German units. Thanks to the successes registered at Zaritchanka and Voinovka, the road was opened to the German panzer group, which forced the Soviet forces to pull back towards the Voltsctya River.

On 27 September, prior to the action at Petrikovka, the Italian units were deployed as follows: the 'Pasubio' was dug in behind the Oril, between Nekvoroshska and Zaritchanka, the 'Celere' was positioned along the right bank of the Dnieper, between the mouths of the Oril and the bridgehead at Dniepropetrovsk, the 'Torino' was at the Dniepropetrovsk bridgehead behind the 'Wiking', with troops across the Dnieper.

The attack opens

The main objective of the German headquarters was to overwhelm the Soviet defenses in the area of the Dniepropetrovsk bridgehead and to make contact with friendly forces coming from the north. To that end, XIV.Armee-Korps was to cross the Oril and march on Novomoskovsk,

A Blackshirt column and trucks on the move along a Russian railway bed, autumn 1941. (USSME)

An L3 light tank, armed only with two 8mm machine guns, of the 'San Giorgio' light tank battalion crossing through a Ukrainian village, autumn 1941. (Authors' collection)

A group of bersaglieri on a bank of the Dnieper in Ukraine, autumn 1941. The raft on the river presumably is carrying Italians or Germans. (USSME)

making contact with III.Armee-Korps, which in turn was to move from the Dniepropetrovsk bridgehead with its divisions against the same objective, then to continue on to the east and take up positions along the Samara River. As part of this plan, General Messe wanted to carry out a pincer movement with the 'Pasubio' from the northwest and the 'Torino' from the southeast, to eliminate any chance of escape by Soviet forces located between the bend between the Dnieper and the Oril. The Petrikovka position played a key role, as it represented the door to open and then to close in order to surround the enemy forces. In order to carry out this maneuver all of the CSIR divisions would be needed and to that end, Messe had to ask the commander of 1.Panzerarmee to return the 'Pasubio' to his subordination. With that done, the CSIR commander was able to plan an offensive action which was to unfold in three phases: on 28 September, 'Torino' would attack the Soviet positions around the bridgehead. On 29 September, a converging action against Petrikovka by the 'Pasubio' from the north and 'Torino' from the south would take place. On 30 September, the Soviet forces trapped in the pocket would be captured, with help from the west by the 'Celere'.

At 7:30 on 28 September, following brief but intense artillery preparatory fire, 'Torino' infantry units attacked, forcing the Soviet forces to withdraw to the west, even though the Soviets put up strong resistance and had to cross several minefields. The bridgehead was expanded and the same day the Obuskvskye-Gorianovskiye line was reached. At the same time, the German divisions successfully moved to the north and northeast. Italian units captured about a thousand prisoners and a large quantity of weapons and equipment.

Towards evening, Messe issued orders for the next day: the 'Torino' division was to continue its attack, moving in two columns as far as the Kurilovka-Petrikovka line. The 'Pasubio' was to move from the Zaritshanka area to the south and to position itself along the Shuligovka-Prodanovkiye-Galuschovka-Petrikovka line, making contact with the 'Torino' and impeding the

Soviet withdrawal. The 'Celere' was to allow two battalions of bersaglieri to cross the river, which would be used to sweep the area between the Dnieper and the Oreli.

Second day of battle

At 5:30 on 29 September, 'Torino' troops advanced in two columns: on the right, two battalions of the 81st Infantry 'Torino' and the Blackshirt Legion, on the left the 82nd Infantry 'Torino'. The column on the right, marching along the Kamenka-Popovka-Petrikovka-Zaritshanka axis, clashed with numerous Soviet forces which were retreating, taking many prisoners. At 18:00, the III/81st, leading the column, after having overrun several Soviet units, made contact with 'Pasubio' units inside Petrikovka. The march of the left-hand column was somewhat slower, not only because of the presence of enemy forces but mainly due to the lack of roads and the swampy terrain; the column commander was forced to continue the march with only foot troops, leaving the trucks and motorized artillery in the positions they had reached the previous day. At 17:00 the column occupied Kurilovka, establishing contact with the XXV Bersaglieri Battalion of the 'Celere'.

Soon after, the 'Pasubio' moved forward with a column consisting of the 79th Infantry Regiment 'Roma', reinforced by two artillery groups and a squadron of light tanks, breaking into Petrikovka with its vanguard around 18:00, where infantrymen from the 'Torino' had arrived shortly before.

Meanwhile the 'Celere', after having transferred the XX and XXV bersaglieri battalions to the other bank of the river on the night of the 28th, quickly engaged the XX Battalion in a sweep of the area between the left bank of the Oreli and Varvarovka and the XXV of the area between the Dnieper and the Kurilovka-Yelissavetovka line. When night fell, the two battalions respectively reached Galuschkovka and Petrikovka, joining the 'Pasubio' and 'Torino' units.

A 47/32 antitank gun in a well-camouflaged position along the banks of the Dnieper, autumn 1941.
(USSME)

Third day of battle and final balance

On 30 September, while troops of the 80th Infantry 'Roma' were taking up positions along the Schuligovka-Galuschkovka line, the other units already in the area were completing their sweeps of the adjacent area and the two bersaglieri battalions returned along the course of the Dnieper. During the operation, heavy losses were inflicted on the Soviets and about ten thousand prisoners were taken in addition to a large quantity of arms and equipment. CSIR losses amounted to 219 men, of which 87 were killed (6 officers), 190 wounded (13 officers) and 14 missing.

The Petrikovka action concluded the first operational cycle of Italian forces on the Russian front. Contributing significantly to the great success of the CSIR units were the bridging and aviation units. For about a month, under constant Soviet artillery fire, the I and IX bridge battalions were directly involved in repairing damage caused by Soviet aerial bombardment, allowing the troops to continue to shift between the two banks of the Dnieper. The CSIR air element, which had already distinguished itself in the defensive battle with reconnaissance and support missions, participated with the 'Pasubio' columns in the fighting at Zaritshanka, maintaining air superiority during the battle for Petrikovka.

There was great satisfaction within the Italian headquarters, above all because they had been able to succeed by themselves where the Germans had failed, even though the Germans had far superior resources. On this occasion the Blackshirts and Italian infantrymen had done much better than had the soldiers of the SS 'Wiking' Division. And so, on 2 October 1941, General Messe wrote to the Chief of Staff, General Ugo Cavallero:

> I was able to initiate, carry out and bring to a close a major offensive operation and contribute in a decisive manner to the victorious conclusion of this recent operation north of Dniepropetrovsk, which was one of the most bitter and hard-fought. It should be borne in mind that the Kleist group had in vain attacked the Dniepropetrovsk bridgehead for several days, incurring heavy losses and achieving very modest results.[1]

The Italian action was also praised in a letter addressed by Adolf Hitler to the Duce, dated 28 October 1941: 'The success of Panzer Group Kleist for the formation of the Dniepropetrovsk bridgehead also gave your divisions, Duce, the occasion to effect for the first time a proper and completely victorious operation in the framework of a great battle of annihilation'.

---

1   Messe's letter was included by General Cavallero in his Diary under the date of 2 October. U. Cavallero, *Diario 1940-1943*, p. 239.

Italian troops attacking the village of Petrikovka, September 1941. (Authors' collection)

A column of Soviet prisoners being escorted by Italian soldiers, September 1941. (USSME)

5

In the Donets Basin

The Dnieper having been crossed and the Soviet forces between the Dnieper and the Oreli annihilated, the next objectives of von Kleist's panzer group were the coast of the Sea of Azov, the Donets Basin and the conquest of Rostov on the Don. For its part, the CSIR was to continue to cover the left flank of the corps and at the same time was to participate actively in the new offensive. After the battle of the Dnieper, the situation in the area where the CSIR was to be employed was as follows:

- XIV. Armee-Korps, moving from the Zaritshanka and Voinovka bridgehead, had managed to seize intact the bridges at Novomoskovsk over the Samara River;
- III. Armee-Korps, moving from the Dniepropetrovsk bridgehead, had taken up positions on the Samara, between Novomoskovsk and the confluence with the Dnieper;
- The CSIR, following the sweeps in the Petrikovka pocket, was regrouping in the Petrikovka-Dniepropetrovsk area.

An Italian L3 light tank and motorcyclists crossing the Dnieper, October 1941. (Authors' collection)

Based on this new disposition of forces, General von Kleist decided to have his XIV. Armee-Korps advance quickly from north to south, while III. Armee-Korps was to protect the exposed flank, advancing deeply and on the left. The CSIR was to advance as far as the Voltsctya River and take positions south of Pavlograd, gradually replacing III. Armee-Korps to protect the panzer group's flank. In particular, by Order Number 59, the headquarters of von Kleist's panzer group ordered the CSIR to redeploy one division across the Samara beginning on 3 October in order to quickly ensure protection of the exposed flank. General Messe chose the 'Celere' for this task, because the 'Torino' had no trucks and the 'Pasubio' was temporarily stalled along the road by torrential rains.

Marching orders

By operations order Number 21 dated 1 October, Messe ordered the 'Celere' to quickly begin its crossing of the Dnieper at Dniepropetrovsk. However, crossing the river by the 'Celere' troops did not go off quickly and meanwhile the German headquarters had slipped the start date for the Italian division to 4 October. At that point Messe ordered the 'Pasubio' to move ahead, followed closely by the 'Celere'. On 3 October, the CSIR headquarters moved to the north of Dniepropetrovsk.

In the meantime, von Kleist's panzer group[1] had begun its movement to the south on 4 October and XIV. Armee-Korps had reached the Orechov area. At the same time, III. Armee-Korps repulsed all Soviet attacks against the XIV. Armee-Korps flank and along with 198.Inf.Div. had reached the Pavlograd area, continuing to protect the exposed flank. The 60.Inf.Div. had meanwhile occupied Zaporozhe.

Beginning on 5 October, the Italian units also began to move towards the Voltsctya River. Their march was slowed by bad weather and by the lack of trucks. On 6 October, the 'Pasubio' was strung out between Pavlograd and Ulianovka. On 8 October, the 'Celere' extended the Italian deployment southward, as far as Yekaterinovka, while the 'Torino' concentrated at Kamenka. The CSIR headquarters moved from Dniepropetrovsk to Sinelnikovo. The new Italian defensive line behind the western bank of the Voltsctya extended for about 100 kilometers. In the 79th Infantry Regiment 'Roma' sector, the line extended further inward because of the presence of the Pavlograd bridgehead, which was tenaciously defended by the Soviets in an attempt to bar the Italo-German forces from the road to Stalino. From the bridgehead, the Soviets fired artillery and mounted counterattacks and patrols, forcing the Italian units to stay constantly on the alert and to engage in many firefights. The bad weather and the first snowfalls made the situation even more difficult.

Pavlograd bridgehead

In order to eliminate the Pavlograd bridgehead and to allow the units to march to the east, the German headquarters ordered an attack against the Soviet positions towards M. Baba and M. Riasnaya-Pavlograd, using the 198.Inf.Div., whose left flank was protected by Italian units. For this new offensive action, on 8 October Messe ordered the formation of a motorized group, the Colonna Garelli, commanded by Colonel Arduino Garelli, consisting of the 63rd 'Tagliamento' Blackshirt Legion (minus the LXIII Battalion which was attached to the 'Pasubio'), a 105/32 group of the 30th Raggruppamento and a motorcycle company. The other groups of the 30th Raggruppamento were engaged in supporting the German 198.Inf.Div.. While the German division attacked, the

1   As of 5 October 1941, it officially became 1.Panzerarmee.

Italian cavalrymen in Russia, autumn 1941. (USSME)

An Italian cavalry column on the march in Russia, autumn 1941. (USSME)

left wing of the 'Pasubio', the 79th Infantry Regiment 'Roma', was also to move to the right bank of the Voltsctya.

The attacks against the Soviet bridgehead which began on 9 October went well, although Soviet counterattacks prevented the German forces from advancing past Mogila Baba. At that point, the German headquarters decided to commit the Colonna Garelli to flank the enemy positions at Pavlograd on the left. As initial objectives, the villages of Miziritc and Mavrina were selected. The attack by the Blackshirts began on the morning of 10 October against Mizritc, finding the position well defended by barbed wire entanglements and trenches. Despite strong resistance offered by troops of the 15th Rifle Division, the position was wiped out by Italian troops around noontime. Seeing the positive results, the commander of 198.Inf.Div., General der Infanterie Otto Röttig, ordered the Italian force to continue the attack towards the village of Mavrina and the railway line. The Soviets resisted doggedly there as well, but in the end their positions were broken into and the Italians also made it across a deep antitank ditch and a thick line of barbed wire. The Soviets were forced to withdraw, suffering heavy losses and leaving behind a large quantity of weapons and equipment.

The attacks resumed the following day with the seizure of the railroad bridge, while German troops reached close to the road bridge that the Soviets had blown up. This unforeseen circumstance prevented the immediate conquest of Pavlograd and it was then that the Italian I Bridge Battalion came upon the scene and was soon able to throw up a bridge allowing other units of the force to cross the river and to take positions on the left bank. The commander of 198.Inf.Div. praised the valor of the Italian units in a special order:

Italian soldiers armed with Model 38 rifles attacking Soviet positions, October 1941. (USSME)

In three days of combat the Colonna Garelli with the 63rd 'Tagliamento' Legion commanded by Consul Nicchiarelli and the 2nd Bersaglieri Motorcycle Company led by Captain Tanganelli – shoulder to shoulder with troops of the 198th Infantry Division – broke into the well-fortified and tenaciously defended bridgehead in front of Pavlograd, clearing out the villages of Mizritc and Mavrina and pushing the enemy out of the Woltscya area. The batteries of the 30th Raggruppamento commanded by Colonel Matiotti effectively supported the action as well as the German infantry and, with the help of their accurate fire, contributed to the victory. I express to the above-named commanders and to their valorous troops my full recognition and at the same time my comradely thanks in the name of my division and give my best thanks for a new military glory until our final common victory.

After having eliminated the Pavlograd bridgehead, the 'Pasubio' replaced the 198.Inf.Div. and extended its defensive sector to the left, while the 'Celere' replaced the 'Wiking', also extending its lines to the south as far as Gulay Pole. In the meantime, 1.Panzerarmee had continued its advance towards the Sea of Azov and its forward elements had reached Berestovoye and Mariupol. In collaboration with 11.Armee, the Soviet 9th Army had been defeated.

Conquest of the Donets Basin

While fighting was still going on in the Pavlograd bridgehead, on 8 October 1.Panzerarmee headquarters had been ordered to continue the offensive towards Taganrog, Rostov and Stalino and in particular, III.Armee-Korps was to occupy Taganrog and establish a bridgehead at Rostov. XIV. Armee-Korps was to protect the left flank of III.Armee-Korps. XXXXIX.Gebirgs-Armeekorps was to attack in the Stalino area. The CSIR was to protect the northern flank of the army and follow the movements of XXXXIX.Gebirgs-Armeekorps.

According to army orders, the CSIR represented the northern wing of 1.Panzerarmee and was to take up positions between XXXXIX.Gebirgs-Armeekorps to the south and 1.Armee to the north. It had a dual mission: cover the army's left flank and along with XXXIX.G-AK invest the Stalino industrial zone, having as its primary objective the major rail hub and its large station.

Stalino Maneuver

The change by the CSIR units from a defensive deployment to an offensive stance was not simple, considering that some troops of the 'Torino' were still bogged down in the Tikonovka area, while the bulk of the unit, after exhausting marches on foot in rain, mud and snow, was regrouping in the Tatarka area. There was also the problem of the few bridges available over the Voltsctya River, most of which had been destroyed by the retreating Soviets. Thus, taking into account the disposition of the Italian divisions on the Voltsctya and the characteristics of the terrain and of the river, General Messe decided to dispatch the 'Celere' to the south with its mobile units that were more capable of marching over rough terrain and to send the motorized and truck-borne forces to the north, where the ground was more suitable for vehicular movement. In particular, the 'Celere' was to advance towards Stalino and surround the city along with XXXXIX-Gebirgs-Armeekorps. The 'Pasubio', further to the rear, was to protect the northern flank and, if necessary, enlarge the CSIR's encircling move. The 'Torino', deployed in the second echelon, was to keep itself ready to intervene in critical areas.

On 13 October, troops of the 'Celere' began to cross the Voltsctya, the next day with the 'Savoia' and 'Novara' regiments reaching near the Yantshal River, ensuring control of the crossings and

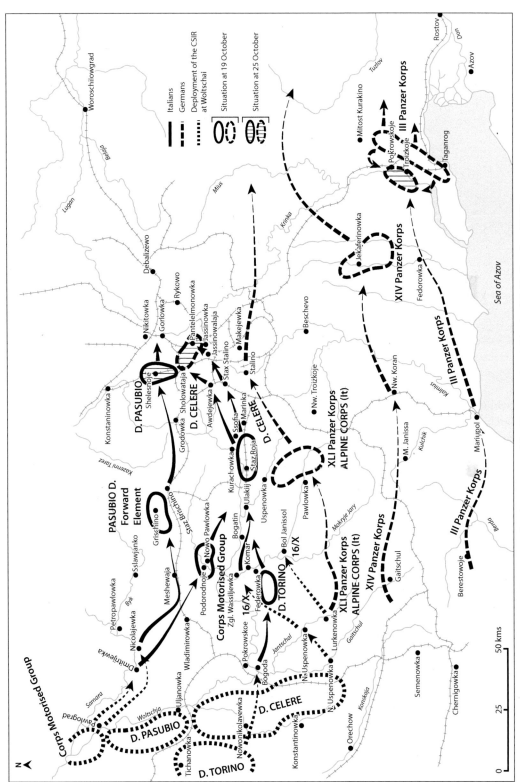

Operations for the capture of the Donets industrial basin (19–29 October 1941)

General Giovanni Messe (center, with binoculars in hand) with officers of the CSIR in Russia, autumn 1941. On the left is Colonel Chiarimonti, wearing glasses. (USSME)

establishing two bridgeheads, at Novo Uspenovka and Turkenovka. The 3rd Bersaglieri Regiment, marching on foot, was halted by bad terrain near the Gaitskul River, as were the motorized elements stalled further to the rear. The movement of 'Pasubio' troops depended on the bridge that had been destroyed at Pavlograd, which was being rebuilt by Italian engineers.

On 15 October, 'Celere' troops resumed their march, despite terribly adverse conditions, while those of the 'Pasubio' were stalled at Pavlograd while awaiting reconstruction of the bridge, which occurred on the morning of 16 October. To speed things up, on the 15th, by order of Colonel Chiarimonti, commander of the 80th Regiment, some of the division's troops, two infantry battalions, one from the 79th and one from the 80th Regiment, were transferred to the other bank of the river by alternate means. The 'Pasubio' headquarters quickly sent two more battalions of the 80th forward.

On the night of 16 October, disposition of the CSIR troops was as follows: the 'Celere' division had reached the Zgl.Vassilievka-Bol. Yanisol line. The 'Pasubio' found itself with the Chiarimonti column at Dmitrievka and Nikolayevka, with the division headquarters and two battalions of the 79th Infantry at Pavlograd. The 'Torino' was still on the march and was quite far behind.

In the meantime, 17.Armee had reached the Nikolayevka-Alexandrovka-Katerinevka line, XXXXIX.Gebirgs-Armeekorps forward elements had reached the Suchiye Yaly River, III. Armee-Korps, despite furious Soviet counterattacks, had managed to establish a bridgehead on the Mius River and XIV.Armee-Korps continued to protect the rear area and the left flank of III. Armee-Korps.

The advance continues

On 17 October, in accordance with new orders issued by Messe, the 'Celere' moved forward with its cavalry regiments, clashing with strong Soviet rear guard elements supported by artillery near the Suchiye Yaly River. The Italian cavalry units attacked Uspenovka with decision with the 'Novara' and at Ulakliy and Yaly with the 'Savoia', forcing the Soviets to retreat after having inflicted heavy casualties and having taken many prisoners. At the same time contact was made with XXXXIX Gebirgs-Armeekorps in preparation for the attack against Stalino.

The 'Pasubio' had reached Nikolayevka, where it was forced to halt because of the atrocious state of the roads and the blown bridge. The Chiarimonti column was however able to proceed, chasing the retreating Soviet troops, thus securing the left flank of the CSIR.

Between 18 and 19 October, there were no noteworthy actions, only shifting and regrouping of various units. On the night of the 18th, Messe issued orders for the attack against Stalino by the 'Celere' and for action by the other two divisions. For the attack against the Stalino station, 'Celere' headquarters formed two columns: the right-hand column, consisting of the 3rd Bersaglieri, which was initially assigned to seize the Sofia position and then Stalino, and a left-hand column, consisting of the 'Novara' Cavalry Regiment, which from the station at Roya was to advance to Kurakovka and Mog.Pereskop.

On 20 October, after an exhausting march under a pouring rain, the 3rd Bersaglieri occupied Sofia around 11:00, after having eliminated or captured Soviet rear guard elements in the position.

Italian bersaglieri entering Stalino, October 1941. (USSME)

Left: Soldiers of the Celere division entering Stalino, October 1941. (USSME)

Below: Italian bersaglieri motorcyclists at Stalino, October 1941. The lead motorcyclist is armed with a Breda Model 30 light machine gun. (Authors' collection)

The regiment then continued to pursue the enemy and around 20:00, with its XX Battalion, took the Stalino railway station and the rail hub. At the same time, the forward elements of XXXXIX. Gebirgs-Armeekorps broke into Stalino.

That same day, the Chiarimonti column of the 'Pasubio' opened the road through the Soviet troops that were in full retreat, reaching the station at Grishino and then towards evening, at Krasnoarmejskoye. The motorized detachment seized the position of Novo Pavlovka and soon after was engaged in fending off several counterattacks by Soviet units which, while pulling back, blew the bridge over the Voltsctya river. The 'Torino' division, by forced marches and amidst a thousand difficulties, reached the Mokrye Yaly River, between Fedorovka and Komar.

With the occupation of the city and station of Stalino, the first phase of the operation for the conquest of the Donets Basin was concluded. CSIR losses amounted to 61 killed, 143 wounded and 8 missing in action.

Gorlovka Maneuver

With Stalino taken, it was necessary to continue operations to conquer the entire Donets industrial basin, with its rich coal and iron deposits and its chemical and metallurgical industrial complexes. In order to secure control of the area the positions of Gorlovka, Rykovo and the Trudovaya station had to be captured. Gorlovjka and Rykovo represented not only important industrial and mining centers the conquest ensured greater security for holding Stalino, while the outlet for the Caspian oil pipeline was at Trudovaya. Headquarters 1.Panzerarmee assigned the capture of these three important locations to the CSIR. Messe thus issued new orders: the 'Celere' was to occupy the Rykovo-Gorlovka-Nikitovka area and the pipeline terminus at Trudovaya. The 'Pasubio' was to continue its advance eastward and then assume positions in the Yekaterinovka, Dylevka and Shelesnoye area, protecting the left flank and rear of the 'Celere'. The 'Torino' was to proceed on foot towards Stalino. At the same time, Messe ordered formation of rear guard detachments, consisting of corps elements, charged with road maintenance and protecting the lines of communication against any attacks by partisans, and also ordered disbanding the corps motorized group.

For the conquest of Rostov, 1.Panzerarmee ordered III. Armee-Korps to assume a defensive posture and to repel all enemy counterattacks, while XIV. Armee-Korps was to continue towards Golodayevka and Schachty and then to the south to encircle Rostov from the east and to XXXXIX. Gebirgs-Armeekorps to move to the Dmirievka-Diakovo area to protect the XIV. Armee-Korps rear area.

These new directives led the CSIR to face on its own the Soviet forces located in the area southwest of Voloshilovgrad, to prevent the occupation of Gorlovka and the threat to the 1.Panzerarmee flank and rear area.

The CSIR units then resumed their move and the 'Celere' Division, after having reached the positions at Jassinovataya and Avdievka on 22 October, respectively with the 'Savoia' and 'Novara' cavalry regiments and after having eliminated strong enemy rear guard elements, especially at Avdievka, on 24 October attacked the Skotovatoye-Panteleymonovka line, where Soviet resistance intensified markedly. According to information reported by recon patrols and gleaned from prisoner interrogations, they were facing at least three Soviet divisions reinforced by mortars and artillery batteries. Considering the presence of these numerous forces, Messe ordered the 'Celere' to assume defensive positions and to intensify reconnaissance activity.

Meanwhile, the Chiarimonti column of the 'Pasubio', after having moved past Grishino on 23 October, continued eastward and on the 25th took Shelesnoye after a tough battle against superior enemy forces. The next day, the Italian troops repulsed several counterattacks mounted by the Soviets. Between 28 and 29 October, the four battalions of the Chiarimonti column (three

Infantry and cavalry moving up to attack, November 1941. (USSME)

battalions of the 80th Infantry 'Roma' and one of the 79th), with a new leap forward, also seized the mineral center of Shelesnoye, taking the Soviets by surprise and forcing them to withdraw in all haste without having time to destroy the factories and distilleries, which were captured intact by the soldiers of the 'Pasubio'.

The advance of the 'Celere' and the Chiarimonti column created the premises for the attack against Gorlovka. The situation improved even more with the arrival of the other two battalions of the 79th Infantry at Shelesnoye. For the action, Messe was not able to count on the support of German units, because XXXIX. Gebirgs-Armeekorps had already begun to move to the south and the 17.Armee troops were still far behind. The 'Torino' division was still marching on foot and was unable to furnish any support. On 30 October, its units concentrated in the Yassinovataya area as corps reserve.

Awaiting the artillery units, which had been stalled along the road by mud, the 'Celere' and 'Pasubio' divisions continued to send out recon patrols to get information on the enemy forces: they were facing three Soviet divisions, the 74th, 262nd and 296th, as well as troops of the 5th, 56th, 62nd and 105th Soviet regiments.[2]

The attack begins

The attack began on 1 November when the 3rd Bersaglieri with a bold action surprised and overran the Soviet positions in the Rykovo industrial district and at 9:00 occupied that city. That same day, the 'Torino' resumed its march and reached the Krinka River in the Im.Karova-Korsuni area,

---

2   AA.VV., *Le Operazioni delle Unità Italiane al Fronte Russo (1941-1943)*, p. 119.

protecting the southern flank of the 'Celere'. The two regiments of the 'Pasubio' then attacked Gorlovka, the 80th Infantry from the west and the 79th Infantry from the south. Furious fighting ensued in the streets of the suburbs, fighting house-to-house against Soviet soldiers who fired from the windows with automatic weapons, but also against the partisans who fired from behind on the Italian troops who had penetrated into the town. On 2 November, 'Pasubio' troops of the 80th Regiment occupied the northern part of the city and the 79th the southern part, while a column of the 'Celere', consisting of the 'Lancieri di Novara', attacked from the southwest. After having been thrown out of Gorlovka, the Soviet troops dug in in Novo Gorlovka, continuing to resist. The 79th Infantry was thrown against them.

Also on 2 November, 1.Panzerarmee headquarters had ordered the CSIR to have a strong force advance as far as the Tschystakovo-Debalzevo Armenskoye station in order to protect the left flank of XXXXIX. Gebirgs-Armeekorps which was engaged in operations to take Rostov. In addition to having to carry out this new mission, at that time the CSIR still had to occupy Nikitovka, north of Gorlovka, and to secure the area between Rykovo and Gorlovka.

After having pulled the cavalry regiments from the front line to let them rest and because of the death of many horses, General Messe decided to assign the 81st Infantry Regiment 'Torino' to the 'Celere' to replace the 3rd Bersaglieri and to transfer the 82nd Infantry Regiment 'Torino' to Kol. Davido Orlovka to cover the flank of XXXXIX. Gebirgs-Armeekorps and to seize the area between Gorlovka and Rykovo with a combined action from the west and east.

On 5 November the 81st Infantry Regiment, led by the 'Celere' commander, reached Rykovo with two battalions, shifting the III Battalion to Solievka, between Rykovo and Gorlovka to protect the wide gap between the 'Pasubio' and the 'Torino'.

On 6 November the 82nd Infantry Regiment occupied Kol. Davido Orlovka, protecting the left flank of XXXXIX.Gebirgs-Armeekorps which was threatened by attacks by Soviet cavalry

Artillery in forward positions on the front line, November 1941. (USSME)

Italian soldiers preparing to attack an enemy position, November 1941. (USSME)

The soldier in the foreground is armed with a Breda Model 30 light machine gun; the other soldier is armed with a Carcano carbine, November 1941. (USSME)

formations coming from the north. The Italian troops were able to draw the enemy attacks on their positions, thus lessening the pressure on the left flank of the German corps.

On 5 November 1941, Rosario Randazzo, a young machine gunner whose origins were from Catania, did not give up fighting even though he had lost an arm after having been hit in full by an exploding mortar round. He was posthumously awarded the Gold Medal for Military Valor: 'Positioned to block a difficult position, he remained alone at a machine gun because all of the rest of the fire team had been put out of action, he continued intrepidly in action. With his right arm completely removed by a shard from a mortar round, he did not abandon his weapon and, while with his left hand he continued to hold onto the pistol grip, the pressed the trigger with his teeth, continuing to fire and slowing the advance of the enemy who had closed to within a few meters of his position until, hit by a burst of bullets, he died at his weapon, which had been dearer to him than life. Nikitovka'. Russian Front, 5 November 1941.

Battle for Nikitovka

Due to the deterioration of the situation on the left flank of the CSIR deployment, the capture of Novo Gorlovka by the 79th Infantry Regiment was not able to be achieved. This was because, after the 80th Infantry had occupied Gorlovka, its troops had continued on to the north towards Trudovaya. But, having reached the outskirts of Nikitovka, they were attacked on their left flank by strong Soviet units: the entire Soviet 74th Infantry Division, after having identified the wide gap existing between the Italian corps and 17.Armee, had attacked the left wing or the CSIR. 80th Infantry troops repulsed the enemy attacks, inflicting heavy losses on the Soviets, including an entire infantry battalion. Thus, on 6 November, Italian troops entered Nikitovka, taking up defensive positions. The Soviets resumed their attack, preceded by artillery fire, especially against the flanks of the 80th Infantry, bent upon surrounding the Italian regiment and wiping it out. But the Italian soldiers defended themselves doggedly, driving off the enemy attacks for five full days, even though ammunition began to run low and there was a shortage of food.[3]

The 'Celere' Division, committing the forces it had available, i.e., the 79th Infantry Regiment and elements of the 'Lancieri di Novara' Regiment, was sent to the rescue of the besieged force at Nikitovka. The I and II/79 were to attack the Rykovo-Gorlovka road towards the railway line, with the Mog. Dinnaya and Mog. Gossuduref positions as their objectives. The III/79 was to move astride the Gorlovka-Nikitovka road and make contact with the 80th. The 'Lancieri di Novara' were to establish a defensive front to the east, in front of Nova Gorlovka. The Italians moved to attack, but the Soviets held fast and were able to hold onto their positions, unleashing a violent fire with their artillery. Orders were given to hold onto the positions that had been reached, while the 3rd Bersaglieri (minus the XXV Battalion which was engaged at Rykovo) and the III/81 were sent in as reinforcements. Two new attacks were made in an attempt to free the 80th from the Soviet grip, but without any success. In the evening of 11 November, the situation remained unchanged.

On the morning of 12 November, help also came from the CSIR's 371st Fighter Squadron, which from Zaporozhe had displaced to the field at Stalino, providing needed help to the besieged force. The attack by Italian units was again halted by violent fire that was unleashed, mainly by machine guns that were well sited in dominant positions. In this latest attack the XVIII and XX bersaglieri battalions distinguished themselves, which, despite artillery and air support, were not able to reach Nikitovka. Some patrols of the III/79 managed to make contact with the 80th and taking

---

3   In order to make up for the lack of food, the soldiers were forced to eat the meat of mules that had been killed in the fighting.

An Italian infantry squad attacking Gorlovka, November 1941. (Authors' collection)

advantage of an unexpected lessening of Soviet pressure, the commander of the 80th attempted to have his men withdraw. The attempt failed because of intense fire thrown by the Soviets against the Nikitovka-Gorlovka road. At dusk, a fresh attempt was more successful and the entire regiment was able to pull back to Gorlovka in good order in the dark, bringing with them all of their wounded and all of their equipment. Losses however were heavy: in operations for the conquest of Nikitovka, the CSIR suffered 68 killed (4 officers), 206 wounded (17 officers) and 6 missing. In operations for the liberation of the besieged 80th at Nikitovka, there were 62 killed (5 officers), 347 wounded (10 officers) and 10 missing in action.

New tasks

Following the occupation of the Gorlovka and Rykovo industrial districts and the fighting at Nikitovka, the CSIR's summer-fall operational cycle was concluded. Since October, on the Voltsctya front, Messe had informed 1.Panzerarmee headquarters, through the German liaison officer, that it was not possible to continue on past the Donets Basin and asked to know what plans the German headquarters had for the future employment of the Italian units. Messe was concerned about the lack of vehicles and winter gear for his troops and was not able to follow the German forces in any further eastward advance. The troops needed a period of rest after the exhausting marches (in part on foot) as far as the Donets, and to be reorganized and to regain their offensive potential. Thus, for the moment, the Italian troops had to be engaged in consolidating the positions they had reached or, at best, to participate in limited operations.

After the fighting for Nikitovka, the CSIR commander decided to eliminate the salient held by the Soviets between Gorlovka and Rykovo in order to stabilize the front line. Meanwhile, 1.Panzerarmee forces had reached the Tuslov River and prepared to invest Rostov from the north and from the west. The XXXXIX.Gebirgs-Armeekorps had crossed the Mius River and further to the north the 97.Inf.Div. had occupied Artemovsk. On the CSIR front the Soviets continued their attacks in an attempt to drive a wedge between the Italian corps and 17.Armee.

On 17 November, 1.Panzerarmee headquarters ordered the CSIR headquarters to exploit the success achieved by the southern wing of 17.Armee in the Artemovsk area, continuing the advance

Italian soldiers attacking a factory in Gorlovka, November 1941. (Authors' collection)

An Italian patrol examining the ground around a recently captured position, November 1941. (USSME)

to the east, with the Gorodicce-Seterovka line as its objective, and to employ at least one division near the Rassipnaya station to protect the northern flank of the army, from that location as far as Gorlovka. General Messe quickly replied to the army commander, stating that based on orders received on the 17th, he could at best deploy some 'Celere' motorized units to the Rassipnaya area and with some elements of the 'Torino' division, make a limited attack towards Ubescicce.

On 18 November, after having informed 1.Panzerarmee headquarters of the condition of the CSIR, Messe ordered the 'Torino' to attack at 9:00 on 19 November, with its right wing, towards Ubescicce in order to hit the Soviet positions from the rear. To that end, the commander of the 'Torino', General Luigi Manzi, set out the following attack plan:

• fix the enemy with the left wing, that is, with the 81st Infantry, and force the Ubescicce sector with the right wing, that is to say the 82nd Regiment;
• pivot on Hill 102.3 and, securing the flank on the east, fall with the 82nd Infantry on the rear of the enemy deployment, which is facing the 81st.[4]

Battle for Ubescicce

During the night between 18 and 19 November, the 'Torino' infantry battalions and artillery groups began to move to their attack positions. Against Ubescicce, acting in the first echelon, were the I and II/82 Infantry, supported respectively by the II and III groups of the 52nd Artillery, and in the second echelon, the III/82. In the Rykovo area were the I and II/81, supported by the I Group of the horse artillery regiment and by the 7th Battery of the 52nd Artillery. In support was the III Group of the horse artillery regiment and the I/52 under the orders of the divisional artillery commander, Colonel Giuseppe Ghiringhelli.

At dawn the completely snow-covered ground was blanketed by extensive fog banks which hampered the artillery, which at a certain point had to cease its preparatory fire in order to avoid hitting friendly troops. The infantry went on the assault and the 81st Infantry troops clashed with the enemy forces on the ridge of Hill 182.2, while troops from the 82nd Infantry eliminated the forward elements of the Soviet line, then closing in on the centers of resistance in Ubescicce. The infantrymen of the I and III battalions of the 82nd attacked with fixed bayonets, seizing the houses on the outskirts of town, taking up positions along the Balavin River. Because of the frozen surface of the lake which the river formed near the village, they had to halt. In addition, heavy machine gun and mortar fire erupted from the southern bank. Attempts were made to overcome this barrier of ice and fire, both frontally as well as with a maneuver on the flanks, but without any success. Towards evening, the intensity of the fighting ebbed. At 20:00, in view of the inability to make any more progress, the regiment was ordered to return to its departure positions. During the night the Soviets sent out several recon patrols and also tried an attack which was quickly repulsed by the Italians.

On 20 November, to satisfy a request by 1.Panzerarmee to send at least one division to the area of the Rassipnaia station, General Messe ordered the headquarters of the 'Celere' Division to form a motorized column with the 3rd Bersaglieri, two 47/32 antitank companies, the LXII Group (105/32), the III Group (75/27) of the 'Torino', two 20mm antiaircraft batteries and to send them to the Rassipnaia station area the next day, with the mission to protect, in cooperation with XXXXIX.Gebirgs-Armeekorps, the left flank of 1.Panzerarmee. The 'Celere' horse-mounted units were subordinated directly to CSIR commander, who used them to form a special group to

---

4   AA.VV.: *Le Operazioni delle Unità Italiane al Fronte Russo (1941-1943)*, p. 128.

Bersaglieri in a defensive
position doing their best
to shelter from the cold,
November 1941. (USSME)

Italian soldiers during an
attack against a Soviet
position, November 1941.
(USSME)

be used in case of emergency. In addition, to ease the connection between the 'Torino' division and the 'Celere' motorized column, Messe assigned a cavalry squadron to the 'Celere', located at Kol. Ivan Orlovka.

Position Warfare

During this period the Italian units were engaged in repulsing continuous Soviet attempts to break through, but at the same time to launch counterattacks to adjust the front line, all of this under extreme conditions, aggravated by the increasingly intense cold and the lack of suitable vehicles and equipment. Soviet attempts to break through were persistent especially on the 'Pasubio' front, where the enemy hoped to envelop the left wing of the CSIR, which was still exposed because of the wide gap that separated it from 17.Armee. Thus, on 27 November, Messe ordered the 'Pasubio' to extend its deployment further west, occupying the station at Shelesnoye. To that end, a tactical group was organized, subordinate to the 'Pasubio', with the 63rd Legion, which had already been assigned to reinforce the 'Pasubio' and deployed north of Gorlovka, with a squadron of the 'Lancieri di Novara' Regiment and with a battery of the II horse artillery group. These units shifted to the new positions on 28 November.

In the meantime, 1.Panzerarmee forces had continued their advance towards Rostov and on 20 November, III.Armee-Korps occupied the city. But this was only a temporary success, because at the same time the Soviets launched a massive counteroffensive, catching the Germans completely by surprise. Committing numerous divisions supported by a large number of tanks, the Soviets forced the Germans to withdraw as far as the River Mius. Enemy attacks continued and began to affect the positions of the CSIR as well.

On 30 November 1941, the CSIR was deployed between 17.Armee to the north and XXXXIX. Gebirgs-Armeekorps to the south, from Shelesnoye station to the station at Rassipnaia with:

- the 'Pasubio' Division, reinforced by the 63rd Legion, a squadron of the 'Lancieri di Novara', a 105/32 group and an 75/27 battery from the horse cavalry regiment, from the Shelesnoye station to Mogila Pavlovskaya;
- the 'Torino' division, minus the III Gruppo (75/27) of the 52nd Artillery, reinforced by a 105/32 group and two groups of the horse artillery regiment, from Mogila Pavlovskaya to the Baskovski station;
- the 'Celere' motorized column, reinforced by a 105/32 group, by the III Gruppo (75/27) of the 'Torino' and by a squadron from the 'Savoia' Regiment, from the Baskovski station to the Rassipnaia station.

The CSIR aviation element was still largely deployed at Zaporozhe, with a fighter squadron, an observation squadron and the headquarters of LXXI Group at Stalino, where antiaircraft assets included the XIX 75/46 group and the 97th Battery with 20mm guns.

On 18 November, the CSIR tactical headquarters had moved to Yassinovataya, where antiaircraft defense was provided by the IV 75/46 group and the 95th Battery with its 20mm guns.

Battle for Kazepetovka

The new CSIR defensive front, about 50 kilometers wide, in addition to not being covered by sufficient forces was also lacking in any type of natural obstacles. The front line passed through the Gorlovka-Rykovo industrial zone, marked by many urban areas and mining facilities, causing a wide dispersion of forces. In addition, there was a 20-kilometer gap between the left wing of the CSIR and 17.Armee. It was thus necessary to plan an offensive action to improve the defensive positions prior to the coming winter. The action, which has passed into history as the battle of Kazepetovka, was the CSIR's final offensive in 1941. In order to activate it, General Messe transferred the 63rd Legion and the III Group of the horse artillery regiment to the 'Celere' sector to reinforce its left wing. The offensive's objective was to shorten the defensive front and with the Italian units to close up the deployment between 1.Panzerarmme with that of 17.Armee. The action was planned as a pincer movement by the right wing of 1.Panzerarmee, represented by 111. Infanterie-Division and the left wing of 1.Panzerarmee, consisting of CSIR units. One was to move from northwest to southeast, the other from west to east. The common objective was the Debalzevo area. To better coordinate operations, 17.Armee was to have begun the offensive a day earlier than the CSIR, which that day was to support the action with its artillery.

The orders to the CSIR units, issued between 3 and 4 December, stated that the objective of the offensive was to eliminate enemy forces facing them and to advance the 'Torino' deployment as far as the line designated as 'Z', on the ridge between the Bolschik gulch and the Sorrotscya gulch, establishing contact to the north with 17.Armee positions in the Debalzevo area and to the south with the positions of the 'Celere'.

On 5 December, while the right wing of 17.Armee began its attack with its objective the Luganskaya-Yekaterinovka line, the left wing of the CSIR also began to move. In the 'Pasubio' sector, numerous patrols of the 79th and 80th Infantry and of the 'Novara' squadron, supported by artillery fire, advance northward, astride the Gorlovka/Nikitovka railway line. Having reached east of the railway, they came under Soviet fire, suffering casualties. To the west of the same line, enemy positions were found empty and a patrol from the 'Novara' managed to push as far as Petrovka, making contact with elements of 17.Armee. In the 'Torino' sector, patrols from the 81st Infantry spotted an enemy position on Hill 128.2, from which massive fire from automatic weapons and artillery emanated. Based on these recon patrols, at 7:00 on 6 December the Italian attack columns advanced towards their respective objectives.

In the 'Torino' division's attack, along the Rykovo-Kazepetkova ridge, astride the railway, the division commander, General Manzi, had divided his forces into two columns and a reserve. The left-hand column, consisting of the 81st Infantry, the XXVI Mortar Battalion, an antitank company, a horse-drawn artillery group, an engineer platoon and a flamethrower squad, was to capture the village of Kazepetovka, to the west of the station. The column on the right, consisting of two battalions of the 82nd Infantry, the III Gruppo of horse-drawn artillery, an antitank company, an engineer platoon and a flamethrower squad, was to seize the village of Kazepetovka to the east of the station. Three battalions and a squadron group were in reserve. Facing the Italians, the Soviets had fielded the 95th Guards Regiment, with three battalions, reinforced by several special companies and two cavalry squadrons.

In the first phase of the attack, due to the cold, most of the Italian automatic weapons jammed and it was only possible to open fire with rifles and 81mm mortars. The left column was able to get close to the ridge of Hill 129.8, but after having been taken under enemy fire coming from Hill 128.2 and from the village of Nekomitovka, it was forced to halt. With a new leap forward, the II/81 was able to reach Hill 135.7 at dusk.

During this latest fighting, Lieutenant Pietro Bernardini of the 82nd was killed alongside his 47/32 antitank guns after having been wounded three times. He was awarded the Gold Medal for Military Valor posthumously with the following citation:

> Commander of an antitank platoon, who had previously distinguished himself in action by his abilities and valor, during bitter fighting he brought his unit quickly and decisively past the line of riflemen to better hit the slits of the insidious enemy positions which were strongly

An 81mm mortar in battery, December 1941. (USSME)

holding up the advance. With one gun destroyed and the crew killed, even though he was first wounded in an arm and then in a leg, he dragged himself to the other gun and personally directed its fire, destroying an enemy position. Assaulted in a counterattack by overwhelming enemy forces who threated to surround him, and wounded a third time, even though weakened by a loss of blood, he remained calmly at his post, encouraging by word and example the only two surviving gun crew to fight to the end. To the enemy, by now very near, who asked him to surrender, he replied with fire. Mortally wounded, he fell alongside his gun which he had strenuously defended.

Wolinzewo, Hill 129 (Russian front), 6 December 1941.

That same day of 6 December, another casualty was Gino Arnolfi, a machine gunner, also from the 82nd, while for the nth time he shuttled back and forth between his position and a bonfire, which was burning behind a small wall, over which he was thawing out his machine gun. He was awarded the Gold Medal for Military Valor posthumously with the following citation:

Machine gunner who had already distinguished himself in previous actions, with his squad having entered in action, at the head of his team he threw himself boldly forward and reached an uncovered and intensely fired upon position from which he could better direct his fire.

A flamethrower in action during an attack against Soviet positions, December 1941. (USSME)

With the operating parts of the automatic weapons frozen because of the intense cold, with great disregard for danger, for four times he carried his machine gun to the rear to thaw it out over the fire, bring it quickly back to the line and resume fire. All of the other members of his team having been killed, and he himself wounded in one arm, he continued to fight animatedly. Seeing that a large enemy force threatened a counterattack against the battalion's left flank, even though in pain and exhausted, he was able by supreme effort to shift the gun and its tripod toward the enemy who he hit even though he was wounded once again. Hit mortally for a third time, he fell with his weapon, the faithful companion to his heroic behavior, in his hands.

Wolinzewo, Hill 129 (Russian front), 6 December 1941.

Still on that same day, the troops of the 'Pasubio' had occupied Sayzevo, Kalininsk, the Nikitovka station and the Novo Kayuta ridge, while the 'Celere' had captured Novo Petropavlovka, Kol. Ivan Orlovka and Ivanovskiy.

On 7 December, at 7:30, the 81st and 82nd Infantry again went on the attack: advancing side by side and making contact at Balka Oskad, the Italians threw the Soviets back thanks in part to artillery fire, then continuing eastward to Kazepetovka. Fighting continued until evening, when the last pockets of enemy resistance in a group of houses southwest of Kazepetovka were eliminated. At the same time, the 79th Infantry took the hamlet of Novo Kayuta.

Killed during the fighting at Balka Oskad was Second Lieutenant Umberto Nicosia of the 82nd Infantry while he was leading his mortar platoon in an assault. He was decorated with the Gold Medal for Military Valor posthumously with the following citation:

He refused a period of rest for physical disability in order to stay with his regiment and in numerous actions was an example of valor. During a prolonged fight, in difficult climatic conditions and even though stalled by violent resistance, at the head of his mortar platoon he drew up close to the enemy's positions. Wounded a first time, down to a few men and surrounded, he fearlessly persisted fighting. Freed by an attack by other troops, having seen a machine gunner killed, he took his place at the weapon in order to maintain continuity of fire. Along with a few survivors, even though weakened by a loss of blood and wounded a second time, he mustered the energy to make another bound forward and to audaciously attack by throwing hand grenades. Having reached the objective, he fell mortally wounded and, before dying, expressed his pride at being able to die for his country with the vision of an enemy in flight.

Balka Oskad (Russian front), 7 December 1941.

On 8 December the attack against Kazepetovka resumed: after overwhelming the Soviet resistance, the 81st and 82nd Infantry made contact with the 79th, which after furious combat with the enemy rear guard, had occupied the village two hours earlier. Patrols also established contact with the 111.Inf.Div., which in the meantime had captured Debalzevo. However, the centers of enemy resistance at Nekotimovka, Sfyno, Rayevka and Yelenovka still had to be eliminated.

With the capture of Kazepetovka, the center of gravity of the fighting shifted to the east and therefore General Messe ordered the 'Pasubio' division to move to Rykovo, in the area southeast of the railway line and for the 'Novara' squadron, as reinforcement for the 'Pasubio', to return to its parent regiment. The 'Torino' division was ordered to complete the occupation of Line 'Z' the next day, eliminating the last pockets of Soviet resistance in the Rykovo area. The 79th Infantry was to remain in Kazepetovka attached to the 'Torino'.

Based on orders he had received, General Manzi, commander of the 'Torino', planned to attack with two battalions of the 81st Infantry towards Line 'Z', making contact with German units near the Bulavin station. To eliminate the remaining enemy forces, he planned a combined action by two columns, one consisting of two battalions of the 82nd Infantry coming from the north, and the other, led by General De Carolis,[5] commander of the divisional infantry, consisting of the II/81 and the I/79, two batteries of the I/52 and of the II/52 Artillery and a flamethrower detachment, coming from the south.

---

5   Ugo De Carolis, born in Capua on 7 October 1887. After having attended the Royal Academy of Modena and having graduated as a Second Lieutenant, he took part in the war in Libya with the 15th Regiment 'Cavalleggeri di Lodi', being wounded in fighting around Zuetina in March 1914. Following a period of convalescence, he returned to service in Libya, this time attached to the 18th Regiment 'Cavalleggeri di Piacenza', where he distinguished himself particularly in fighting in July 1915 at Gabr Abdalla, earning a Bronze Medal for Military Valor. At the beginning of the Great War and with promotion to captain, De Carolis was placed in command of the 19th Bombard Battery of the 30th Artillery Field Regiment. On Monte San Michele, which was bitterly contested, in August 1916 he earned a second Bronze Medal for Military Valor. Between October and November 1916, deployed with his unit on the Veliki, he was awarded the Silver Medal for Military Valor. Before the end of the war, he also received a War Cross for Military Valor during the fighting which followed the defeat at Caporetto near Dosso Faiti. With the war ended, he was promoted to major and then to lieutenant colonel, De Carolis was given new and increasingly prestigious postings: first as commander of the 9th Regiment 'Cavalleggeri di Firenze' and then of the 14th Regiment 'Cavalleggeri di Alessandria'. He was also given the added role of judge at the Military Tribunal of Florence and, from 1935, command of the 19th Regiment 'Cavalleggeri Guide'. The outbreak of the Second World War found him, as a brigadier general, commanding the 'Celeri' Troops School. Then, in June 1941, he was assigned command of the 'Torino' Infantry Division's infantry troops.

A Breda Model 37 machine gun of the 3rd Bersaglieri in position, December 1941. The Model 37 proved to be reliable even under harsh conditions in Russia. (USSME)

On 9 December, at 8:00, the Italian troops attacked, quickly running into stiff resistance near the enemy positions. Thanks to action by the flamethrowers, the 81st Infantry managed to repel an enemy counterattack and to dig in for the night in the area of the railway gate crossing about two kilometers east of Kazepetovka. Meanwhile, while the 82nd Infantry was marching towards Sofyno Rayevka, the column under De Carolis attacked the village of Volinzievo, passed through it and continued on to the Sofyno Rayevka and Yelenovka basin, occupying it along with troops of the 82nd. The Soviets, who were well positioned along the ridges that dominated the basin, temporarily stalled the Italian advance. Furious house-to-house fighting ensued, with the Italian soldiers finally able to conquer the villages of Nekotimovka and Sofyno Rayevka.

In the morning of 10 December, fighting resumed, particularly in the northern area, where the 81st Infantry was engaged in fending off violent enemy counterattacks, thanks to support by artillery and mortars. Also in the Yelenovka basin, the Soviets continued to resist doggedly, putting a brake on progress by Italian units. In order to give momentum to the offensive, Messe ordered a battalion of the 80th Infantry to move from Rykovo and to occupy Vessieli, making contact with troops of the 'Celere'. On 11 December, the troops settled in to the positions they had reached, awaiting further orders from Messe, which arrived around noon and which set out the actions for the following day: the 'Torino', reinforced with the 79th Infantry, was to resume the attack against line 'Z'. the 'Pasubio' was to ensure formidable fire support with its artillery. The 'Celere' was to conduct recon patrols along the entire front. The aviation element was to protect the attack by 'Torino' and carry out reconnaissance in front of the 'Celere' sector.

Italian soldiers fighting in a village, December 1941. (USSME)

Final assault

For the final attack, three columns were organised:

- a northern column, commanded by Colonel Rocco Biasioli, commander of the 79th Infantry, consisting of two battalions of the 79th, one battalion of the 80th, two battalions of the 81st, the XXVI Mortar Battalion, a 105/32 battery, an engineer platoon and a flamethrower squad, which was to deploy along the line of Hill 144.2 and Hill 187.9 and to make contact at the Bulavin station with the German troops at Debalzevo.
- a central column, commanded by Colonel Evaristo Fioravanti, commander of the 82nd Infantry, consisting of two battalions of the 82nd, the III Gruppo of horse artillery, the II Gruppo of the 52nd Artillery (minus one battery) and a flamethrower squad, which was to seize the northern ridge of the Yelenovka basin and the stretch between the eastern edge of the village and Hill 114.3, making contact with the northern column on Hill 187.9.
- a southern column, commanded by Major Buglione, commander of the II/81, consisting of the II/81, the II/82, a battery of the I/52 artillery and a battery of the II/52, which was to complete

Cover of the Domenica del Corriere, 21 December issue, commemorating the death of General de Carolis. (Authors' collection)

the capture of the southern ridge of the Yelenovka basin, then to reach that same village from the southwest.

General De Carolis was assigned to coordinate the actions of the central and southern columns.

On the other side, the Soviets fielded two regiments of the 73rd Division along the railway line between Kazepetovka and Debalzevo and the 95th Guards Regiment in the Grosniy-Yelenovka area.

On the morning of 12 December, the Italian columns moved to attack their respective objectives. A heavy fog hampered the advance of the troops. The leading elements of the northern column, advancing under massive fire from Soviet mortars, reached the area of the Bulavin gate crossing, where they were attacked by two squadrons of Cossack cavalry which appeared unexpectedly out of the fog. The Italians reacted quickly and after a wild clash, the Cossacks were eliminated. Meanwhile, two companies of the II/79 advanced towards Grosniy, where they were stalled by heavy enemy resistance. The men of the central column also ran into significant difficulty in the capture of Yelenovka because of the fog, as did the southern column.

General De Carolis then decided to shift Major Buglione's column to the north and along with the central column, was able to reach the ridge and the mines north of Yelenovka. During this last move, General De Carolis himself was killed while he was personally leading a reconnaissance patrol. For valor shown in the field, he was awarded the Gold Medal for Military Valor posthumously. 'Noble and heroic figure of soldier and commander, during five months of war he was a constant and luminous example of bravery and heedless of danger. Divisional infantry commander, during a bitter battle which lasted seven days, he lived every hour amongst his soldiers. On the seventh day of the strenuous fight, while, as always, in the front line with the infantrymen, spurring them on by example and action, a machine gun burst cut off his life. He sealed with supreme sacrifice in the field his noble existence which was all dedicated to duty and to the ideal of the motherland. Russian front, July-December 1941.'

His death elicited much admiration in Italy, so much so that La Domenica del Corriere of 21 December 1941 dedicated its cover with the following caption: 'The heroic death of General Ugo De Carolis. In the fields of the Donets, while proceeding in the front line, at the head of a point patrol, the 'Torino' Division infantry commander was hit in the chest by a bullet. The soldiers called him General Avanti [General Forward, translator's note] because always, during the fighting, he went ahead of the artillery, ahead of the mortars, ahead of the machine gun teams, ahead of the recon patrols. He went to see, he went to see where his troops would pass'.

The German headquarters also recognized De Carolis's valor and sacrifice, awarding him the Knight's Cross of the Iron Cross posthumously on 9 February 1942.

End of the fighting

After having lost the railway crossing and the Bulavin station and Yelenovka, the Soviets began to withdraw in the Olkovatka area. Other clashes followed and between 13 and 14 December the northern column occupied the villages of Grosniy and Savielevka, while the central and southern columns, occupied the villages of Yelenovka and Usbescicce. Thus, after almost ten days of hard and bitter fighting, the battle for Kazepetovka was over: CSIR losses amounted to 135 dead (11 officers), 523 wounded (31 officers) and 10 missing (1 officer). There were also 915 cases of frostbitten limbs.

While the Italian units were still engaged in the final sweeps between the positions that had just been taken, an order came from 1.Panzerarmee headquarters for the CSIR to make a new leap forward to the east to shorten the front line and to establish contact with IV.Armee-Korps in the

Debalzevo area. Naturally, Messe was strongly opposed to this new order, claiming logistic difficulties that could not be easily overcome.

Meanwhile, the corps deployment was readjusted, with the 'Pasubio' to the north, the 'Torino' in the center and the 'Celere' to the south. In the days that followed, the Italian troops were engaged in reinforcing and improving their positions in order to defend themselves from any enemy attacks but to defend themselves from the cold as well.

6

The Christmas Battle

With fighting at a halt in order to reorganize the front line in early December, General Messe took advantage of a few days of relative calm in an attempt to reorganize the troops and their positions in preparation for the winter season. However, the intelligence services reported alarming news regarding an imminent new Soviet offensive in the CSIR sector during the Christmas timeframe. In reality, during that time the Soviets had launched a massive counteroffensive across the entire Eastern Front, from Leningrad to Rostov. In particular, in the southern sector the Soviets intended to overwhelm the German forces in the Kharkov area and then eliminate the other Axis forces as far as the Black Sea.

In the CSIR sector, the sector that was most vulnerable to enemy attacks was that of the 'Celere', not only because in that sector had a linkup been made with XXXXIX. Gebirgs-Armeekorps, but mainly because a breakthrough in that direction would have opened the way for the Soviets along the major Kharzysk highway, making it possible to quickly reach Stalino and to threaten the rear area of 1. Panzerarmee. In addition, there were not enough forces to defend the wide stretch of the front even though the militia legion had been attached to the 'Celere'; in practice, to defend more than twenty kilometers of the front there were the 3rd Bersaglieri Regiment (three reduced strength battalions), two militia battalions and four artillery groups.

On the other side, the Soviets had two infantry divisions, reinforced with other units and artillery batteries. Since 20 December, air reconnaissance had reported numerous trains coming from the east as well as having spotted strong enemy troop concentrations in the Tchernukino-Nikischin area, facing the 'Celere' and at the juncture point with XXXXIX. Gebirgs-Armeekorps. As mentioned previously, the intelligence services continued to claim that a Soviet attack was imminent at the juncture point. Enemy intentions were to break through the center, between Petropavloka and Novo Orlovka, aiming directly at Alexievo Orlovka and to sweep through the left flank of the CSIR with cavalry as far as Krinka.[1]

Because at that time the CSIR had no reserves, 1.Panzerarmee moved a counterattack force into the 'Celere' sector, consisting of Infanterie-Regiment 318 (213.Sicherungsdivision), a parachute regiment and a panzer unit being formed with 75 tanks.

On 23 December, in anticipation of the Soviet attack, operations order Number 63 was issued by 1.Panzerarmee headquarters, which called for the formation of two operational groups:

- one defense group, led by the commander of XXXXIX.Gebirgs-Armeekorps, General der Gebirgstruppe Rudolf Konrad, including the forces deployed in the 'Celere' sector, which were to hold out to the last man;
- a counterattack group, led by the CSIR commander, with the 'Pasubio' and 'Torino' divisions.

---

1   AA.VV.: *Le Operazioni delle Unità Italiane al Front Russo (1941-1943)*, p. 154. This information was later confirmed by documents found on several Soviet prisoners captured during the battle.

Colonel Aminto Caretto on the left, speaking with the deputy commander of the Celere division, Colonel Carlo Lombardi. (USSME)

By a following order by Messe issued on 24 December, the counterattack group was divided into two subsectors: the subsector on the right was led by Colonel Aminto Caretto,[2] commander of the

---

2   Aminto Caretto was born in Crescentino in the province of Vercelli on 7 October 1893. Having joined the Regio Esercito, in 1914 he was promoted to second lieutenant in the bersaglieri corps. During the Great War, he fought with the 4th Bersaglieri Regiment. Promoted to captain in the 14th Bersaglieri Regiment, he was wounded on Monte Zebio in June 1916. He returned to active service in 1917, and the following year he was assigned to an arditi unit, the XXVI, and distinguished himself during the Battle of the Solstice in June 1918. In 1922 he was transferred to the Regio Corpo truppe coloniali d'Eritrea (Royal Colonial Troop Corps of Eritrea), assigned to the X Eritrean Battalion, taking part between 1923 and 1926 in military operations in Cyrenaica and for the reconquest of the Gebel. After having received high praise, he returned to service with the 4th Bersaglieri and in 1928 was promoted to the rank of major. Transferred to the 11th and then to the 3rd Bersaglieri Regiment, once promoted to lieutenant colonel he was assigned to the Inspectorate of 'Celeri' Troops. Promoted to colonel on 1

3rd Bersaglieri, and that on the left, led by Colonel Carlo Lombardi, deputy commander of the 'Celere'.

The attack begins

At 6:40 on 25 December 1941, after a brief preparatory artillery fire, the Soviets attacked with infantry supported by tanks against the extreme left of the front held by the CSIR, in the sector held by the 63rd 'Tagliamento' Legion and later, against the center and the right, defended by the 3rd Bersaglieri. At the same time, perhaps as a diversionary move, two cavalry squadrons and an infantry company attacked the forward position at Vessieli, on the 'Torino' front. The forces defending there reacted quickly and mounted a counterattack with a company which moved from Yunyi Kommunar, forcing the Soviets to pull back. On the 'Celere' front bitter fighting broke out. After being able to breach the external defenses, the Soviets broke into the Italian positions, where several strongholds, after having been surrounded, continued to hold out until death. The battle broke up into furious close-quarter fighting. The Novo Orlovka position, held by a reinforced company of the 63rd 'Tagliamento' Legion, resisted to the end, not giving way until all of the officers had been killed or wounded.

'Novo Orlovka, held by a reinforced company of the LXXIX Battalion of the 63rd 'Tagliamento' Legion, attacked by two Russian battalions, was overwhelmed after tenacious and heroic resistance. All of the officers were killed or wounded. Lieutenant Ezio Barale, the only remaining officer, in the final moment of the fighting crawled to counterattack with a handful of men. Separated from his unit and surrounded by the enemy, he fought valorously until a burst felled him. Only a few men from the strongpoint of Novo Orlovka were able to pull back to Michailovka.[3]

Having taken Novo Orlovka, the Soviets continued on towards Krestovka; to avoid being surrounded, the forces defending it, headquarters of the 63rd Legion and a horse-drawn battery, withdrew fighting to Malo Orlovka. On this new position, thanks to supporting fire by nearby units of the 'Torino', the Italians halted the enemy advance.

At Ivanovskiy, defended by the XVIII Bersaglieri Battalion, the Soviets attacked with two infantry regiments and several cavalry squadrons; the bersaglieri fought for ten hours along with the gunners of the 5th Horse Battery, which after having fired all of their ammunition, continued to fight hand-to-hand. At 16:00, the defenders were able to open a breach between the Soviet units surrounding them, managing to withdraw towards Michailovka, where they continued fighting. Other Soviet troops attacked the village of Stosckvovo but were thrown back by the XX Bersaglieri Battalion.

In the right-hand sector of the defensive front, an infantry regiment from the Soviet 136th Division and cavalry squadrons attacked the positions at Petropavlovka and Rassipnaia. In the latter locality, defended by the XXV Bersaglieri Battalion, the Soviets were repulsed, while at Petropavlovka, held by the motorcycle battalion, after a bitter fight and attacked by clearly superior enemy forces, the Italians were forced to pull back to Rassipnaia.

While this fighting was going on along the 'Celere' front, units of the 'Pasubio' and 'Torino' engaged the Soviet 74th Infantry Division to prevent them from participating in an attack against the 'Celere'.

January 1940, in October of that year he assumed command of the 3rd Bersaglieri Regiment. In May 1941 he took part in the invasion of Yugoslavia and in the successive operations in the Balkans.

3   G. Messe, *La guerra al fronte russo*, pp. 138-140.

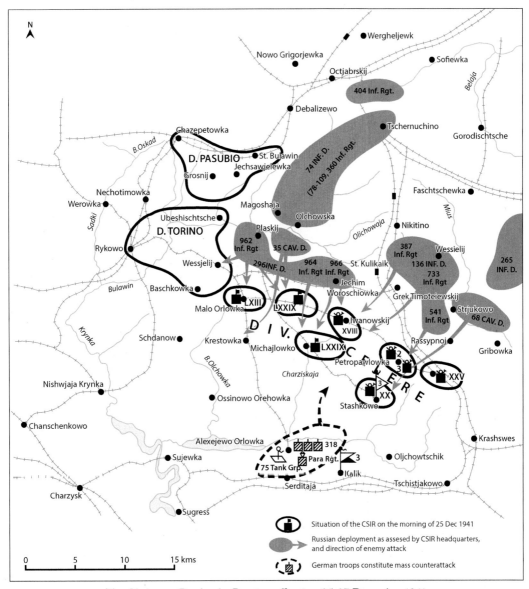

The Christmas Battle, the Russian offensive, 25-27 December 1941.

German counterattack

Around noon, XXXXIX.Gebirgs-Armeekorps headquarters issued orders for a counterattack that was to begin at 13:30 by Infanterie-Regiment 318 and by a detachment of the XVIII Bersaglieri Battalion, supported by tanks. The troops were to attack in two columns: two German battalions and the bersaglieri detachment were to move against Ivanovskiy, while the other German battalion was to move against Petropavlovka. The action at Ivanovskiy was successful, with the troops reaching the eastern edge of the village. The column that was aiming for Petropavlovka was, however, forced to fall back, stalled by the snow and by enemy resistance. When night fell, the

Blackshirts of the Tagliamento Legion in combat, December 1941. (USSME)

situation was as follows: the positions at Novo Orlovka, Krestovka and Petropavlovka had fallen into Soviet hands. Half of the position at Ivanovskiy had been retaken by the Italo-German force. The positions at Rassipnaia and Michailovka were still holding out.

In this latest round of fighting, bersagliere Guido Cassanelli of the 6th Regiment distinguished himself, falling at Novo Petropavlovka. He was awarded the Gold Medal for Military Valor post-humously, with the following citation:

> Ammunition bearer for an antitank gun during an attack by overwhelming enemy forces, he stubbornly defended his gun in obstinate resistance which he prolonged courageously, even though he had an arm seriously wounded by a shell fragment, engaging in a supreme effort against the enemy who surrounded him. Remaining alone, rather than surrender, he continued the unequal fight managing before being overcome to kill, in tragic hand-to-hand fighting, seven enemy soldiers on top of which he fell dead, riddled with wounds. This heroic sacrifice galvanized the resistance of the survivors allowing the situation to be stabilized.
>
> Novo Petropavlovka (Russian front), 25 December 1941.

At Petropavlovka, the chaplain of the 3rd Bersaglieri, Don Giovanni Mazzoni, bearer of the Gold Medal from the First World War, also fell. A bersagliere had been seriously wounded past the front line; two of his companions went forward to help him, but also came under enemy fire. Don Mazzoni then came to the rescue; while he was trying to climb over the top of the trench to give aid to the wounded soldier who continued to moan, the soldiers stopped him, warning

Soldiers with a Breda light machine gun in combat on a frozen river. (USSME)

him of the grave danger he was risking: 'But do you really think I can stay here, indifferent to the moaning of a man who is dying?' he said to the soldiers, who then answered, 'Then we are coming with you!'. Don Mazzoni looked them in the eye and then peremptorily said: 'No, I am going alone'. He threw himself out of the trench, running. Hit a first time, he continued to move forward until, hit again, he found the strength to drag himself as far as the sounded soldier, embracing him and dying with him. He was awarded the Gold Medal for Military Valor posthumously with the following citation:

Gold Medal for the War of 1915-1918, after having proudly requested and obtained assignment to a front-line unit engaged in bitter fighting, he gave continuous and clear testimony of his fervor as an apostle and of his temperament as a soldier fused together in a display of the most noble priestly attributes and of the highest daring and unparalleled self-denial. In days of desperate fighting, he shared with a rare spirit of sacrifice the heroism of a bersaglieri regiment bringing everyone, even in the greatest danger, the burning words of faith and the stirring voice of his courage. In an episode during the furious fighting, he became aware that a wounded soldier who had been stranded alone was calling for aid and, despite the fact that other attempts to reach the man had been bathed in blood, with admirable recklessness and awareness, rushed to aid the soldier, nor did he cease from his noble intent even when a bullet hit him in the side. Wounded once again mortally, with his last reserve of life, he surrendered to the sublime mysticism of his bravery and finally dying by his side. Admirable example of the highest virtues and of sublime awareness of the patriotic ideal.

Rassipnaia, Petropavlovka (Russian front) 1-26 December 1941.

That same day, Second Lieutenant Angelo Vidoletti[4] of the 3rd Bersaglieri also was killed, executed in cold blood by the Soviets after having been taken prisoner. He was awarded the Gold Medal for Military Valor posthumously, with the following citation:

> He twice refused to be repatriated so that he could remain in command of his platoon, which he had forged into a block of granite and led with skill and bravery in all of the actions during his battalion's long operational cycle. During a day of bitter fighting, heedless of the violent fire of enemy automatic weapons and mortars, by his enthusiasm he motivated his soldiers, going where the threat was the greatest. Wounded in the throat, he persisted in the action. Hit again in the chest by a burst from a machine gun, he refused to be brought to an aid station and continued to urge his surviving men to resist. Left on the field because of his serious wounds and captured by the enemy, facing a Soviet commissar who sought to question the officer, who proudly declined. Threatened with a revolver, he disdainfully lowered the armed hand of the commissar, bared his chest, showed his wounds and told him he was ready to follow him, but after having taken a few steps with extreme effort, he was barbarously executed by the vile adversary. Shining example of heroism and strong virtues as an Italian.
>
> Ivanovski (Russian front), 25 December 1941.

On 26 December, 'Celere' troops went on the counterattack along with German reserve units. At the same time, the 'Pasubio' attacked the Soviet positions between the high Bulavin and Timofeyevskiy to hit the flanks of the enemy who had left from the Olkovatka and Kurgan Ploskiy area. Meanwhile, soldiers from Inf.Rgt. 318 and the XVIII Bersaglieri Battalion recaptured a large portion of Ivanovskiy, with the Soviets still dug in in its northern part. The battalions of the 63rd Legion moving towards Novo Orlovka were stopped by a violent enemy attack. The II/Inf. Rgt. 318 and the XX Bersaglieri Battalion retook Petropavlovka, but the Soviets counterattacked shortly after, forcing the Italo-German troops to abandon the position. At Rassipnaia, the XXV Bersaglieri Battalion continued to successfully ward off all enemy attacks. Despite some local lack of success, the situation of the Axis forces appeared to have been restabilized, but most of all the impetus of the Soviet offensive had been blunted.

On 27 December, 1.Panzerarmee headquarters ordered XXXXIX.Gebrirgs-Armeekorps to pursue the enemy forces along the Ivanovskiy-Nikitino line, as far as the Grabova-Nikitino line. The CSIR was to continue to support the action of the 'Celere', first along the line Voroshilova-heights southwest of Olkovatka, then to advance as far as the heights west of Nikitino. Based on these new orders, General Messe ordered an attack for the following day. Thus, on 28 December the 'Celere' troops moved forward and occupied Rasinopnoy, Timofeyevjskiy and the station south of Nikischin-Voroshilova. The 'Torino', grouped into two columns, with the southern column, consisting of the 82nd Infantry, occupied Kumschazkiy, Ploskiy and Mogila Ostraya and with the northern column, consisting of the 81st Infantry, reaching as far as the area of Kurgan Ploskiy, where the Soviets were well entrenched. The Italian troops attacked these positions and were on the verge of eliminating them when a fresh counterattack launched by the Soviets forced them to

---

4   According to other sources, Vidoletti was caught up in a massacre by Soviet soldiers, involving wounded soldiers at the field hospital of the XVIII Battalion, in which bersaglieri and legion-naires who were survivors from Nova Orlovka were being treated. The first to be killed was Second Lieutenant Angelo Vidoletti who was trying to defend the wounded men, then the other were massacred one by one with a bullet in the back of the neck. A wounded bersagliere who managed to escape and who was hidden by a Ukrainian woman recounted the unfolding of the event when, 48 hours later, Ivanovka was retaken by Italian troops.

Angelo Vidoletti's sacrifice reported in the pages of the *Tribuna Illustrata*. (Authors' collection)

Torino Division infantrymen preparing for a new attack, moving to the front lines. (USSME)

withdraw to Novaya Orlovka. The troops of the 'Pasubio' supported the attack of the 'Torino' and of the 'Celere' with a diversionary attack.

Throughout these latest attacks, Second Lieutenant Gino di Curzio of the 81st Infantry fell while leading his rifle platoon during a bayonet charge. He was awarded the Gold Medal for Military Valor posthumously, with the following citation:

> Commander of a rifle platoon, already having distinguished himself in many actions by his indomitable courage and bravery, he again showed his valor in a bloody action carried out under extremely adverse weather conditions. Leading his platoon, with a bold maneuver, he attacked a strongpoint by surprise, capturing it in close-quarter fighting and forcing the enemy to fall back with heavy losses. He then held out heroically, with his men, against three successive enemy counterattacks, until, out of ammunition, he calmly awaited the enemy, standing on the captured fort, and refusing to surrender, engaged in the final unequal hand-to-hand fight. He fell dying, shouting: 'Forward 81st Infantry, long live Italy'.
>
> Novaya Orlovka area (Russian front), December 1941.

On 29 December, the Soviets mounted new counterattacks with the intention of regaining the ground they had lost. In the 'Celere' sector, attacks were made from Striukovo, Vessieli, Nikitino and from the Olkovatka gorge, all of which were repulsed. The Soviets were able to break through at only one point, near Hill 331.7, defended by a German unit. Because the position was strategically important, on 31 December, a coup de main by the XVIII Bersaglieri Battalion, supported by German tanks, retook the position. Another position that was strongly contested was Voroshilova, defended with great determination by the LXIII Blackshirt Battalion, and later by the LXXIX as well. In the end, the Soviets were thrown back.

Fighter aircraft of the CSIR aviation element were also engaged in the actions, managing to shoot down at least 15 Soviet planes.

At the end of the fighting, which achieved fairly positive results for the Italians, CSIR losses were 168 killed (13 officers), 715 wounded (14 officers), 207 missing (9 officers) and 305 cases of frostbite (6 officers).

The fighting at Voroshilova

Soon after the Battle of Christmas, the Soviets suspended any new large-scale offensives, limiting themselves to harassing actions and local attacks. Only in the Voroshilova sector were there any actions of some import, which involved shifting the positions of the 'Celere' along a more forward line. In particular, the German headquarters ordered that Voroshilova be held until Hill 331.7 could be fortified, whose loss would have threatened the 'Celere' sector. For all of the first half of January 1942, the Soviets bombarded Voroshilova, defended by the 63rd Blackshirt Legion, with artillery, mortars and aircraft. Then on 18 January they launched an attack in force; combat went on for two full days, but in the end the Soviets withdrew. On 20 January, the Blackshirts were relieved by a detachment of the XVIII Bersaglieri Battalion.

On 23 January, the Soviets resumed their attack against Voroshilova, this time managing to break through the bersaglieri defensive line, forcing them to fall back onto Hill 331.7. On 25 December, the bersaglieri attempted a counterattack against Voroshilova, but without any success. The 'Celere' losses were 24 killed (6 officers), 86 wounded (2 officers), 42 missing (1 officer) and 180 cases of frostbite (4 officers).

Knight's Cross for Giovanni Messe

On 23 January 1942, General Giovanni Messe was awarded the Knight's Cross, for valor shown while leading the Italian Expeditionary Corps in Russia. We do not have the official document which proposed the award of the prestigious German decoration but are able to cite an annotation of the Kriegsmarine staff about the first year of the CSIR's employment in Russia[5]: 'In the Russian front three Italian divisions are engaged which fight in a praiseworthy manner. The good showing by the Italian forces was also attributable to Messe who knew how to motivate his troops and at the same time was able to be inflexible towards demands that did not meet his expectations, and for this received recognition even from German headquarters'.

---

5   Thomas Schlemmer, *Invasori, non vittime – La campagna italiana di Russia 1941-1943*.

7

Izyum Front

In late January 1942, the Soviets continued their counteroffensive on the Ukrainian front, in particular in the 17.Armee sector, creating a wide salient west of Izyum that was 100 kilometers deep and 80 wide. Once the breach had been opened, the Soviet forces spread to the west, south and northwest. The German headquarters reacted quickly, organizing a line of fortified positions protecting the main road and railway hubs, later attempting several counteroffensives with two large units, the Gruppe von Mackensen, consisting of the Hube, Kohlermann and Sanne groups, and the XI.Armee-Korps coming from Pavlograd. In addition, on 29 January, 17.Armee and 1.Panzerarmee were consolidated into a new army group commanded by General von Kleist. The objective was to throw the Soviet forces back, attacking with the Gruppe Hube from south to north, having as its objective the hub of Alexandrovka on the Samara River and with Gruppe Kohlermann, which moving from Petropavlovka along the source of the Samara, was to attack the enemy's left flank and move towards Alexandrovka.

To block any threats to the Stalino-Grishino-Dniepropetrovsk railway line, the only route for resupply of 1.Panzerarmee and the CSIR, special qick reaction units were created, and to that end the German headquarters, although knowing that the Italian corps had no reserves, requested Italian units to reinforce these reaction units.

The Musinu Tactical Group

General Messe certainly could not take any men from the defensive line itself, which was already lightly garrisoned, so he decided to draw upon men from the only units that were not engaged, namely, the cavalry and the 'San Giorgio' light tank group. To recover other forces, after having sent on foot a group from the 'Novara' Regiment to Meschevaia-Slavjanka, he also pulled the I Bridging Battalion from the front line, followed by a group on foot from the 'San Giorgio' and by the IX Bridging Battalion. To comply with the pressing German requests, in the end a 75/27 battery was also detached from the 'Pasubio'. All in all, the CSIR had to furnish 1,340 men to the Germans, who were gathered together on 6 February 1942 in a tactical group commanded by Colonel Giuseppe Musinu. As this was a heterogeneous group, not well trained to fight as infantry and with insufficient armament, initially it was charged with guarding a stretch of the railway line between Dniepropetrovsk and Stalino, between Ulianovka and Grishino. Later, with a deterioration of the military situation, the Germans also committed the Musino tactical group in battle, putting it alongside German units engaged in the capture of the Samara line. After having been engaged for several days as a link between the Hube and Kohlermann assault groups, it took part in the attack against enemy positions in Sofievka, Tschervonnyi, Brodi, Nikolayevka and Petrovka. The Soviets then regained the initiative by mounting new attacks against the Samara line, against the very positions defended by the Musinu group. Bitter defensive fighting ensued, during which the Italian soldiers held out for three days against continuous Soviet assaults.

Italian soldiers on a reconnaissance patrol, January 1942. (USSME)

Italian defensive position with a Breda Model 37 machine gun, January 1942. The assistant gunner, with a carbine slung over his shoulder, has a fresh feed tray ready to insert into the gun. (Authors' collection)

At the same time, on the right of XI. Armee-Korps, Soviet tank forces were able to penetrate the Romanian positions, threatening the left wing of Gruppe Kohlermann. In an attempt to stem the threat and to block the penetration, the Germans formed a new alert group, reinforcing it with the 75/27 group from the 'Pasubio' and formation of a new tactical group, to be kept in reserve, formed by the 6th Bersaglieri Regiment and by the 120th Motorized Artillery Regiment, which had just arrived from Italy, at Dniepropetrovsk, placed under the command of Colonel Lombardi. Then a counterattack was made with the 1.Gebirgs-Division, supported by tanks, against the flank of the Soviet forces that were advancing between the Samara and Ternovka. The action was successful and the Germans seized Ossatschiy, a major communications hub in the area between the two rivers, forcing the Soviet cavalry corps to withdraw after having inflicted heavy casualties on it. Soviet pressure on Pavlograd, Petropavlovka and Slavyanka was thus lessened, even though the Izyum salient had not yet been eliminated.

In the meantime, General Messe decided to replace the bridging units of the tactical group, which were not well suited to fight as infantry, with a group from the 'Novara' on foot, which along with the other 'Novara' group reconstituted a regimental unit. A group of the 'San Giorgio' tank unit on foot was attached to the 'Lancieri di Novara' and both units were reinforced with other miscellaneous personnel. This new tactical group, formed on 28 February, numbered 28 officers, 61 NCOs and other ranks, two 47/32 guns, two 81mm mortars, 10 machine guns and 35 light machine guns and was led by Colonel Egidio Giusiana, commander of the 'Novara'. Naturally, this formation of this new group meant that the Musinu group was disbanded.

Monte Cervino Alpine Ski Battalion

With the worsening of the military situation on the Eastern Front, above all after the failure to capture Moscow and Leningrad and the Soviet counteroffensive that followed, Hitler asked Mussolini to send additional troops, especially alpine troops which could be employed in the Caucasus area, having also been impressed by the brilliant results of the CSIR. The first request was dated 1 January 1942, when Hitler sent the Duce a message in which he praised the combat spirit of the Italians and adding that a new contingent of troops would be advisable, if possible, during the course of the winter.[1] This naturally was not deemed possible by the Italian General Staff, which sent, while awaiting dispatch of the rest of the force, which was to arrive in Russia in the spring and summer, only one unit, the 'Monte Cervino' alpine ski battalion. The unit traced its origins to the 'Monte Cervino' alpine battalion, constituted in the winter of 1915 as part of the 4th Alpine Regiment, which fought in the First World War and whose flag was decorated with a Silver Medal for Military Valor. In 1919, the battalion was disbanded. It was not until 1940 that a ski new battalion was reconstituted at the central military alpine school at Aosta, from the ashes of the disbanded 'Duca d'Aosta' battalion, commanded by Major Gustavo Zanelli and taking the name 'Monte Cervino': in order to be accepted into the unit, the men had to be volunteers, unmarried, and know how to ski. In January 1941, the battalion was transferred to Albania to fight against the Greeks and was engaged in bitter fighting, especially in the Mali Scindeli area. At the conclusion of operations on the Greek-Albanian front, the battalion had only about sixty survivors.

In November 1941, the reconstituted battalion was placed under command of Lieutenant Colonel Mario D'Adda and received adequate weapons and equipment. Recruitment was based on the ten best skiers from each alpine battalion as long as they were volunteers and unmarried. More than

---

1   E. Faldella, *L'Italia nella Seconda guerra mondiale. Revisione dei giudizi*, p. 406.

Prince Umberto of Savoy meets with alpini of the Monte Cervino ready to leave for Russia. To his left is Lieutenant Colonel D'Adda. (Authors' collection)

Russia, March 1942. A Monte Cervino patrol equipped with camouflage tunics and two Italian infantrymen in grey-green uniforms. The stark difference between the equipment of the 'Cervinotti' and their comrades is readily apparent. (Authors' collection)

a third of the recruits volunteered, while the others were chosen by headquarters. On 13 January 1942, the battalion was officially incorporated into the CSIR and was the first alpine unit to be sent to the Russian front, at Yasinoataya along the Don River, where it arrived on 21 February. On 2 March, it was shifted to Rykovo and to Ploskiy, directly subordinate to the corps headquarters, but slated to be used to reinforce the 'Torino' and 'Pasubio' divisions in recon and patrol activities.

New Soviet attacks

After having stabilized the situation between the Samara and the Ternovka, thanks to the intervention of 1.Gebirgs-Division, the Soviets shifted their attacks against the left wing of 17.Armee and in particular against the sector of 97.Infanterie-Division. In order to stem this new threat, the commander of the army group, von Kleist, transferred the 60.Infanterie-Division and the Lombardi group, consisting of the 6th Bersaglieri and the 120th Artillery, to that area, between Pavlograd and Postishevo. Because of that, successive Soviet attacks around the middle of March were held in check.

Attacks continued as well against the CSIR defensive front, in particular in the Novaya Orlovka sector, defended by troops of the 'Torino'. At dawn on 27 February, after massive artillery preparatory fire, the Soviets attacked with the entire 541st Infantry Regiment and two battalions of the 387th; the fire of all of the weapons of the I/81 Infantry defending Novaya Orlovka, as well as divisional artillery and fire from the 'Pasubio' and 'Celere' artillery was unleashed against the advancing enemy units. Under this hurricane of fire, the Soviet forces broke up even before being able to reach the proximity of the village and the attack failed. Having reorganized their units,

An antitank gun of the Monte Cervino alpine ski battalion . Note the camouflaged helmet covers and accoutrements. (USSME)

around 10:30 the Soviets resumed their attack, concentrating on the eastern side of the position. Bitter fighting followed, lasting until late afternoon and ending with the defeat of the Soviets, who were forced to withdraw, after having left at least 700 men dead and wounded on the field as well as much equipment and many weapons. Losses to the I/81 were 5 killed and 12 wounded.

The Soviets returned to attack soon after near the stronghold of Malo Orlovka, also defended by elements of the 81st Infantry. The attack was driven off. Two days later, a new attack was made against Novaya Orlovka, which was also repulsed. During the night of 6 March, an entire Soviet infantry battalion, supported by mortars and artillery, attacked the same position once again. And, once again, the massive blocking fire unleashed by Italian artillery and mortars was decisive in breaking the impetus of the enemy offensive, which was followed by an Italian counterattack that completely stopped the Soviet forces.

On 11 March, the Soviets attacked along the 'Pasubio' front, in particular against the strong-point on Hill 277.4, defended by soldiers of the 79th Infantry. The attackers were repelled, leaving several prisoners in Italian hands.

Attack on Olkovatka

In an attempt to ease enemy pressure and to determine his next moves in advance, CSIR headquarters ordered a series of reconnaissance actions and several local attacks against the Soviet forces that faced the Italian positions. Thus, on 22 March, purposely to provoke a reaction by the Soviets and at the same time to lessen enemy pressure in the Izyum sector, an attack was made by elements of the 'Pasubio' and the 'Torino' against Olkovatka to capture prisoners and weapons. The 'Pasubio' employed the 'Monte Cervino' alpine battalion, reinforced by a company of 81mm mortars and by two machine gun platoons from the 80th Infantry, by recon elements of the 79th and 80th Infantry, supported by III Gruppo of the 8th Artillery. The 'Torino', which was to attack towards Vessieli and from Hill 261.4, employed the I/82 Infantry reinforced by an 81mm mortar platoon and by a 47/32 platoon, supported by II Gruppo of the 52nd Artillery.

In order to better coordinate the two offensive moves, the 'Monte Cervino' was ordered to attack at dawn, then to be followed in action by the 'Torino' which was to hit the village of Olkovatka with its weapons for about ten minutes and then to attack soon after with artillery support. Air support overhead was to bomb Olkovatka and hit any enemy reinforcing columns.

At the appointed hour, the Italian troops moved forward and despite the harsh temperature, around 30 degrees Celsius below zero [-22 Fahrenheit], the enemy's security zone was overcome quickly, forcing the Soviet forward elements to fall back. The Italians, attacking from two different directions, converged on the Olkovatka basin. The Soviets attempted to react quickly, bringing in reinforcements and at the same time attacked the 'Celere' front. In particular, the positions of the XVIII Bersaglieri Battalion were attacked repeatedly, but to no avail. At that point the enemy began to withdraw. Meanwhile, troops of the 'Pasubio' and the 'Torino', their mission completed, pulled back to their respective positions.

Monte Cervino's baptism of fire

The 'Monte Cervino' alpine skiers, upon their baptism of fire in Russia, handled themselves rather well, but they incurred heavy losses because of the lack of adequate support from heavy weapons. The action was carried out in conditions of intense cold, with temperatures around thirty degrees below zero and over ground characterized by many gullies, the famous balkas, with no reference points. The 2nd Company of the 'Cervino' began to march on their skis, finding

Monte Cervino alpine skiers consulting a map prior to an action. (USSME)

themselves between the Soviet defensive positions and under fire from mortars and machine guns Having lost the element of surprise, the attack still had to continue and the alpini had to use hand grenades, because their carbines and light machine guns had all jammed because of the low temperature. Stalled under enemy fire and threatened by a Soviet encircling maneuver on their left flank, the situation was saved by the intervention of the 1st Company, and in particular, by the actions of Sergeant Gualdi from the Ski Training Center, who had managed to pick up a heavy machine gun from the 80th infantry, thanks to which it was possible to protect the withdrawal of the 2nd Company to its line of departure. The 'Cervino' suffered six killed and about a dozen wounded, in addition to about thirty men who returned to Rykovo with symptoms of frostbite due to the prolonged time spent on the snow and ice. The fighting at Ollovatka led to the decision to add a support weapons company to the battalion, led by Captain Egidio Bassi consisting of two 81mm mortar platoons with four mortars, led by Lieutenant Enrico Merlini and Second Lieutenant Giuseppe Modigliani, two antitank platoons with four 47/32 guns led by second lieutenants Francesco Audino and Luigi Grigato, and by two machine gun platoons led by second lieutenants Francesco Caruso and Giampiero Marini. Leaving Aosta on 14 April, the 80th Company reached the 'Cervino' on 24 April in the Krisino area, bringing the battalion's effective strength up to more than 400 men.

Reorganization of the CSIR

With the approach of springtime and the imminent resumption of operations on the Eastern Front, in December 1941 General Messe had sent the Supreme Command several proposals to improve the organization and the effectiveness of the CSIR; among these were the transformation of the 'Celere' Division into a motorized division, assigning two alpine divisions to replace the two autotransportable divisions, which in turn were to be transformed into motorized divisions, reinforcement with new armoured and artillery units, and most of all, issuing a greater number of motor vehicles. But from among all of these proposals, in the end, only the transformation of the 'Celere' was enacted, which as of 15 March 1942 became a motorized division which received as reinforcements the 6th Bersaglieri Regiment, the XLVII Bersaglieri Motorcycle Battalion, the IC Mortar Battalion, the 272nd 47/32 Cannon Company and the 120th Motorized Artillery Regiment. In the summer of 1942, the division had assigned to it the LXVII Bersaglieri Armoured Battalion, equipped with L6/40 light tanks and the XIII 47/32 'Cavalleggeri di Alessandria' self-propelled group. At the same time, the "Savoia' and 'Novara' cavalry regiments, which had formed the 'Raggruppamento truppe a cavallo', led by Colonel Guglielmo Barbò, the former 'Savoia' commander, were detached. The horse artillery regiment also was part of the group. The III Gruppo of L.3 tanks was also repatriated.

With the coming of spring and the progressive improvement of the weather, the CSIR units began to resume the work of consolidating the front lines in anticipation of the impending moves to the east. In particular, in the 'Pasubio' sector the Savielevka-Usbescicce ridge was occupied, while the strongpoint at Ploskiy became a simple observation post. The continuity of the line between the 'Torino' and the 'Pasubio' was also established with two new intermediate strongpoints between Usbescicce and Yunyi Kommunar.

General Messe, wearing the German Iron Cross, visiting Italian trenches, March 1942. (USSME)

L6/40 light tanks of the LXVII Bersaglieri Armoured Battalion on the Russian front, spring 1942.
(Authors' collection)

The MVSN Croat Legion

During this period, the Croat Legion was assigned to the CSIR. The independent state of Croatia, born in 1941 following the dissolution of the Yugoslav state after the invasion of Russia by Axis forces, desired to unite in the fight against Bolshevism by forming the volunteer legion which was integrated into the Wehrmacht as the Verstärktes (kroatisches) Infanterie-Regiment 369 and later a naval legion and a Croat air legion were also formed. In July 1941, creation of a similar unit was arranged, to be assigned to the Italian expeditionary corps in Russia, mainly in an attempt to ease the tensions between the new Croat state and Italy over the Dalmatian territories. Thus, on 26 July 1941, thanks to the work of the Italian Military Mission in Croatia of General Giovanni Battista Oxilia and later of pressure exerted by the Chief of General Staff, Ugo Cavallero on his counterpart Slavko Kvaternik, the Croatian Army arranged for the formation of the Lako prevozni zdrug (Light Motorized Brigade), based on the reserve battalion of the 369th Regiment and designated in Italian as the Croatian Autotransportable Legion. The designation as 'autotransportable' indicated that the antitank cannon company and logistic services were completely motorized, while the rifle companies were only set up for motor transport and thus had to resort to vehicles furnished from time to time by higher echelon transportation groups.

Despite the designation of 'light brigade', in reality the unit was structured as a regiment, with a Legion headquarters, a rifle battalion (consisting of a headquarters company and three rifle companies), a support weapons company, an 81mm mortar company, a support gun company and a reserve company. Stationed at Varaždin, near the Hungarian border, the Legion was placed under the command of Lieutenant Colonel Stjepan Neuberger and on 26 July 1941, the Light Motorized Brigade numbered 1,121 men of whom 45 were officers and 67 were NCOs. For political reasons the unit was subordinated to the Milizia Volontaria Sicurezza Nazionale as far as organization, weapons and equipment. The Croat volunteers wore the Italian Model 1940 uniform with black

Arrival of the Croat Legion of the MVSN on the Russian front. (USSME)

Blackshirts and Croat legionnaires fraternizing, April 1942. (USSME)

The truck-borne Croat Legion being reviewed by General Messe, commander of the CSIR. A 47/32 antitank gun is in the foreground. (Authors' collection)

flames and Militia insignia on their collar tabs. The Croatian insignia was sewn on the right jacket and coat sleeves with the word 'Hrvatska' on a white and red field. The Croat legionnaires wore a black shirt but not the fez, which was replaced by the Italian garrison cap with the M.V.S.N. badge. While in Italy awaiting their transfer, the Croat legionnaires, subordinate to the Italian 2nd Army, were employed in operations against Tito's partisans. In November a training cycle began with eight Italian officers, eight NCOs and some corporals, in order to familiarize the Croats with Italian weapons, vehicles and tactics of the Regio Esercito. On 17 December 1941, the Legion was moved within Italy, at Riva del Garda, where its depot unit was located, for further training and to assimilate Italian combat tactics. Once training was completed, the legionnaires swore allegiance to the Duce and to Poglavnik Ante Pavelić, in the presence of Cavallero and Kvaternik. In March 1942, the legion was declared combat ready and in early April began its transfer by train to the Soviet front. Having reached the Ukraine, the troops gathered at Wladimirovka on 16 April. On 18 April 1942, the unit was assigned as the CSIR corps reserve and then was subordinated to the 3rd 'Celere' division, replacing the 63rd CC.NN. Legion 'Tagliamento', which was to be reorganized because of the losses it had suffered.

German counteroffensive

In view of the new summer offensive, the German high command decided to complete occupation of Crimea and to eliminate the Izyum pocket. The offensive in Crimea began in early May and ended after bitter fighting, with a total conquest of the peninsula. On 12 May, however, the Soviets launched on offensive against Kharkov, thus forestalling the Germans in their action against the

Izyum pocket. Nevertheless, this unexpected Soviet attack did not worry the German headquarters very much and the offensive that they had planned was kicked off on 17 May along the Samara front, employing 17.Armee and Gruppe von Mackensen (III.AK). 17.Armee moved to the line of the Donets as far as its confluence with the Bereka, while Gruppe von Mackensen established a bridgehead along the same river at Petroskaya. These attacks forced the Soviets to withdraw from the pocket, without, however, being able to do successfully because of an encircling move by the German forces. On 18 May the Barbò tactical group was also engaged in combat on the extreme left of Gruppe von Mackensen, being given the mission of capturing the dorsals of Mal Rostol, Klynovoy, Ivanovka and the position at Lugovoy. In the latter locality it was to make contact with the Romanian 20th Division. The group was given two German battalions as reinforcement which on the morning of 18 May attacked the Mal Rostol ridge, encountering strong enemy resistance. The 'Monte Cervino' alpine battalion and a bersaglieri company were able to penetrate into the village of Klinovoy, a position that was captured following furious close-quarter combat.

After having occupied the village, the alpini had to face a Soviet counterattack made by four infantry battalions and several squadrons of Cossack cavalry. Out of ammunition and to avoid being surrounded, the commander, D'Adda, ordered the 1st Company to fall back, covered by fire from Lieutenant Modigliani's mortar platoon. The fighting lasted until 12:30 to eliminate several enemy elements that had taken up positions around the village. The alpini suffered 15 killed, among them two officers, second lieutenants Frascoli and Audino and 45 wounded. Not a single alpino fell into Soviet hands alive and Lieutenant Vitaliano Frascoli was not even left on the field although dead. While the battalion withdrew while still fighting, his orderly, alpino Domenico Caspani, himself wounded, saw the officer fall dead and turned back. He took the dead corpse on his shoulders and ran to join his companions. Every once in a while, he had to stop to catch his breath and to fire against some Soviet soldiers who were chasing him. Exhausted and by now out of strength, he set

A bersagliere motorcyclist with a Breda Model 30 light machine gun, spring 1942. (USSME)

Alpini defensive position with an antitank gun in a semi-revetted position, 1942. A fresh 47mm round is ready to be loaded into the breech. (Authors' collection)

the officer's corpse down in an out-of-the way spot and returned to friendly lines. The next night, he went out into no-man's-land and retrieved the officer's body.

Two days later, the battalion returned to resume the attack against Klynovoy, but this time there was no fighting as the Soviets had already abandoned the position and the advance could continue towards the villages of Riassnoy and Andrievka.

Meanwhile, the action by III and XI. Armee-Korps against the Izyum pocket had unfolded successfully, with Soviet forces making a last desperate attempt to break out of the encirclement, with attacks from inside the pocket and from the left bank of the Donets. In order to contain these final enemy gasps, the German headquarters requested that Messe make other Italian units available. Thus, two tactical groups were transferred to von Kleist's army group, one from the 'Pasubio', consisting of the I/80 Infantry and the II/8 Artillery and one from the 'Torino', consisting of the II/81 Infantry and the II/52 Artillery, which moved on 26 May to Barvenkovo. At the same time, to make up for the loss of these units, Messe transferred the 'Tagliamento' Legion to Rykovo, for eventual employment in the 'Pasubio' and 'Torino' sectors.

On 28 May, fighting for the Izyum pocket ceased, with the annihilation of two Soviet armies: German war bulletins reported the capture of 240,000 prisoners as well as a large quantity of arms and equipment. The Italian units were engaged in sweep actions. On 7 June, the two artillery groups returned to their regiments, while the two infantry battalions continued to be engaged in protection of a stretch of railway while subordinate to a German group until 26 June. On 26 May, the Barbò tactical group also returned to CSIR subordination, as did the 'Celere' Division.

Final defensive fighting

On 3 June 1942, the CSIR was subordinated to 17.Armee, continuing to remain in a defensive mode until 10 July. Throughout this period, the Italian forces continued to defend themselves from local enemy attacks, of small size, especially in the 'Pasubio' and 'Celere' sectors. It was not until 27 June that there was a larger attack against the forward outposts of the 'Celere' at Greco Timofeyevkiy and against Hill 11.7, defended by the VI Bersaglieri Battalion. At dawn that day, Soviet artillery began to shell the outpost on Hill 311.7 and after about 40 minutes, an enemy battalion attacked and was able to occupy two forward positions after the defenders had fallen at their weapons. A hasty counterattack made by a reserve company threw the Soviets back. The enemy left at least a hundred dead on the field as well as some prisoners. Italian losses were 15 dead (1 officer) and 33 wounded (4 officers).

8

Italian 8th Army in Russia

Ever since the formation of the CSIR in the summer of 1941, the Italian Supreme Command had already begun to plan to expand the Italian expeditionary corps with at least another army corps. This decision had been dictated by Mussolini himself, who was desirous to send a greater number of Italian troops to the Eastern Front to increase the political impact of the undertaking. Nevertheless, it was necessary to wait until the summer of 1942, more precisely until 9 July 1942, when the CSIR headquarters was replaced by headquarters of the Italian 8th Army, commanded by General Italo Gariboldi,[1] consisting in addition to the CSIR (renamed as the XXXV Army Corps), the II

1   Italo Gariboldi was born in Lodi on 20 April1879. At twelve years of age, he began attending the Military College in Milan, four years later moving to the military college in Rome. Joining the Regio Esercito, beginning in October 1896 he attended the Royal Military Academy of Infantry and Cavalry at Modena, graduating with the rank of second lieutenant in October 1898. Assigned to the 2nd Infantry Regiment, he became a lieutenant in June 1902, and after marrying, returned to active service in October 1904, assigned to the 70th Infantry Regiment. In October 1909, he was admitted the War School in 'Torino', at the end of which he was promoted to captain, leaving for a brief operational tour in Libya assigned to the 40th Infantry Regiment. Returning to Italy, he was assigned to the VI Army Corps staff. Promoted to major, at the beginning of the Great War he served on the staff of the 4th Army under Lieutenant General Luigi Nava, who four months later was replaced by General Matio Nicolis de Robilant. Twice promoted for wartime merit, on 6 January 1918 he became a colonel and was assigned as Chief of the Operations office of the Army of the Grappa. Assigned to army corps headquarters in Bologna, in 1919 he assumed the post of Chief of Staff of the 77th Division stationed in Volosca di Fiume, taking part in the clashes involved with the Fiume question. From 1920 to 1923, he was President of the Italian delegation for drawing the border with Yugoslavia. In December 1923 he assumed command of the 26th infantry Regiment and later was an instructor at the War School. Promoted to brigadier general on 15 December 1931, he successively commanded the 5th Infantry Brigade stationed in San Remo, the Modena Military Academy and the Parma Application School. On 1 January 1935 he was promoted to major general and became a member of the Army Council, leaving for the war in Ethiopia in 1936, assuming command of the 'Sabauda' Division, assigned to General Ruggero Santini's I Army Corps. He took part in the battle of Amba Aradam, the first battle of Endertà and that of Tembien, entering Addis Abbaba on 5 May. After the end of the war, he assumed the post of Chief of Staff for the Governor General of Italian East Africa. On 1 July 1937 he was promoted to lieutenant general for exceptional merit. Returning to Italy in February 1938, he became Commander of the Military Order of Savoy and High Officer of the Colonial Order of the Star of Italy, assuming in March 1939 command of the V Army Corps in Trieste. On 11 June 1940, Gariboldi assumed command of the 5th Army in North Africa on the border with Tunisia. Following the death of the Governor of Libya, Italo Balbo and the arrival of Graziani, Gariboldi took part in the advance of the 10th Army against Sidi El-Barrani, then replacing General Mario Berti on 15 December. After the British counterattack that led to the destruction of the Italian army, on 11 February 1941 he was nominated as the Commander-in-Chief in North Africa, replacing Graziani. On 24 March he became governor of Libya, but on 19 July left that post because of his disagreements with General Erwin Rommel, commander of the Deutsches Afrikakorps. He then returned to Italy at the disposition of the Comando Supremo. In the spring of 1942, he was assigned to command the new Italian 8th Army deployed to the Russian front.

General Italo Gariboldi, commander of the Italian army in Russia (ARMIR), reviewing troops at the Stalino (Donetz) airfield in June 1942. (USSME)

Army Corps, commanded by General Giuseppe Zanghieri, consisting of the 2nd 'Sforzesca', 3rd 'Ravenna' and 5th 'Cosseria' divisions and the Alpine Army Corps, led by General Gabriele Nasci, consisting of the 2nd 'Tridentina', 3rd 'Julia' and 4th 'Cuneense' alpine divisions. Units directly subordinate to the corps were the 156th Infantry Division 'Vicenza'[2], the horse-mounted grouping (two cavalry regiments and a horse-drawn artillery regiment), the army artillery grouping, engineer units, infantry units, the chemical group, air units (an observation group and a fighter group) and the Croat Legion.

The presence of Militia units was also notably increased, with the formation of two raggruppamenti, directly subordinate to II and XXXV Army Corps. In particular, subordinate to II Corps, was the Raggruppamento CC.NN. '23 Marzo',[3] commanded by Lieutenant General Enrico Francisci, consisting of the CC.NN. 'Valle Scrivia' Battalion Grouping (V and XXXIV CC.NN. battalions and the XLI CC.NN. Support Weapons Battalion) and the CC.NN. 'Leonessa' Battalion Grouping (XIV and XV CC.NN. battalions and the XXXVIII CC.NN. Support Weapons Battalion).

Subordinate to the XXXV Army Corps was the Raggruppamento CC.NN. '3 gennaio',[4] under Lieutenant General Filippo Diamanti, consisting of the CC.NN. Battalion Grouping 'Tagliamento' (LXII and LXXIX CC.NN. battalions and the LXIII CC.NN. Support Weapons Battalion) and the CC.NN. Battalion Grouping 'Montebello' (VI and XXX CC.NN. battalions and XII CC.NN. Support Weapons battalion)

These two ragruppamenti were in reality two small divisions, lighter than army divisions, but better armed and trained. With the transformation of the 63rd Legion into Battalion Groupings, Console Niccolò Nichiarelli was promoted and left the command to Console Domenico Mittica.

---

2   The division was employed as an occupation force and in protecting the ARMIR rear area, then in December 1942 it was subordinated to the Alpine Army Corps.

3   On 23 March 1919 the Fasci di Combattimento (Combat Fasces, a Fascist organization) were founded in Piazza San Sepolcro.

4   On 3 January 192, Mussolini made a speech in the Chamber considered to be the beginning of the Fascist regime as a totalitarian regime.

Unit Transfers

The departure of new units of the Italian army began in the first week of June and it was established that the Alpine Army Corps would be the last to leave. The German headquarters had designated the area southwest of Kharkov as an unloading and assembly area for II Army Corps, while for the Alpine Army Corps the area north of Taganrog had been chosen. The Italian Supreme Command quickly made it clear that the 8th Army was to be employed in a cohesive manner, without subdividing its forces, as had already happened with the CSIR. Between 17 June and 7 July, a large portion of II Corps units reached the area of Kharkov, including the headquarters with most of its directly subordinated units, the entire 'Ravenna' Division and half of the 'Sforzesca'. Shortly afterwards, the order was given to move the troops towards the Donets, to approach the XXXV Corps operational area and to begin to assemble the Army.

While the move of new units arriving from Italy was being completed, in light of the resumption of the offensive, the Army commander decided to reinforce the XXXV Corps artillery groups, which since 3 June had been subordinated to 17.Armee, because they were already on the line and about to be committed to combat once again. In addition, also transferred to the same corps was the 'Sforzesca' Division, which had just arrived from Italy, which replaced the 'Torino'. The cavalry raggruppamento and the 'Monte Cervino' alpine ski battalion fell under direct subordination of the Army headquarters. The Alpine Army Corps was still in Italy.

New German summer offensive

German plans for the summer of 1942 were focused mainly on the southern sector of the Eastern Front. Attacks against Moscow or Leningrad were temporarily put off until a later date. For the prosecution of the war, which by now had become worldwide with involvement of Japan and the United States, the Third Reich was urgently in need of raw materials and oil. The objectives of the new offensive, code named Fall Blau (Case Blue), defined by Hitler in Directive Number 41 dated 5 April 1942, called for wiping out the Soviet forces located between the Donets Basin and the Don, the conquest of the passes in the Caucasus and seizure of the rich oil fields on the Caspian Sea. There was also another objective, much more ambitious, which was a linkup of the Italo-German forces from Egypt with Japanese forces from India, in order to directly strike at British interests in the Middle East and in Asia Minor. The offensive, which was to involve Army Group South exclusively, had been subdivided into four distinct operational phases: initially the enemy defensive line on the Don at Voronezh (Blau 1), then conquer the entire Don Basin as far as the Donets (Blau 2). Soon after, German forces were to be engaged in the conquest of the entire area between the Don, Stalingrad and Rostov (Blau 3). At that point the offensive was to shift to the south with the objective of conquering the entire Caucasus region, including the areas between the Caspian Sea, the Black Sea and the Volga River and the mountainous chain of the Caucasus, with its rich oil deposits (Blau 4). Prior to launching this new offensive, the Germans were engaged in eliminating several dangerous Soviet salients which were wedged along the German front, at Kharkov, Izyum and the Kerch peninsula. In early May, Soviet forces had launched an offensive in the Izyum area but were surrounded and completely wiped out, losing more than a thousand tanks and 2,500 guns, as well as more than 240,000 men taken prisoner, not counting dead and wounded. On the Crimean front, the German 11th Army under General von Manstein was able to conquer the entire peninsula. Between 10 and 26 June, other offensive actions were mounted with which the Germans established a bridgehead on the eastern bank of the Donets River to the east of Kharkov. These moves made it possible to establish the departure points for the new offensive.

An Italian defensive position with an antitank gun, summer 1942. (USSME)

Case Blue began officially on 28 June and from the earliest clashes it seemed that the rapid advances of the preceding summer were being repeated, with the Germans attacking and the Soviets being overrun or forced to withdraw. The first forces to move were those deployed in the Voronezh sector and at the beginning of July German armoured thrusts crossed the Don. This time, however, the Soviets withdrew in time, along a new defensive line further to the east. This sudden withdrawal avoided the loss of major forces but most of all forced the Germans to continue the offensive along two different axes, with the resultant separation of the forces involved. On 9 July Army Group South was split into two new Army Groups: Army Group A, under Marshal Wilhelm List, and Army Group B, under Marshal von Weichs. Army Group A consisted of Ruoth's 1.Armee, Hoth's 4.Panzer-Armee and von Kleist's 1.Panzer-Armee. Army Group B consisted of von Salmuth's 2.Armee, 6.Armee under Paulus, the Romanian 3rd and 4th Armies, the Italian 8th Army and the Hungarian 2nd Army. Hitler's new directive, Number 43 dated 23 July 1942, fixed the objectives of the German offensive along two very distinct routes: Army Group B was to rapidly seize Stalingrad (Operation Fischereiher: Heron) and secure the left flank of Army Group A which was to push to the Caucasus (Operation Edelweiss: Alpine Star).

Occupation of the Krasny Lutsch mineral basin

According to agreements established between the Italian and German headquarters, while awaiting the assembly of all of the 8th Army's units, it had been decided to initially commit to combat only the XXXV Army corps, subordinate to 17.Armee, for the new summer offensive. As previously mentioned, the corps had been reinforced with the 'Sforzesca' Division and with 111.Infanterie-Division, in addition to receiving strong artillery support in view of its action on the Donets front. The corps also received the cavalry raggruppamento and the 'Monte Cervino' alpine ski battalion as reinforcements.

The so-called Krasny Lutsch maneuver, carried out between 11 and 22 July, developed in three phases:

1) Initially, the Soviet front between Debalzevo and Nikitino was to be broken with the CC.NN. Battalion Grouping 'Tagliamento', with a converging action by 'Pasubio' and the 111. Infanterie-Division from the north and by the 'Celere', the 'Sforzesca' and the horse-mounted raggruppamento from the south, towards the Fatschevka station, then proceeding to Ivanovka, which had been abandoned following the Christmas Battle.
2) Having reached Ivanovka, the Soviet defensive line between Voroshilovgrad [now Luhnask] and Krasny Lutsch was to be eliminated.
3) Finally, it was necessary to make an encircling move around all of the Soviet forces present in the Krasny Lutsch-Bokovo Pitovo-Bokova Antrazit area.

During the morning of 11 July, the 'Celere' Division headquarters sent out two reconnaissance in force detachments, the first conducted by the Croat Legion on the ridge of Hill 253.4 towards Vessieli and the second by the LXII CC.NN. Battalion (of the 'Tagliamento' group) toward the town of Nikitino, with the aim of stabilizing the situation on the ground and overrunning the enemy's forward positions, stabilizing the departure points for the attacks that were to follow. The two recons, adequately supported by divisional artillery, were successful and by nightfall orders for an offensive action were issued.

At dawn on 12 July, the 3rd Bersaglieri Regiment, reinforced by the 3rd Bersaglieri Motorcycle Company and a 75/27 group of the 120th Artillery Regiment, after having left Nikitino and Vassieli in the hands of the forces that had occupied them the day before, advanced in two columns: on the left the XX Battalion and the 3rd Motorcycle Company moved towards the station at Fatschevka and on the right the XVII Battalion advanced towards Hill 333.5 (Mogila Ostraya). The rest of the division followed close behind in four echelons in the two directions cited. A sudden storm hampered the movement of the motor vehicles and slowed the advance of the troops, who at the same time were engaged in overcoming enemy resistance that had been left as rear guards, as well as many minefields. At 18:00, the division commander ordered a new column, designated the Salvatores column, led by Colonel Umberto Salvatores,[5] consisting of the VI Bersaglieri Battalion of the 6th Regiment, the XLVII Bersaglieri Motorcycle Battalion and a 100/17 group of the 120th Artillery to march on Petrovenki, leapfrogging the 3rd Bersaglieri force. Some hours later, this new column was stalled by strong enemy resistance near the crossroads at Artema. In the event, contact was made with German units on the flanks, in particular on the left at Utkino with Inf.Rgt. 308 (111.Inf.Div.) and on the right with Inf.Rgt. 217 (198. Inf.Div).

On the morning of 13 July, General Messe, following the 17.Armee plan, ordered the 'Celere' Division to attack Scevshenko-Malaya Nikolaevka and Ivanovka-Krasnaya Polyana to prevent the Soviets from withdrawing and to set up in defensive positions along the Voroshilovgrad-Krasny Lutsch line. At the same time, the 'Pasubio' and 'Sforzesca' divisions, in the second echelon, were to follow the movement to the east. Thus, the 'Celere' commander, General Mario Marazzani, ordered the Salvatores column to eliminate Soviet resistance at the Artema crossroads, occupy the Petrovenki railway station and continue on to Krasnaya Polyana.

The recon patrols that had been sent ahead reported that the Sveschenko position on the left was strongly defended while on the right, near Hill 367.1, the Soviet rearguards had stalled the advance of 198.Inf.Div. The division commander, Generalmajor Albert Buck, thus requested aid from Italian units and the VI Bersaglieri Battalion attacked and took the hill.

---

5   Commander of the 6th Bersaglieri Regiment.

Bersaglieri motorcyclists on a recon mission, summer 1942. (USSME)

A Monte Cervino mortar crew in action, summer, summer 1942. (USSME)

Italian artillery in action, summer 1942. (USSME)

A Blackshirt machine gun team with a Breda Model 30 during an attack, summer 1940. The soldier on the right has an ammunition chest and two spare barrels on his back. (USSME)

Towards evening, the bulk of the 'Celere' formed into two columns near the Kommendantski railway station. During the night, Soviet cavalry units supported by artillery and mortars, attacked Hill 367.1; the Italians counterattacked and pushed back the Soviets who left many dead and wounded on the field.

At dawn on 14 July, the attacks resumed; troops of the German 111.Inf.Div. attacked towards Yelisabetovka and Malaya Nikolaievka, while the 'Pasubio' was ordered to take up positions between the 111.Inf.Div. and the 'Celere'. At 3:30, the VI Bersaglieri Battalion, supported by III horse artillery group, with the aid of dusk, made a surprise attack against Hill 360.2, a vital position needed for the advance against Ivanovka. After half an hour of fighting the hill was taken and more than 200 prisoners were captured in addition to a large quantity of equipment.

At 6:00 all of the units moved forward and were soon challenged by Soviet infantry supported by artillery, mortar and Katyusha rocket launchers. To overcome the stiff enemy resistance, intervention by the Luftwaffe was requested; due to an error, at least initially, the Stuka dive bombers hit the Italian columns, causing several wounded. Later, the Stukas hit the Soviet positions. Between 8:00 and 9:00, Ivanovka was captured following furious house-to-house fighting. The Soviets pulled back to the heights to the east of the village, continuing to target the position with their artillery.

On the XXXV Corps left wing, the 111.Inf.Div. occupied Malaya Nikolaievka, while on the right wing, 198.Inf.Div. was stalled in its attack, leaving the right flank of XXXV Corps exposed. General Messe ordered the horse cavalry group to provide cover. Initially, the 'Celere' headquarters had sent the 'Tagliamento' group and the Croat Legion to the sector previously occupied by the 198.Inf.Div.. These two units stayed to defend the positions of the German division and were integrated into the 'Pasubio' Division.

Between 15 and 16 July, all unit moves were suspended so that XXXV Corps would be able to reorganize its units. It was planned to deploy the 'Pasubio' and 'Sforzesca' in the area between the

A section of Brixia mortars manned by Blackshirts supporting an attack, summer 1942. The officer on the left is armed with a Beretta MAB 38A submachine gun. (USSME)

Blackshirts in an attack, summer 1942. (USSME)

A Breda Model 30 in action against enemy positions, summer 1942. (USSME)

'Celere' and 198.Inf.Div. on 17 July, while the units that has replaced the German division were to remain in the positions that they had occupied.

At 7:00 on 17 July, responsibility for the Krasny Lutsch sector was assigned to the 'Sforzesca' Division. This freed the 'Celere' to be used to exploit its success. Throughout the day of 17 July, recon patrols continued to meet with stiff enemy resistance. In the 111.Inf.Div. sector there was a tank attack that was repulsed.

Blackshirts attack

On the morning of 17 July, the LXXIX 'M' Battalion[6] had been ordered to carry out a recon mission and to take the village of Shterovka and Hill 342. Thus, at 11:00 in the morning, without any preparatory artillery fire so as not to alert the Soviet defenders, two recon squads led by capomanipolo [Lieutenant] Mario Zago moved towards Shterovka. After having gone about 500 meters, the Blackshirts came under fire from automatic weapons and mortars. Italian artillery quickly came into action in an attempt to ease the pressure, while the Blackshirts of the 2nd Company of Centurione [Captain] Rota moved forward in support of Zago's patrols. The offensive action thus was able to continue and the legionnaires reached the outlying houses of Shterovka, where Soviet riflemen were entrenched and supported by numerous machine gun positions. Among the first to fall to enemy fire was Lieutenant Zago, along with other Blackshirts. The officer lay on the ground, badly wounded. It was in that moment that one of his Blackshirts, Mario Paolucci, having seen his commanding officer wounded on the ground, brought himself closer to save him. In the morning he had already been wounded in his right arm but had taken part in the attack by pulling ammunition chests along with his other arm. When Paoloucci approached the officer on the ground, a burst from a Soviet machine gun wounded him in the left arm. Finding it impossible to drag Zago with either arm, despite the pain, Paolucci decided to grab his commander's jacket with his teeth, managing to drag his body for a long stretch, until he was once again hit in the chest by enemy fire and dying. He was the Legion's first recipient of the Gold Medal for Military Valor, with the following citation:

> Unable to wait, even though he was a retired officer, he enlisted as a simple soldier. Always a volunteer for the riskiest actions, during violent fighting, he went on the attack against well-fortified positions using hand grenades, an example to all of his fellow soldiers. Seriously wounded in his right arm, he did not desist from the action, continuing to fight with lion-like courage. Having reached the enemy position and during a violent counterattack, because ammunition was running out, he crossed the area under fire bringing several ammunition chests with him using only his left arm. Seeing his officer fall, while enemy reaction became

---

6   The 'M' battalions (where the 'M' referred to Benito Mussolini) were elite units of the Milizia Volontaria per la Sicurezza Nazionale (MVSN) and were created in October 1941 as a transformation and upgrading of the MVSN mountain assault battalions that had distinguished themselves in combat. The Blackshirts of the 'Tagliamento' Group were not originally an 'M' unit but were promoted to that category in recognition of valor shown during operations on the Eastern Front. The men of the 'M' battalions wore the normal MSVN uniform, the only difference being the black collar tabs on which the silver lictor's fasce used by MSVN units in place of the stars used by the Regio Esercito was replaced by a fasce entwined with a small letter 'm' in red enamel, reproducing Mussolini's handwriting. The pennants of the various battalions repeated the same symbology: on them, configured as a swallowtail, were embroidered the same red 'M' with the lictor's fasce, and the word 'Seguitemi' [Follow me] (which expressed loyalty to Italy and to Fascism) with the same calligraphy of the 'M' and the unit number.

increasingly furious, he quickly went to him to offer aid. Hit by a machine gun burst which immobilized his left arm as well, he dragged himself to his officer and, seizing part of his jacket with his teeth, with supreme effort was able to drag him for a short stretch until, mortally wounded, he consecrated his indomitable heroism on the field of battle.

Shterovka, Russian Front, 17 July 1942.

The Blackshirts of the 2nd Company also suffered some losses. At 13:00 Console [Colonel] Mittica ordered all the recon patrols to return, which withdrew bringing their wounded and all of their equipment along with them. During the withdrawal the 2nd Company commander, Captain Rota, was also wounded. All of the other officers of the company were also wounded. Shortly after, the Soviets attacked, exerting maximum effort against the 1st Company's positions. The men of the 2nd Company went to its aid, led by Centurione Alberto Mingiardi, and those of the 3rd Company, led by Seniore [Major] Silvio Margini. The Soviet riflemen were forced to withdraw and during the night they abandoned the entire sector. On the morning of the following day, under a driving rain, the legionnaires of the LXXIX 'M' Battalion captured Shterovka first and then Surayevka, capturing two hundred prisoners and a large amount of arms and munitions.

New orders

The next day, Heeresgruppe A headquarters issued an order to XXXV Corps to attack the positions at Krasnaya Polyana and Rovenki. These two objectives were assigned respectively to the 'Pasubio' and the 'Celere', while the 'Sforzesca' was to advance on Bokovo Platovo. The horse raggruppamennto was to approach the industrial center of Krasny Lutsch from the south and also aim for Bokovo Platovo. At that time, the bulk of the Soviet forces were pulling back towards the Donets, leaving strong rear guards behind.

On 18 July, movement continued to be slowed down by bad weather conditions. The 111.Inf. Div. was subordinated to III.Armee-Korps. The 'Celere' division occupied Shterovka, Kolpakovo and Krasnaya Polyana, where the 'Pasubio' arrived in the evening. After having passed through Krustaliny, the 'Sforzesca' continued on to Hill 347, north of Krasny Lutsch. After an exhausting 60-kilometer march slowed down by mud and minefields, the horse raggruppamento reached the Krasny Lutsch area.

Towards evening, the German headquarters ordered XXXV Corps to assemble at Bokovo Platovo to sweep the entire mining area. Between 19 and 22 July, the troops were engaged in these sweeps, capturing about 4,000 prisoners.

On 23 July, 8th Army headquarters, which had become operational, ordered XXXV Corps to move to Luganskaya on the Donets River, near Voroshilovgrad.

9

March Towards the Don

On 23 July 1942, Heeresgruppe A headquarters ordered the Italian units to move towards the Don and at the same time, the Italian 8th Army was subordinated to Heeresgruppe B. The Italian divisions thus had to quickly cross the Donets to support the German divisions engaged on the right bank of the Don. The retreating Soviets had left behind wrecked bridges, roads and railway lines sabotaged and mines of all types. The Italian engineers were soon busy throwing bridges across the Donets at Luganskaya and Veselaya Gora in order to allow rapid crossing by the units. At dawn on 26 July, 8th Army troops began to cross the Donets on bridges at Luganskaya. The last division to cross was the 'Cosseria', on 31 July 1942.

The intention of Heeresgruppe B was for the Italian troops to deploy along the Don, to act as a defensive flank for the German forces that were pushing on towards Stalingrad. Because of a sudden shortage of fuel, the move of the units was significantly delayed and it was not until 4 August that most of the 8th Army troops took up positions along the Rossoch-Millerovo railway line. The final deployment of all of the troops was completed on 13 August, when General Gariboldi assumed

Bersaglieri motorcyclists crossing a pontoon bridge across the Donets River in the Ukraine in the summer of 1942. (USSME)

operational responsibility for the entire 8th Army sector, from Pavlovsk to the mouth of the Chopër on the Don. From mid-August, the first contingents of the Alpine Army Corps also began to arrive in Russia, also slated to be deployed along the Don front and no longer planned to be used in the Caucasus.

Employment of the 'Celere' in the Serafimovich bend

In order to move the Axis units to the line of the Don it was necessary to eliminate all of the Soviet bridgeheads on the right bank of the river. For this operation, the Italian 8th Army was requested to commit some forces, with plans to deploy them along the Don to the left of 6.Armee under Paulus. Accordingly, the 'Celere' Division, which was completely motorized and which at that time was still halted in the Mius mining basin, was made available to 6.Armee: its orders were to move quickly, passing through Voroshilovgrad, Millerovo and Bokovskaya to eliminate the Soviet bridgehead on the right bank of the Don at Serafimovich, which threatened the left flank of the German army. On 27 July, after having reached the Bokovskaya-Ponomarevka-Nizne Astakov line, the division was subordinated to XVII.Armee-Korps led by General Karl Hollidt. In the evening of the 28th, the division was ordered to reach the area south of Serafimovich, between Baskowski and Ribni the next day in order to prepare for an attack against the Soviet bridgehead. Inf.Rgt. 578, already on the spot, engaged in holding a 25-kilometer front with only two battalions each of which was down to 400 men and with only a few artillery pieces, was assigned as reinforcement.

On the morning of 29 July, while General Hollidt reported to the 'Celere' headquarters at Karaghishev to define the final attack details, the Soviets had thrown the Inf.Rgt. 578 troops out

Italian troops crossing a pontoon bridge built by Italian bridging engineers across the Donets in the Ukraine, summer 1942. (USSME)

A long column of Italian troops crossing a pontoon the Donets in the Ukraine, summer 1942. (USSME)

of Baskovski and Bobrovski and occupied them. In the afternoon, new attacks forced the Germans to also abandon Hill 207.9. During the course of the day, the commander of the 'Celere', General Mario Marazzani, went to the Inf.Rgt. 578 command post on Hill 210 to see the situation first-hand. While on the right of the regiment there was weak contact with 79.Inf.Div., on the left, towards Ribni, there was a gap of about 30 kilometers towards the XXIX.Armee-Korps. The Soviets occupied all of the localities in the bridgehead, from Baskovski to Satonski, with about 3,000 men and were also awaiting fresh reinforcements in order to attempt an offensive action to the south and southeast to free the Soviet units that had been surrounded by 6.Armee forces and at the same time to ease the German pressure on Stalingrad.

That same day, General Marazzani ordered the 6th Bersaglieri Regiment to recapture Hill 207.9 and to occupy the heights in front of the village of Baskovski. Thus, at dawn on 30 July, the XIX/6 rooted out the Soviets from Hill 207.9, continuing the advance against Hill 122.7. At the same time, the VI/6 attacked towards Baskovski, occupying Hill 149.1 and the positions at Belosoin and Belonemukin, relieving some German units. The XIII/6 attacked towards the northern extreme of the balka of Verh. Fominski. The 3rd Bersaglieri Regiment and the artillery followed the moves of the other units.

Around 14:00 on 30 July, the Soviets made two attacks: from the north towards Hill 210.1 with 24 T-34 tanks and from the east against Hill 176.7 with 15 T-18 tanks. For the first time, the 'Celere' troops found themselves facing an enemy armoured attack and, not having adequate antitank guns, concentrated their fire mainly against the Soviet infantry that was following behind the tanks. The artillery, which also consisted of two sections of the 75/39 battery, saw to it, firing at close range and knocking out 12 enemy tanks. The units suffering the highest losses were the XIX/6 and the II/120, swamped by the enemy attack while they were getting into position. In particular, the II/120 suffered the loss of 12 guns, 7 tractors and 13 trucks.

At dawn on 31 July, Inf.Rgt. 578 attacked the Soviet positions at Satonski, then taking positions on the western slopes of Hill 197.4. At the same time, the 3rd Bersaglieri attacked the eastern slopes of the hill, then aiming towards Serafimovich. After having overrun the first Soviet defensive line, as soon as the bersaglieri approached the second line, the ran into a violent enemy counterattack. The regiment was forced to send the XXV Battalion to Byelavelski, where Soviet reaction

A column of Italian troops moving through Voroshilovgrad in the summer of 1942. (USSME)

Bersaglieri marching across the Ukrainian steppe in the summer of 1942. (USSME)

seemed to be a greater threat. Between 10:00 and 12:00 the Soviets counterattacked again with tank support, but to no avail.

At 14:00, with Inf.Rgt. 578 now in Satonski and with 3rd Bersaglieri which had almost reached hills 197.4 and 180, the Soviets counterattacked again stride the Serafimovich-Popov line. The German and Italian troops held out well but this did not stop Soviet tanks from getting close to the artillery positions, only to be driven off and suffering the loss of almost all of the infantry accompanying the tanks. On the right, the 6th Bersaglieri had overcome enemy resistance, reaching the ridges of hills 176.7 and 122.7, thus protecting the right flank of the two attacking columns. After having counterattacked at Bobrovski with tank support, the bersaglieri had held fast and repulsed the enemy, inflicting heavy losses, thanks in part to fire by the III/120 Artillery and by the 75/39 antitank battery. Some Soviet tanks that had managed to pass through the artillery positions and had made it close to the divisional command post were knocked out by 75/39 antitank guns that were well sited in a sunflower field. Towards evening, all Soviet counterattacks had been fended off. During the fighting Colonel Caretto was wounded in the leg. He died on 5 August at Field Hospital No. 6. Colonel Ercole Felici took over command of the 3rd Bersaglieri.

In the early hours of 1 August, the attack resumed: Inf.Rgt. 578 moved from Satonski along the Don, while XX Battalion of the 3rd Bersaglieri moved up onto Hill 180. The Soviets reacted with violent artillery and mortar fire. At dawn, supported by German air sorties, the XX attacked and seized Hill 197.4, thus assisting the action of Inf.Rgt. 578, which at 5:30 broke into Serafimovich from the south, while the XX and XVII broke in from the east.

The XXV Battalion which was attacking towards Byelayevski was not able to make contact with the VI/6 and began to shift too much to the southeast, distancing itself from the regiment's other battalions. The division commander then threw in the XLVII Motorcycle Battalion to fill the gap and to capture Byelayevski. Meanwhile, the XIII/6, after bitter fighting, captured Hill 121.8 and other heights north of Baskovski.

Bersaglieri troops attacking, summer 1941. A Breda Model 37 heavy machine gun in the foreground is being prepared for action. (USSME)

A column of bersaglieri motorcyclists on the move, summer 1942. (USSME)

By the night of 1 August, the situation was as follows: Serafimovich and Byelayevski had been occupied, but there were still Soviets hidden in the woods to the east of Serafimovich. The 6th Bersaglieri had settled in on the ridge in front of Bobrovski and Baskovski.

On 2 August, the attacks resumed: the 3rd Bersaglieri were engaged in completing the occupation of Serafimovich and Byelayevski, carrying out sweeps, while other elements of the 3rd and 6th Bersaglieri, split into two columns, were engaged in the occupation of Bobrosvski and Baskovski. The 3rd Bersaglieri column cleared the woods east of Serafimovich and after having reached the Don had to ward off a strong Soviet counterattack. The 6th Bersaglieri column, led by Colonel Salvatores, captured Bobrovski at 3:00 and also had to face and repel a strong Soviet counterattack. The VI/6 column led by Lieutenant Colonel Trevisani attacked Baskovski, meeting stiff resistance and it was not until 12:00 that the village was taken.

In the afternoon, the Soviets brought in fresh forces and made repeated attacks, with no success. Southeast of Baskovski, the Italians finally made contact with 79.Infanterie-Division, which had captured Raspopinskaya. In the evening of 2 August, General Marazzani ordered the formation of two sectors for the following day: a 'Lombardi' sector from Serafimovich to Byelayevski with the 3rd Bersaglieri (minus the XXV Battalion), the XLVII motorcylists and other reinforcing elements, and a 'Salvatores' sector, from Byelayevski to Baskovski with the 6th Bersaglieri (minus the VI Battalion) and reinforcing elements. In divisional reserve were the VI and XXV battalions, to the east of Hill 210.1. At the same time, in both sectors clearing operations had to be completed to the east of Serafimovich and the woods between Bobrovski and Baskovski.

On the morning of 3 August, the XVIII/3, a German infantry battalion and the 3rd Motorcycle Company, after having eliminated the last pockets of enemy resistance, cleared the woods east of Serafimovich. In the 6th Bersaglieri sector, the Soviets attacked Bobrovski; heavy fighting continued, at the end of which the XII Bersaglieri were forced to withdraw to the ridge east of the village. A counterattack was mounted by the VI/6 and after more furious close-quarter fighting which lasted almost eleven hours, Bobrovski was retaken. Baskovski, which had been temporarily abandoned, was recaptured after a hard-fought battle.

Bersaglieri thrown into an attack on the Ukrainian steppe, summer 1942. A ubiquitous, although notoriously unreliable, Breda Model 30 light machine gun can be seen to the right of center. (USSME)

Gold Medal for Military Valor

Distinguishing himself in this latest defensive fighting was Second Lieutenant Bruno Carloni of the 6th Bersaglieri Regiment (2nd Company, VI Battalion), who defended Hill 210 with his men. After having been wounded in one arm, the young bersagliere stayed at his post while continuing to fight under Soviet fire. He did not stop urging his men to persevere in their action until a burst of machine gun fire, hitting him full in the chest, dealt him a mortal blow. He was awarded the Gold Cross for Military Valor posthumously, with the following citation:

> A very young, enthusiastic and valorous officer, previously decorated with the Silver Medal for Military Valor in the field. During the bitter and bloody fighting, when the enemy had managed to break into the lines, threatening the left flank of one of our battalions, at the head of his men he went on the counterattack. Wounded in one arm, he refused all aid and having summarily bandaged himself, he continued with unaltered bravery, throwing back the enemy in hand-to-hand fighting. While standing erect in front of his men, he defended his position with hand grenades against renewed and increasingly furious assaults, a machine gun burst felled him. To the bersaglieri who ran to his aid he responded with a supreme effort, raising his feather [a cockerel plume worn on bersaglieri headgear] high: 'My father gave this to me, tell him I wore it with honor'. Magnificent figure of a soldier, who in the light of his sacrifice consecrates and exalts the example of the purest bersaglieri passion.
>
> Russian front – Bobrovski, 3 August 1942.

During the course of the same action, also killed were Lieutenant Colonel Enrico Rivoire who was awarded a Silver Medal for Military Valor, and soldier Berardino Leoni, also awarded the Gold Medal for Military Valor, with the following citation:

> Machine gunner, during a bitter fight, his squad leader having fallen, on his own initiative he gave his weapon over to another gunner and assumed command of the surviving team

Bersaglieri carrying two prisoners to the rear aboard Benelli a motorcycle. (USSME)

members, revealing his uncommon character and abilities. With a second and more violent attack by preponderant enemy forces, calmly, heedless of danger, he urged his fellow soldiers to continue to resist. The machine gunner having fallen, he placed the weapon on the edge of the position for a better field of fire, and he handled it with rare ability, cutting down the attackers. Out of ammunition, pressed closely by a renewed enemy wave and with almost all of his fellow soldiers dead or wounded, while standing in the contested trench line he threw all of his hand grenades. Wounded, bleeding from various places and having run out of grenades, he threw himself against the enemy, shouting 'Savoia' while throwing stones. In a supreme holocaust, he immolated his proud youth in a supreme act of victory.

Russian front – Bobrovski, 3 August 1942.

Sweep operations

Because there were still some Soviet soldiers taking refuge in the woods between the two villages, on 4 August General Hollidt ordered the 'Celere' to sweep the woods and to push the Italian units as far as the right bank of the Don. In particular, worried about the existence of a wide space between the 'Celere' positions and those of XXIX.Armee-Korps, Hollidt asked the Italians to keep watch over a stretch of the right bank of the Don about thirty kilometers wide. In order to sweep the woods, a combat group was formed led by Major Siegfried Schuchardt, commander of I/Inf. Rgt. 226, consisting of two German battalions of 79.Inf.Div., and the Italian XII/6 and XIX/6, and the III Gruppo of the 120th Artillery, the remainder of the II (75/27 guns) and the LXIII 105/32 group. Stukas were to support the action. The Soviets reacted against the attacks begun on 6 August, setting off desperate fighting, with heavy losses on both sides, but towards evening the Italo-German force reached the right bank of the Don. That same day, Generalleutnant Richard Graf von Schwerin, commander of 79.Infanterie-Division, meeting with the commander of the 6th Bersaglieri Regiment on Hill 176.7, Colonel Umberto Salvatores, stated to him that 'You bersaglieri are marvelous. Even without adequate means, you stopped the Soviet tanks. In your condition, we Germans ourselves would not have been able to fight even one day of war'.[1]

During the night, the Soviets attempted to recapture the ground they had lost but were again beaten and pushed across the Don. In the night of 8 August, despite heavy losses sustained the previous days, the Soviets returned to attack the wooded area, forcing the Italians and Germans to withdraw to the heights again. At that point, General Hollidt became convinced that he had to abandon the woods to the enemy and ordered the Italo-German units to continue to hold out to the last on the dominant heights in order to preclude any new Soviet offensives.

Distinguishing himself in the fighting between 7 and 8 August was Second Lieutenant Enzo Michelini, a platoon leader in the 6th Bersaglieri, decorated with the Gold Medal for Military Valor posthumously, with the following citation:

> During a long period of bitter fighting, he distinguished himself by his superb courage. Finding himself with his platoon in a critical counterassault situation at the head of his platoon, he led by example and word against an enemy who had overwhelming men and equipment. Having repulsed the enemy he continued on to the objective that had been assigned to him, reaching it and defending it at the price of enormous sacrifice. Although badly wounded in the chest, he still urged his platoon to resist. He defended himself with his pistol against the enemy who was closing in, killing several of them. Out of ammunition, he shouted the battle cry 'Savoia' to his bersaglieri and, before being cut down by a new machine gun burst, threw his pistol at the fleeing enemy.
>
> Russian front – Bobrovski, 7-8 August 1942.

On 13 August, 'Celere' troops were finally relieved by the 79.Infanterie-Division, to be transferred to Italian 8th Army reserve. Only the raggruppamento Lombardi remained on the line, subordinate to 79.Inf.Div. and on 21 August was transferred to the 'Sforzesca' division sector.

---

1   AA.VV.: *Le operazioni delle Unità Italiane al Fronte Russo (1941-1943)*, p. 227.

10

First Defensive Battle of the Don

In mid-August 1942, the Italian 8th Army, as part of Heeresgruppe B, was deployed along the Don, with the Hungarian 2nd Army on its left and the German 6.Armee on its right. Army headquarters had divided the defensive front into three sectors; from left to right were II Army Corps (294.Inf.Div., 'Cosseria', Ravenna), the XXIX.Armee-Korps ('Torino', 62.Inf.Div.) and XXXV Army Corps ('Pasubio', 'Sforzesca'). Beginning on 12 August, the Soviets began to make small-scale incursions against the Italian defensive line which cost a dozen or so killed and many wounded. The purpose of these actions was to find the weakest spots in the deployment and then to attempt to penetrate the line; one of these points was determined to be in the sector defended by the 54th Regiment 'Umbria' of the 'Sforzesca' Division.

The Soviet attack

At 2:30 on 20 August, following a brief preparatory bombardment by artillery and mortars, three regiments of the Soviet 197th Rifle Division crossed the Don on ferries and attacked the positions of the 54th Regiment of the 'Sforzesca', in particular, those of the II/54 on the heights south of Simovski and between Simovski and Krutovski and those of the III/54 between Satonski and Tyukovnoski. The Italians warded off the attacks twice. At 4:30, the Soviet attacks also hit the positions of the 53rd Regiment 'Umbria', at the boundary with the 'Pasubio' division near Pleshyakovski. At the same time the attacks intensified against the II/54 which was deployed on the right wing at Simovski, which soon found itself surrounded. Division headquarters sent the battalion a company of the I/53 as reinforcement. At 7:30, XXXV Corps headquarters sent as reinforcements to the 53rd Infantry an antitank company and two flamethrower platoons, while to the II/54, which faced a greater threat, the LXII Battalion of the 'Tagliamento' Blackshirt group was sent as reinforcement; this battalion took up positions along the balka that from Krutovski ran from the Don to the southeast, managing to reestablish continuity of the defensive line and contact with the III/54. At the same time, the I/54 was ordered to move to the north and to counterattack, aiming at Hill 163.1 and Simovski. Further to the right the Conforti[1] column was engaged, which was to push to the north towards Bobrovski to protect the right flank that had been left exposed by German units. To add greater strength to the counterattack, General Messe also made available to the 'Sforzesca' the LXXIX Blackshirt battalion, reinforced by the 3rd Battery of 75/32 guns.

At 15:30, after desperate fighting that lasted at least twelve hours, the men of the II/54 were able to free themselves; of the 680 soldiers present at dawn, only 72 managed to cross back into friendly

---

1   From the name of the commander of the squadron group, Major Gerardo Conforti (1 squadron group and 2 machine gun platoons of the 'Savoia Cavalleria', 1 47/32 antitank platoon, 3rd Horse Battery)

Blackshirt troops on the march, August 1942. (USSME)

lines, moving to Hill 163.1 south of Bobrovski. The Soviet offensive thrust was temporarily kept in check.

At 16:00, without the planned aerial bombardment against the opposite river bank, the I/54 mounted its counterattack, pushing Soviet forces back as far as Hill 142.4, while the 'Tagliamento' group and the 'Savoia Cavalleria' Regiment protected its flanks. A few hours later, fire from Soviet heavy weapons deployed on the right bank of the river stalled the counterattack about three kilometers south of Simovski. The Conforti column got as far as Bobrovski, but also was taken under enemy fire and was forced to withdraw.

At the end of that first terrible day, Italian losses had been heavy, especially for the 54th Infantry. The continuity of the front line had, however, been maintained and a counterattack was planned for the following day to reestablish it completely. On the XXIX.Armee-Korps front, late in the evening, the 'Torino' threw back an enemy attack near Monastirshina. All of the attacks made against II Army Corps positions were also repulsed with minimum losses.

Episodes of courage were not lacking, such as that of Sergeant Major Eraldo Cabutto of the 54th Infantry who, when he saw the Soviets break through the Italian defenses, gathered together a group of soldiers assigned to various service units, not from the front line, and leading them in a counterattack. Despite being badly wounded he refused to leave the front line, fighting to his death. He was awarded the Gold Medal for Military Valor posthumously, with the following citation:

A payroll NCO, having noted during heavy fighting that irresistible enemy pressure was about to make a breach in his battalion's line, with quick initiative and having gathered a group of bold soldiers from the administrative and service personnel, he led them in an attack, motivating them with his heroic example. During the fighting, badly wounded in his legs, he continued the unequal struggle and, even though immobilized on the ground, he refused aid

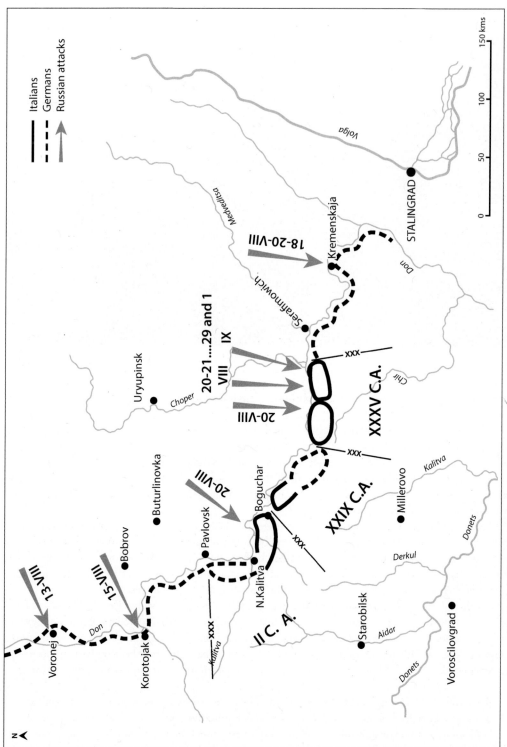

The First Defensive Battle of the Don: Russian attacks from Voronezh to Kremenskaya. (August 1942)

A Breda 30 manned by Blackshirts, August 1942. (USSME)

and continued to fight with tireless valor. Hit once again, he proudly resisted all attempts by those who tried to get him out of the line of fire, and aware of his fate, stubbornly wanted to remain on that ground which he had defended so audaciously and with so much sacrifice. Out of ammunition and having thrown his last hand grenade, he fell to the ground calling with desperate love his far-off country to which he had dedicated his flowering youth.

Russian front, 20 August 1942.

Cavalry participation

As previously mentioned, a counterattack on 21 August was planned by the 'Sforzesca' headquarters in order to stabilize the line of resistance along the Don; in particular, the I/54 was to attack on the right towards Simovski and in the center the III/53 and the XV Sapper Battalion were to move from Hill 190.1 and attack towards Nizne Matveyevski and Tyukovnovski while the I/53 was to attack towards Satonski and on the left, the II/53 reinforced by the 16th Chemical Company was to attack towards Pleshyakovski. But the Soviets attacked first; after having had about a dozen infantry battalions cross the Don (elements of the 14th Guards Division and the 203rd Rifle Division), at dawn these forces moved to attack, preceded by preparatory artillery fire. The main Soviet effort focused mainly on the center of the 'Sforzesca' defensive front, against the III/53, which supported by two sapper companies, was able with great effort to hold its positions. On the right, however, the planned counterattack was made around 7:00, even knowing that the action would not reach its objectives. At the same time, the counterattack against Pleshyakovski was cancelled in order to defend the line of heights that dominated the Don.

Around 10:00, the I Gruppo of 105/28 guns of the division's 17th Artillery, after having defended itself by firing point blank with its guns, was forced to withdraw, protected by the desperate resistance of the III/53. Shortly after, the infantry also pulled back, reestablishing some degree of continuity of the defensive line. In an attempt to close the gap that had been created between the two regiments of the 'Sforzesca', the Corps sent the LXXIX Blackshirt battalion of the 'Tagliamento', with orders to occupy positions between Hill 191.4 and Hill 188.6 to maintain contact between the 53rd and 54th regiments. However, during the advance, near Hill 193.7, the Blackshirts clashed with an enemy force and were surrounded. After managing with great tenacity to contain the attack, the Blackshirts fell back to the right-hand sector on Hill 193.7.

The ferocious resistance by the Blackshirts of the LXXXIX Battalion avoided the worst, preventing the Soviets from surrounding the right wing of the Italian deployment. The legionnaires fought to the end, as General Messe[2] himself attested:

> Thus the LXXXIX Blackshirt battalion, which had been sent in the early hours of the afternoon from the extreme right towards the center of the divisional sector with the mission of establishing a new strongpoint, was attacked during its move by enemy forces dug in on the heights of Hill 232.2, a central point of the watershed between Kriutscha and Zuzkan. Heavily engaged from the front and at the time threatened on its right flank, the battalion heroically faced the critical situation: it is because of the knowing sacrifice of its soldiers that the enemy, due to having been stalled, was not able to overcome the right wing of the deployment until the late afternoon. The battalion, although with serious difficulty, was then able to withdraw.

In order to stem the tide of the Soviet offensive against the center of the 'Sforzesca' positions, General Messe transferred and subordinated to 'Sforzesca' the horse-mounted units that were still available. Thus, at dawn the 'Lancieri di Novara' moved from Gorbatovo to Bakmutkin and to Yagodnyi, marching for 65 kilometers reinforced with mortars, antitank guns and a horse drawn battery group. The horse-mounted units, organized in two columns, with the Morcaldi column on the left and the Dal Re column (Major Dal Re) on the right, sent to support the 'Sforzesca' infantrymen, soon clashed with the advancing Soviet forces.

The regimental commander ordered the recon detachment to take positions from the northern slopes of Hill 187.1, making contact on the left with the II/53, to the northern slopes of Hill 218.9, establishing contact on the right with the 'Savoia Cavalleria' Regiment. The horse artillery group displaced to southeast of Yagodnyi, while the regimental headquarters was in the same village with the rest of the available forces, grouped in the Pagliano column (led by Colonel Carlo Pagliano).

The 'Savoia Cavalleria' Regiment was to be committed on the right of the 'Sforzesca', in the valley of the Zuzkan, where from the preceding day the Conforti column had already been in place and which at dawn on 21 August was engaged on Hill 163.1, along with the LXIII CC.NN. Battalion. The rest of the regiment, grouped together in the Bettoni column, led by Colonel Alessandro Bettoni Cazzago[3] and consisting of the regimental headquarters, II Squadron Group and half of the machine gun squadron, two antitank platoons and one horse battery, at 13:00 moved from Kotovski towards Ceboratevski. A patrol sent out on recon to Hill 232.2 found about a hundred

---

2   Messe, *La guerra al fronte russo*, p. 206.
3   Alessandro Bettoni Cazzago was born in Brescia on 7 November 1892. He studied the classics at the Carlo Alberto royal college in Moncalieri and then enlisted as a volunteer in the cavalry. A captain in the Great War, he fought on the Carso and was awarded the Silver Medal for Military Valor and two Bronze Medals. In 1920 he was assigned to the 3rd Regiment 'Savoia Cavalleria'. An equestrian athlete, in the 1930s he participated in more than 65 international and 141 Italian national equestrian competitions, winning 384 prizes, 253 cups and 62 trophies between 1929 and 1939. In 1942, he was given command of the 'Savoia Cavalleria' Regiment with the rank of colonel.

A Savoia Cavalleria patrol with Soviet prisoners, summer 1942. (USSME)

infantrymen led by a captain, retreating in panic. General Barbò ordered them to deploy to new positions in the same area.

Meantime, the Bettoni column, on the march from Ceboratevski to the same Hill 232.2, clashed with Soviet troops and soon after assumed defensive positions along with an infantry unit that was deploying in defense of Ceboratevski.

At 16:00, Messe officially attached the horse raggruppamento to the 'Sforzesca', which acting in concert with the LXXIX CC.NN. Battalion and two companies of the 53rd Infantry, was to reach the positions from the Hill 109.1 front to Hill 188.6. On the right the Conforti column was ordered to pull back, continuing to fight against the Soviets and at 19:00 set up along the new 'Sforzesca' defensive positions. During the night, the troops were consolidated on the two strong-points at Yagodnyi and Ceboratevski.

On the II Army Corps front, the troops of the 'Ravenna' division repulsed three enemy attacks, while the 'Cosseria' division was not attacked.

At dawn on 22 August, deployed at the Yagodnyi strongpoint were the 53rd Infantry Regiment, part of the III/54, the remnants of the XV Sapper Battalion and the 3rd Flamethrower Company, for a total of about 3,500 men, with 71 light machine guns, 30 machine guns, 16 81mm mortars, 6 47/32 guns and 31 flamethrowers. The I/54 was gathering at the Ceboratevski strongpoint, while already present there were the II/54, part of the III/54 and the 'Tagliamento' CC.NN. Group, totaling about 1,000 men with 9 light machine guns, 21 machine guns, 27 81mm mortars and 2 47/32 guns. The 'Sforzesca' headquarters set itself up in Gorbatovo.

Charge of the 'Lancieri di Novara'

At 14:00, the Soviets attacked the Yagodnyi strongpoint, also attacking the positions of the 'Lancieri di Novara' between Hill 224.4 and Hill 218.9. Thanks to quick reaction by a squadron on foot (1st Squadron) which engaged the enemy frontally and by a charge on horseback by another squadron, the Soviets were thrown back. The squadron on horseback was the 2nd squadron led by Lieutenant Mario Spotti who was ordered to charge against the enemy's flank. Shortly after 14:00, the 2nd Squadron advanced cautiously with its horses at a walk covered by a modest dip in the ground; as soon as they were out in the open, Lieutenant Spotti ordered the charge, shouting to his lancers: 'Boys! It's our day!. God and the standard are with us! Draw sabers…trot..gallop…charge!' The entire squadron of 100 men and 100 horses, as if on exercise with the points of their sabers at the oblique so as to hit from the top down, threw itself against the left flank of the enemy on Hill 224.4; it was unsheathed blades and horses charging against Soviet soldiers armed with automatic rifles, submachine guns and hand grenades. Lieutenant Spotti was among the first to be hit by enemy fire and although wounded, continued to charge while hanging on to his horse until, with his horse also hit, he fell in the midst of the Soviets who surrounded him and he continued to fight to the end with his pistol. The close-quarter fighting lasted only a few seconds. When his lancers, after a wild fight, managed to down all of the enemy around him, they found him dead, his body and face marked by dozens of bullets and bayonet wounds.

With the lieutenant dead, command of the squadron was assumed by Second Lieutenant Mario Guerrieri, but the charge by the lancers, following the initial bold and overwhelming rush, had been transformed in the meantime into a series of ferocious close-quarter encounters. After having charged against the Soviet infantry with their sabers, the lancers were isolated amongst them in small groups. Most of them were surrounded little by little, with their horses knocked from under them by rifle fire or by bayonets. Many instances of bravery characterized this bitter struggle, which saw the Italian cavalrymen unhorsed and their mates rushing to their aid at the gallop, throwing back the enemy and helping them back into the saddle. In the end, Lieutenant Guerrieri and the 2nd Squadron got the better of it, putting the enemy battalion to flight. Losses for the 2nd Squadron were 1 officer, 1 NCO and 9 lancers killed, 24 wounded and 51 horses lost, of which 12 were killed.

Lieutenant Mario Spotti was awarded the Gold Medal for Military Valor with the following citation: 'Even though exempt from military service, he insistently requested and was able to be sent to a mobilized unit. Attacked and on the point of being overrun by overwhelming enemy forces, he threw himself at the head of his squadron in a charge, sweeping away the first enemy ranks. Wounded, in order to stay in his saddle, he clung to his horse and continued to fight, giving his men an example of sublime will and heroism. Having fallen to the ground and with his horse mortally wounded, he managed to get up on his feet. Surrounded by enemy soldiers who asked him to surrender, he pulled out his pistol, kissed it and emptied the clip against his enemies. Then, after once again urging his squadron, which by then had repulsed the enemy, he fell dead while praising his country'. Hill 224.4, Yagodnyi (Russian front), 22 August 1942.

The truce lasted only a short while because the enemy returned shortly after, attacking with greater forces. Some Soviet units, after having managed to infiltrate in the balka of the Krisaya, were on the verge of taking Yagodnyi but were driven back thanks to personal action by Colonel Carlo Pagliano, who after having gathered all of the available men including horsemen, infantrymen, engineers and gunners, launched a counterattack. Around 18:00, the Soviets ceased their offensive action, leaving about a hundred prisoners and a large quantity of arms and equipment in Italian hands.

The strongpoint at Ceboratevski was also attacked by the Soviets for about four hours, but without any success. More than 400 dead Soviets were counted in front of the Italian positions.

Poster from the first page of the period magazine *Cronache* Number 40 of 1943 which shows Lieutenant Mario Spotti leading his lancers in the "Charge at Jagodniy". (From a drawing by G. Bertoletti)

In the afternoon, in addition to the 'Celere', the 'Monte Cervino' alpine ski battalion, the IX Engineer Bridge Battalion and the German Inf.Rgt. 179 were transferred to XXXV Army Corps.

Italian counterattack

At dawn on 23 August, the Yagodnyi and Ceboratevski strongpoints were again attacked by Soviet forces but were again repulsed with heavy losses, thanks mainly to Italian artillery barrage fire. At the same time, to restabilize the situation on the right bank of the Don, a counterattack was planned, moving on the left of the 'Sforzesca' division's sector and that of the 'Pasubio' division. General Messe, who wanted to coordinate the action himself, had fixed the heights that dominated the River Don as the objective of the attack. Two columns were organized for the counterattack:

- a column on the left, under General Roberto Olmi, commander of the 'Pasubio' divisional infantry, consisting of the III/80, the Croat Legion, Inf.Rgt. 179 and two German artillery groups from 62.Inf.Div., which was to move from the area of Hill 219 to the west of Verhiniy Krivoskoy.
- a column on the right, led by General Mario Marazzani, commander of the 'Celere' Division, consisting of the entire division, which was to move from the area west of Bachmutkin towards hills208.4, 188.6 and 191.4.

The 'Monte Cervino' Batttalion, still deployed in the Gorbatovo area, was to take part in the counteroffensive on the right, while the horse raggruppamento was to join in to exploit the success.

The attack began at 9:45: at 12:00 the left column, after having gotten past the balka at Olkovatka, occupied the village of Verhiniy Krivskoy and Hill 197.2, while the III/79 advanced

Cavalry troopers charging in an attack, summer 1942. (USSME)

Alpini of the Monte Cervino engaged in combat, August 1942. (Authors' collection)

on the ridge southeast of Rubeschinski. The right column attacked with the Felici column, led by colonel Ercole Felici, commander of the 3rd Bersaglieri, consisting of the 3rd Bersaglieri, with the XX/3 and XXV/3 in the lead, followed by two battalions of the 6th Bersaglieri and reinforcing elements. The Felici column advanced as far as Hill 208.4, where it was stalled by massive enemy barrage fire. In the early afternoon, the Italian troops skirted the hill from the east, reaching the area between hills 232.2 and 224.4, while the reserve units reached Hill 208.4 and the Otbelaize kolkhoz. At 16:00, XX and XXV/3 battalions attacked Hill 224.4, followed by the VI and XIII/6. The Soviets responded with massive barrage fire from artillery, mortars and machine guns. At 17:00, the summit of the hill was captured with bayonets and hand grenades.

Meanwhile, the Salvatores column, which had just reached Hill 208.4, was attacked repeatedly and suffered heavy casualties. Further to the north, Inf.Rgt. 179 was also attacked on Hill 197.2; after having been pushed off the hill, the Germans counterattacked and retook the hill.

In late evening, Colonel Felici had his troops withdraw further to the south, onto Hill 218.9. At the end of the day the losses were counted: the 3rd 'Celere' reported 28 killed (2 officers) and 263 wounded (17 officers), while the 'Pasubio' had 31 dead, 213 wounded and 65 missing.

General Messe ordered the transfer of Inf.Rgt.179 to the 'Celere' and resumption of the attack against Hill 224.4, in three columns: Oberst Konrad von Alberti's Inf.Rgt.179 was to move from Hill 197.2, the Salvatores column (6th Bersaglieri) from Hill 208.4 and the Felici column (3rd Bersaglieri) from Hill 218.9.

Bersaglieri motorcyclists engaged in tough fighting in a village, summer 1942. (Vicenzo de Gaetano collection)

Cavalry action

Late in the morning of 23 August, General Messe had ordered the horse raggruppamento to focus on the enemy's left flank, moving to Hill 213.5, passing south and southwest of Tchebotarevski, in order to participate along with the 3rd 'Celere' in the capture of Hill 191.4 and then to proceed towards Krutovski. The 'Lancieri di Novara' were to reach Hill 191.4, passing Hill 232.2, but were only able to get as far as Hill 211.8. Threatened with being surrounded, during the night they pulled back to the area northwest of Tchebotarevski. The 'Savoia Cavalleria' Regiment was to reach Hill 213.5 (situated about seven kilometers southwest of the village of Izbushensky) and the following dawn to move to Hill 193.7 so as to threaten the rear of the Soviet units that were pressing on Tchebotarevski and at the same time protect the right flank of the Italian deployment. After having sent out reconnaissance patrols, it was found that the northwest slope of Hill 213.5 was occupied by strong enemy forces. With nightfall, the horse-mounted units made camp on the northern slope of the hill, bivouacking on the steppe and forming themselves into a square. The Bettoni column, led by colonel Bettoni Cazzago, consisting of the 'Savoia Cavalleria' reinforced with the II horse artillery group and by antitank guns (a total of about 700 men), while heading towards Hill 213.5, was spotted by the Soviets on the night of 23 August. Accordingly, to deal with the threat, during the night the Soviets shifted three battalions of the 812th Siberian infantry regiment of the 304th Infantry Division (about 2,500 men) to within about a kilometer of the Italian positions. The Soviets dug in between the sunflowers, forming a wide semicircle from northwest to northeast, waiting to attack the Italian troops.

Italian cavalry deploying prior to an action, summer 1942. (Gaetano de Vincenzo collection)

Horse cavalry on the march, passing a horse artillery piece. Horse-drawn artillery of the cavalry units were also called "Voloire', a word in the Piedmontese dialect that literally means 'Flying'. (Authors' collection)

Charge at Izbushensky

At first light, before moving to attack, a horse patrol was sent out, led by Sergeant Ernesto Comolli, to check out a 'suspicious' cart full of hay that had been noticed the prior evening in front of the Italian positions. A member of the patrol, Corporal Aristide Bottini, quickly spotted a soldier amongst the sunflowers. Initially, thinking of the presence of German soldiers, Bottini called out to him. But when the soldier turned towards them, they immediately spotted the Soviet red star on his helmet. Cavalryman Petroso immediately opened fire, hitting the enemy soldier in the head. The Soviets reacted promptly with massive mortar and machine gun fire which hit the Italian square and caused some losses; among these was Lieutenant Colonel Giuseppe Cacciandra, the regimental deputy commander, wounded in the leg, and Captain Renzo Aragone, hit in the knee. The commander, Bettoni Cazzago, had a bullet go through his overcoat.

Once having gotten past the surprise over the quick enemy reaction, while the squadrons were preparing to attack, the howitzers of the horse artillery battery, under Lieutenant Giubilaro, responded quickly to the fire, as did also the antitank guns and machineguns still in place from the night before. The prompt Italian fire forced the Soviets to lessen the intensity of their fire and to fall back on their own lines, which were too close to the Italian lines. Having noted the Soviet maneuver, the commander to the 'Savioa' decided to commit the 2nd Squadron on horseback into an attack, led by Captain Francesco Saverio De Leone, against the Soviet flank.[4] After having made a wide detour, the 2nd Squadron fell upon the first Soviet battalion in close ranks and with sabers drawn, completely overrunning it and continuing the charge against the other two battalions. As the Italian horsemen passed them, many Soviet soldiers hid in their holes, then raising their heads and fire upon the cavalrymen from the rear. At that point, the 2nd Squadron doubled back, making a second charge, this time throwing hand grenades. The Soviet battalion on the left, before being overrun by the charge, was almost wiped out and its survivors, while withdrawing to the southeast, were captured by troops of the German 79.Inf.Div.

> The squadron came out of the slight depression in the ground unexpectedly, very close to the enemy's left flank; there was a moment of hesitation, followed by 'Galopoooo!' [Gallop], and right after that by 'Caricaat!'[Charge], a yell which was answered by a loud chorus of 'Savoia!'; the howl drowned out the din of the charge and was heard as far away as the regiment. The gallop then became an unleashed charge and the platoons erupted like a river overflowing its banks against the enemy lines, yelling, slashing with sabers, throwing hand grenades. The horses seemed to have overcome their tiredness and raged on in a froth, jumping over trenches and machine gun nests, heading in droves towards the objective indicated by the spurs and disappearing in enormous clouds of dust, followed by the noise of their hooves and by the furious chattering of weapons.[5]

The other two Soviet infantry battalions, having suffered lighter losses, tried to react, at which point Colonel Bettoni had the 4th Squadron dismount, led by Captain Silvano Abba,[6] and ordered

---

4   According to some reports, it seems that commander Bettoni at first wanted to have the entire regiment make the charge, with the standard unfurled, but was then convinced by his adjutant, Major Pietro de Vito Piscicelli di Collesano, to echelon his forces as the situation developed.

5   Lucio Lami, *Isbuscenskii, l'ultima carica*, page 230.

6   Silvano Abba was born in Rovigno on 3 July 1911. After having attended the Rovigno Technical institute, he entered the Royal Military Academy of Modena, graduating with the rank of second lieutenant and assigned to the cavalry branch. He then attended advanced courses at the Application School in Pinerolo and later at the school at Tor di Quinto (Rome). At the end of his studies, he entered service with the 10th Regiment 'Lancieri di Vittorio Emanuele II', stationed in Bologna,

Savoia cavalry troopers on the move, August 1942. (USSME)

it to engage the Soviet forces frontally in order to ease the pressure on the 2nd Squadron on horse-back. The action was successful but Captain Abba was killed in the attack, hit by a burst of subma-chine gun fire while he was leading his men in the assault. Abba was later decorated with the Gold Medal for Military Valor posthumously, with the following citation:

> Squadron commander of exceptional valor, in days of bitter fighting, while other units were n action on horseback on the flank of a large enemy deployment, with his squadron on foot he made a frontal attack against strong enemy positions. Quickly overcoming the enemy first defen-sive line defended by numerous machine guns, in furious close-quarter fighting he again led his troopers against the next enemy line. Wounded once and having fallen heavily to the ground, he got up again with great energy and went on to wipe out other enemy fire positions, thus deciding the victorious outcome of an epic day. In the final superb dash, hit mortally a second time, he died proudly in the field. A shining example of heroism and of every military virtue.
>
> Hill 213 at Izbushensky (Russian front), 24 August 1942.

Despite the two charges and the frontal attack by the 4th Squadron on foot, the other two Soviet battalions continued to fight back, inflicting notable casualties among the Italian troops. It was then that Major Dario Mansuardi, who had taken part in the 2nd Squadron's charge, went to Colonel Bettoni to ask for commitment of another horse squadron for a new charge. Accordingly,

---

showing his talent as an athlete, so much so that he was chosen to participate in the Olympic games in Berlin in 1936. On 2 August 1936, he took first place in the equestrian competition in the modern pentathlon, which earned him an overall third place and a bronze medal, thus becoming the first Italian to step onto the podium in this discipline. During the civil war in Spain, as a lieutenant in the 1st Tank Battalion, leading his company he was first to enter Mazaleón Gandesa and Tortosa and was awarded the Silver Medal for Military Valor. Following Italy's entry into the war, on 10 June 1940 he was assigned to the 3rd Regiment 'Savoia Cavalleria', as part of the 3rd 'Celere' Division' Principe Amadeo Duca d'Aosta', with which he fought on the French front and then in Yugoslavia in April 1941. During 1940, between the two military campaigns, he became the Italian modern pentathlon champion and won the Ceccarelli Cup. Promoted to captain, he left for the Russian front as commander of the 4th Squadron of his regiment, assigned to the Italian expeditionary corps in Russia.

First aid for those wounded at Izbushensky, prior to their transfer to a field hospital. (Authors' collection)

the 'Savoia' commander ordered the 3rd Squadron, under Captain Francesco Marchio, to attack. Joining the squadron in the attack were the commander of the II Squadron Group, Major Alberto Litta Modignani and his headquarters personnel.

When, however, the 3rd Squadron went forward it reached a bottleneck between the folds in the ground and ended up coming under massive fire from Soviet machine guns and mortars well sited on the flanks. Following is testimony of Lieutenant Franco Toja: 'Seeing them arrive we stopped for an instant to watch that tremendous charge in awe, but soon fire fell upon them with incredible accuracy; I saw Ragazzi fall first, then Sergeant Mentasti, then Ardito, the major's orderly, then Sergeant Major Fantini who was riding Albino, then Sergeant Bonacina and Dossena and so many other troopers cut down like grain by the bursts. I saw Marchi who, bloody, cried in pain and in rage, and I picked up Bussolera who was wounded in the abdomen'.

Major Litta Modignani was wounded in the leg by a burst that had also killed his horse; the officer then tried to mount on his corporal's horse, but he was too weak. Dragging himself along the ground, he approached a machine gun position, pointing out to the machine gunner the targets to engage. He was soon hit mortally by another enemy bullet.

Litta Modignani was killed in the charge, along with his aide, Second Lieutenant Emilo Ragazzi; both were later awarded the Gold Medal for Military Valor. Following is the citation for Alberto Litta Modignani:

> A cavalryman who had elevated the purest ideals as a norm in his life, fulfilling his desire to be in command of a troop, the imbued his squadron group with the unshakable faith that motivated him. In a day of bitter, extremely violent battle in which the entire regiment was sorely engaged, at the head of his cavalrymen, he attacked the overwhelming enemy forces with great boldness. With all of the men who were closely following him having fallen, having his horse killed and he himself badly wounded, with singular courage he had himself put in the saddle again on another horse and continued on with the epic charge. Weakened, he fell to the ground but still managed to find the energy, with his saber in his hand, to impart to his troopers the last objective of the attack and directed the fire of a group of troopers on foot. A burst of enemy fire struck him in the heart at the moment in which the last of the enemy resistance fell under the impetus of the squadrons which he prepared and led superbly. A pure and expressive figure of an Italian soldier who unalterably linked his most noble name to the ancient regimental banner.
>
> Hill 213.5, Izbushensky (Russian front), 24 August 1942.

Despite the heavy losses, in the end the charge by the 3rd Squadron put the last of the enemy to flight, pursued by saber blows and hand grenades; the two Soviet battalions were completely overrun and at 6:30 the battalion could be considered over. Captain Marchio was badly wounded in both arms and would later have his left arm amputated.

The battle had cost the Soviets dearly, losing an entire battalion, with at least 250 killed and 300 prisoners in Italian hands as well as those captured by the nearby Germans. Many heavy weapons and machine guns were also captured. From the tactical point of view, the victory served to ease Soviet pressure on the Ceboratevski strongpoint and to free the position at Izbushensky, which was occupied by the Germans. It was only after the battle did it become known that the 650 'Savoia' cavalry troopers had clashed with 2,000 Siberian soldiers. Italian losses were 32 killed (3 officers), 52 wounded (5 officers) and about a hundred horses out of action.

The 'Savoia Cavalleria' Regiment was awarded the Gold Medal for its banner, in addition to two posthumous Gold Medals, two Military Orders of Savoy, 54 Silver Medals, 50 Bronze Medals, 49 Military Crosses and several field promotions.

New defensive fighting

Thanks to the capture of Hill 213.5 by the 'Savoia Cavalleria', the posture of the XXXV Corps forces was improved considerably. However, Soviet attacks did not cease and at 13:00 three battalions of Soviet infantry attacked Hill 208.4, moving from the north and the east, supported by mortar and artillery fire. The men of the XVIII/3 and XIX/6 beat back the attack. However, the Soviets once again returned to attack the same positions for some hours, setting off attacks and counterattacks which cost the Soviets heavy losses: the 889th Rifle Regiment of the 197th Division came out of it almost completely destroyed.

Around 21:00, the enemy attacks shifted to the 'Celere' sector, where another three Soviet battalions attacked Hill 219.9; under cover of darkness, enemy troops broke into the positions defended by the XIII/6, taking the Italians from the rear. During the fighting, the commander of the 3rd Bersaglieri, Colonel Ercole Felici, was wounded, as well as two battalion commanders. Command of the 3rd Bersaglieri was temporarily assumed by Lieutenant Colonel Luigi Gianturco.

At the same time, the Soviets attacked the positions held by the III/120 Artillery and the I/120 Antitank Artillery, whose crews defended their guns with hand grenades. The troops were ordered to withdraw to Hill 187.1. The bersaglieri of the 3rd Regiment defended this position to the last, all of the men dying with their weapons in their hands.

The fighting also involved the II Corps sector; in particular, at 8:00 the Soviets attacked Krasno Orechevo, on the western side of the bend of the Verhniy Mamon, defended by troops of the 'Ravenna'. After two hours of fighting, the Soviets were able to reach the village; a counterattack by a battalion of the 'Cosseria' sent to reinforce the III/89 'Salerno' enabled Krasno Orechovo to be recaptured in the early afternoon.

At dawn on 25 August the Soviets resumed their attacks against the sector that the 'Sforzesca' was sharing with the 'Celere', in particular against the strongpoint at Tchebotarevski and Hill 209.6. The Tchebotarevski strongpoint was attacked from the north, east and west, clearly demonstrating the enemy's desire to isolate it completely. Its defenders, nevertheless, reacted well and were able to fend off the attack. The artillery gunners were however, forced to displace their guns to positions further to the rear. Shortly after, the Soviets broke into Tchebotarevski, where house-to-house fighting broke out. The battle also spread further south to Kotovski, drawing anyone who could hold a weapon, including non-combat personnel, into the fight. The horse-mounted units were also caught up in the fighting in order to push back against the enemy attacks. General Messe requested assistance from XVII.Armee-Korps units, but no aid came from the Germans, despite the fact that a dangerous gap was opening between the Italian 8th Army and the German 6.Armee; if the Soviets had managed to capture Gorbatovo, they would have been able to envelop the strongpoint at Yagodnyi from the south and thus the left wing of 8th Army. Messe then decided to pull the defenses back to the western valley of the Kriuschya and to organize a new strongpoint at Gorbatovo, south of the Yagodnyi position, to establish a defensive flank for all of the 8th Army and a base from which to mount a new counteroffensive across the Don.

During that same day, the forces of the 3rd 'Celere' were also attacked, beginning in the morning; initially the positions of the XXV/3 on hill 187.1 were attacked, north of Yagodnyi, but the Soviets were warded off. In the meantime, under protection of the alpini of the 'Monte Cervino' Battalion it was planned to withdraw Inf.Rgt.179 from Hill 109.2 to Verhniy Krivskoy.

The alpini of the 'Monte Cervino' had also been engaged in the recapture of Hill 187.1 and when on 25 August they reached the positions which had been defended to the bitter end by the bersaglieri, they found themselves facing a scene that showed just how tenaciously the boys of the 3rd Regiment had fought: '...no one had evaded death, all of them had been massacred with bayonets, the machine gunners still had their fingers clutched to the triggers of their weapons that had run completely out of ammunition and in front of them were piled, one on top of another, the corpses of dead Russians...The alpini were joined by another small group of bersaglieri, and together they quickly moved up the hill, overcoming the resistance of the occupants using hand grenades'.[7]

Disagreements with German headquarters

The withdrawals ordered by General Messe between 24 and 25 August, carried out to avoid destruction of the entire army corps, led to protests by Army Group B headquarters. To avoid any further withdrawal orders, the 'Sforzesca' division was subordinated to XVII.Armee-Korps. Messe protested this decision to General Gariboldi, which represented a clear lack of trust in the Italian commanders, but the 8th Army commander was able to do nothing. On the morning of

---

7   L.E.Longo, *I Reparti speciali italiani nella Seconda Guerra Mondiale 1940-1943*, page 231.

An antitank gun crew ready to open fire, August 1942. (USSME)

Alpini during an attack with a Breda heavy machine gun, summer 1942. (USSME)

Tanks of the LXVII Bersaglieri Armoured Battalion on the move, August 1942. (USSME)

26 August, headquarters of XVII.Armee-Korps ordered the 'Sforzesca' to occupy a new stretch of the front line from Yagodnyi to Bolshoi. General Barbò, commander of the horse group, met with General Conradt, commander of XXXXIX.Gebirgs-Armeekorps to avoid shifting the Italian units, considering that enemy attacks were still in progress.

At 8:30 on 26 August, numerous Soviet infantry attacked the positions of the 3rd 'Celere', first from the north and then from the east, but were driven back thanks to artillery support and action by Italian and German aircraft. The Soviets resumed their attacks, attempting to circle around the Italian positions from the southeast; around 11:00, after having occupied the village of Bachmutkin, the Soviets continued to the southwest against Hill 204.2, threatening the artillery positions and the strongpoint at Yagodnyi. The XLVII Motorcycle Battalion was then thrown into a counterattack to retake Bachmutkin, moving from Hill 204.2, while the 'Savoia Cavalleria' group with the remnants of the II/54 and the 1st Motorcycle Company attacked from north to south. Caught between two fires, the Soviets withdrew from the hill and from the village of Bachmutkin, pursued by II Gruppo of 'Savoia Cavalleria'. In the afternoon, other enemy attacks developed against Hill 204.8 defended by the I/79 and against Ribni, defended by the III/79, all of which were repulsed. At the end of the day, 'Celere' losses amounted to 300 men killed and wounded. The Italians took 500 prisoners and a large quantity of heavy and light weapons.

At dawn on 27 August, the eastern side of the Yagodnyi strongpoint was again attacked. After having been driven off, the Soviets attacked yet another time from the northeast, but were also repelled in front of the positions of the XXV/3 Bersaglieri.

In the afternoon, the LXVII Bersaglieri Armoured Battalion (consisting of two companies of L6/40 light tanks), recently arrived in Russia, arrived to reinforce the 3rd 'Celere'. Towards evening, the Army Group B commander cancelled the order transferring the Italian units to XVII. Armee-Korps.

The Yagodnyi strongpoint

On 28 August, the Soviets attacked Yagodni from all sides with two rifle regiments, reinforced by a machine gun battalion and an NCO cadet battalion of the 213th Rifle Division. Also attacking from the north were elements of the 899th Rifle Division. The Italian positions were attacked from all sides, except from the south. After having managed to silence several Italian fire positions, thanks to artillery fire and a counterattack by the 3rd Bersaglieri, the Soviets were driven back after having lost hundreds of men, 400 prisoners and large quantities of equipment. Worn out by the fighting, the XXV Bersaglieri Battalion was replaced during the morning by the 'Monte Cervino' ski battalion. From the strongpoint at Gorbatovo, the remnants of the II/54 counterattacked against Hill 226.7, ejecting the Soviets. An attack by the II Gruppo of 'Savoia Cavalleria' followed against the left flank and rear of a Soviet column that was advancing on Bachmutkin, forcing the enemy to retire.

In the afternoon, the remnants of the 'Tagliamento' group occupied Hill 288.0, taking the enemy by surprise and forcing them to withdraw. The I/54 was quickly sent to the hill to bolster its defenses.

The Alpini arrive

The same day, 28 August, the Soviets also attacked in the 'Pasubio' sector against the positions of the II/79 in the area of Hill 188.8 and against Hill 204.8, defended by the Croat Legion.

A 20mm Breda 35 antiaircraft gun position, August 1942. The 20mm Breda was an excellent weapon and was widely distributed to Italian forces. (Vincenzo de Gaetano collection)

Both attacks were repulsed. Also arriving as reinforcements in the sector were the 'Vestone' alpine battalion, which joined alongside the 'Morbegno', both subordinate to XXXV Corps headquarters. Thanks to the arrival of these reinforcements a counteroffensive was planned which was to involve all of the alpine units of the 'Tridentina', the armoured battalion and all other units present in the area. Participating in the action were also some forces from XVII.Armee-Korps. The attack was initially planned for 29 August, but on the evening of the 28th, the German headquarters reported that it would not be able to commit its own forces (22.Pz.Div. and elements of 79.Inf.Div.). The attack was then postponed to 1 September. Between 29 and 30 August, the Soviets continued to make attacks against the Italian positions, without committing large forces, and thus were all repulsed.

In the evening of 30 August, the directives for the combined attack by Italian XXXV Corps and 79.Inf.Div. were established; the main objective of the German forces was the capture of hills 220 and 206.3, after which armoured units were to continue on to Kotovski to make contact with the Italian units. XXXV Corps had as its objectives the ridge from Hill 236.7 to Hill 228.0, as far as the village of Kotovski, in order to make contact with the German armoured units north of that village.

The attack begins

At dawn on 1 September, after a brief bombardment by the Luftwaffe and by artillery, the Italian units moved to attack: the 'Vestone' alpine battalion advanced with its 54th Company against Hill 195.8, running into strong opposition. Its 55th Company, supported by the tank company, was able to capture the position of Ferma Number 4 at 8:00, making contact near Hill 195.8 with the 'Val Chiese' battalion which had come from Kotovski. With the Soviet troops in flight and having received the news that the Germans had occupied the village of Kalmikovski, the commander of the 6th Alpini Regiment, Colonel Paolo Signorini, ordered the 'Vestone' battalion to continue its attack towards hills 236.7 and 209.6. This latter hill was initially attacked by the L6/40 tanks, but strong Soviet fire caused them to withdraw. The assault by the alpini was more successful and at 10:30 the hill was captured.

Distinguishing himself in this round of fighting was Lieutenant Giuseppe Baisi of the 'Vestone', who was posthumously awarded the Gold Medal for Military Valor with the following citation: 'Commander of an alpine company who had already distinguished himself by exceptional valor and courage, he threw himself decisively in an attack against a hotly contested enemy position. Having reached the objective assigned to him and having captured many prisoners and automatic weapons at the cost of much blood, he was the target, along with his unit, of dangerous enemy reaction. Although during the desperate battle he had lost touch with part of his company, he sought to stabilize the situation, facing the enemy by himself. Wounded once by a machine gun burst, he threw himself with extreme decision and desperate courage against an enemy group that was attempting to surround him, scattering them. Wounded a second time, he did not give up fighting and, although weakened because of the copious amount of blood he had lost, he still urged his alpini and kept them together with the example of his bravery. In an attack that followed, he threw himself resolutely, along with a few survivors, against the enemy and was mortally wounded'. Kotovski (Russian front), 1 September 1942.

Another posthumous Gold Medal for Military Valor was awarded to Second Lieutenant Giovanni Tarchini of the 'Vestone', with the following citation: 'An officer of exceptional valor, in bitter offensive combat, the company commander having been killed, although wounded, he led the company again against strong enemy positions that were dug into the hostile terrain. Wounded again, this time badly, he continued unshaken in his leadership with skill and admirable firmness.

General Gariboldi, second from the left in the foreground, during an inspection of the front line. (USSME)

Alpine troops marching towards the Don, summer 1942. (USSME)

Heedless of his physical suffering, he went where the danger was greatest and where his presence was most needed. Cut down by a machine gun burst, he fell amongst his heroic alpini with the vision of a beaten enemy. A tenacious fighter, with his valorous behavior and sacrifice he held the glorious traditions of the Italian alpini in great honor'. Kotovski – Middle Don (Russian front), 1 September 1942.

The Soviet attacks that followed were all defeated. At the same time, the 55th Company of the 'Vestone' surprised a Soviet battery on Hill 236.7; its crew were felled and four 76mm guns were captured. The attack against Kotovski by German armoured units had not yet happened. Shortly afterwards, the news came that the German units, instead of occupying Kalmikovski, had halted at the edge of the village. As a result, the company of the 'Val Chiese' battalion engaged at Kotovski was forced to withdraw and the other company of the same battalion that had already occupied Hill 178.1, after having suffered strong enemy counterattacks, was obliged to do the same. At the same time, the 'Vestone' company on Hill 236.7 was subjected to violent counterattack. To avoid having the bulk of the 'Vestone' surrounded, at 14:30 the 'Sforzesca' headquarters ordered the withdrawal of the units from hills 236.7 and 209.6.

Particularly difficult was the situation of the L6/40 tank company of the LXVII Bersaglieri Armoured Battalion: of the 14 tanks engaged along with the 'Vestone', six were damaged; of the seven tanks employed with the 'Val Chiese', two were damaged and five had jammed guns.

Despite heavy enemy pressure, the withdrawal of the 'Vestone' was orderly, which allowed the alpini to bring the prisoners they had captured back to Italian lines. The battalion suffered the loss of 443 alpini (4 officers) dead and wounded. The 'Val Chiese' suffered 44 killed (4 officers) and 146 wounded (3 officers). The 54th Infantry of the 'Sforzesca' reported 21 wounded (1 officer).

The action ordered by Army Group B to try to reinforce the linkage between the Italian 8th Army and 6.Armee was not successful, mainly because of the lack of help from the German armoured units of XVII.Armee-Korps. With the 1 September action, the first defensive battle of the Don was concluded. For the Italians it was undoubtedly a tactical success, but losses were heavy.[8] The battle also led to a profound crisis in relations between the Italian and German headquarters, mainly because of the initial dissolution of some of the 'Sforzesca' troops, accused of having abandoned their positions without fighting (while in reality it had been the German units that left the division's flank exposed, enabling the Soviets to easily break into the Italian lines).

---

8   The 8th Army as a whole lost 2,704 killed and missing and 4,212 wounded.

11

New Defensive Battles

In early September 1942 General Messe ordered that the positions at Bolshoi and all of the Italian line to the west as far as Yagodni be reinforced, including use of the 'Verona' battalion that had just arrived and which took up positions between the 'Vestone' and the 'Val Chiese'. Later, beginning on 12 September, the 'Tridentina' alpine division, with the alpine units reinforced by the cavalry group and by a company of L6/40 light tanks, assumed the defense of the sector on the right wing of the Italian army, between Hill 228.0 and Bolshoi, which was about 15 kilometers wide. To be resolved was the problem of the 'Celere', which had suffered heavy losses in the earlier fighting and which needed to be reorganized. The overall combat force of the division amounted to about 2,000 men, so it should have been pulled from the front line. However, considering the overall situation, it was not possible to pull any of the units out of the front line.

Attacks on II Corps

Between 11 and 12 September, the Soviets mounted a new series of attacks against the II Corps sector, engaging the 'Cosseria' and 'Ravenna' divisions. At dawn on 11 September, after artillery preparatory fires and with the help of fog, the Soviets attacked in the sector between Dereskova and Hill 158.0, breaking through along the eastern side of the hill, held by the I/90 Infantry on the right wing of the 'Cosseria' division. The fog prevented the heavy weapons and artillery from laying down effective barrage fire and at 8:00 the Soviets were able to capture the strongpoint on Hill 158.0, thus

An alpini defensive position on the Don front (1 September 1942). (Vincenzo de Gaetano collection)

145

Alpini marching towards the Don, September 1942 They are armed with the Carcano Model 1891 rifle.
(Authors' collection)

threatening the divisional artillery's forward positions. In an attempt to block them, at 8:30 the division commander, General Enrico Gazzale, ordered the transfer of the III/89 to Dubovikov and of the CV divisional mortar battalion coming from Orobinski. At 8:40 the Soviets attacked Dereskova, forcing the defenders to fall back. At 9:10, the III/90 counterattacked against Hill 158.0. At 11:00, part of the battalion advanced towards Krasno Orekovo, clashing bitterly with the Soviets and incurring heavy losses. At 12:35 the II Corps commander, General Giovanni Zanghieri, placed the 'Leonessa I' tactical group at the disposition of the 'Cosseria'. Hill 158.0 and its northern slope were recaptured, and only to the west of the valley of Krasno Orekovo was an Italian position still under enemy attack. In the early afternoon, the Soviets tried to recapture Hill 158.0, but were driven off by artillery fire. A new attempt to break through south of Dereskova was similarly repulsed.

Distinguishing himself in the tough fighting on Hill 158 was Lieutenant Colonel Guido Agosti of the 90th Infantry, who was awarded the Gold Medal for Military Valor posthumously, with the following citation: 'A battalion commander, a most valorous veteran of three wars, wounded and decorated with a Silver Medal for Military Valor in the Great War for admirable behavior while leading a company, with burning passion as an experienced higher officer he prepared his infantrymen for the very hard challenges of the Russian front. With rare skill, in an exceptionally difficult environment and situation, he organized the position assigned to him to defend along the Don. Faced with an unexpected attack by overwhelming enemy forces, he quickly took command of a reserve company and, heedless of the intense fire by enemy machine guns and mortars and led the company so boldly and impetuously that he multiplied the effectiveness of his force in repeated counterattacks using bayonets and hand grenades. In the final and most violent attack while his men were led by his example and by his inspiring action, they threw the enemy back, he fell mortally wounded, a burning example of heroism practiced with the unbroken passion of a soldier, thus closing his most noble life. Exemplary sacrifice as a soldier and commander'. Hill 158 at Dereskova (Russian front), 11 September 1942.

A 47/32 antitank gun manned by alpini on the Don front, September 1942. Note the empty shell casings on the ground and the loader whose camouflage helmet cover also sports the traditional alpini feather. (Vincenzo de Gaetano collection)

Also distinguishing himself was Second Lieutenant Vincenzo De Michel, also of the 90th Infantry and also awarded the Gold Medal for Military Valor posthumously, with the following citation: 'In a counterattack by his company against an enemy with overwhelming numbers and equipment, he threw himself irresistibly into the attack at the head of his unit under the furious fire of enemy machine guns and mortars. After several hours of bitter fighting, having repulsed the enemy, he pursued them with renewed vigor past the line of the earlier positions and, with an encircling move, attempted to cut off their retreat. Left with only a few men and attacked violently by fresh groups of the enemy, he faced them calmly with hand grenades until, overwhelmed by numbers and mortally wounded, he fell proudly. A shining example of heroism, of personal valor and of love of country'. Dereskova (Russian front), 11 September 1942.

Around 14:00, the 'Leonessa I' tactical group moved to Dubikov. At 18:00, the III/89 counterattacked to stabilize the situation on Hill 158.0. At dawn on 12 September, the Soviets attacked again in the area south of Dereskova but were driven off by artillery fire and a counterattack by the II/90.

In the morning of 11 September, the Soviets also attacked the positions of the 37th Infantry 'Ravenna' between Krasno Orekovo and Hill 218.0, first with several patrols and then with infantry detachments. During the morning, the fire positions of the III/37 west of Hill 218.0 were surrounded. The reserve company was sent to free them, but it too became surrounded. Around noon, attacks were made against the extreme right strongpoint of the 'Cosseria' and the extreme right of the 'Ravenna', as likewise against Hill 218.0. At 16:30, a counterattack by the III/37 was able to free the reserve company surrounded west of Hill 218.0. Towards evening, the situation was completely restabilized in the stretch in front of the 'Ravenna'. At dawn on 12 September, the Soviets resumed their attack against the left-hand 'Ravenna' strongpoint, but barrage fire by 'Cosseria' and by 'Ravenna' cut the enemy action short as soon as it began.

Left: Italian soldiers moving
quickly along a trench on
the Don, September 1942.
(USSME)
Below: A Breda 37 machine
gun manned by a Blackshirt
crew, September 1942.
(USSME)

During the day of 11 September, the sector held by the III/38 was also attacked by the Soviets who crossed the river with about a dozen boats. Some of the boats were sunk by artillery fire, whilst others were able to make it to the opposite bank. Another attempt further downstream, near the islet of Kusmenkin, was warded off. Around 7:00, the Soviet forces that had managed to make it to the river's western bank seized Solonzi. A counterattack by the III/38 around 9:00 restored the situation. Around noontime, General Zanghieri attached the 'Valle Scrivia I' tactical group to the 'Ravenna'. In the afternoon, the Soviets attacked in the Solonzi woods but were repulsed by a counterattack by the III/38. At 16:00, the II Corps commander also attached the 'Leonessa II' tactical group to the 'Ravenna'.

In the morning of 12 September, the Italians launched a counterattack, employing the III/38 and the 'Valle Scrivia I' tactical group in the first echelon and the 'Leonessa II' tactical group in the second echelon. The Soviets were thrown back and at 8:00 the right bank of the Don was cleared. II Corps losses in these two days of fighting were 678 men killed, wounded and missing. Soviet losses were 2,500 killed and 104 prisoners.

New force dispositions

After having successfully stemmed Soviet attempts to break through the Don front, Army Group B headquarters, having received the requests by Italian 8th Army headquarters relating to a new disposition of forces, decided as follows:

- Shortening of the Italian 8th Army front
- Dividing the new front line among the four army corps, from north to south, the Alpine Corps, II Corps, XXXV Corps and XXIX.Armee-Korps
- Transfer of 294.Inf.Div., the 'Celere' and the 'Sforzesca' to the second line
- Maintaining 22.Panzer-Division in its current positions
- Moving another panzer division to the Tchertkovo-Diogtevo sector, subordinate to 8th Army

Iron Crosses

Throughout September until early October, the Soviets limited themselves to local attacks with small forces, all of which were defeated. In late September, Army Group B headquarters awarded 40 Iron Crosses First and Second Class to Italian XXXV Corps soldiers who had particularly distinguished themselves during the first defensive battle of the Don. The awards ceremony took place on 28 September at Gorbatovo, at the 'Sforzesca'[1] headquarters, during which the German liaison officer at 8th Army, General Kurt von Tippelskirch, made the following speech:

> In bitter fighting, shoulder to shoulder with their German comrades, all of the late August attempts by the Bolsheviks to break through the lines of the allies were ripped apart by the heroic and generous resistance by the 'Sforzesca', 'Celere' and 'Pasubio' divisions and by the irresistible momentum of the 'Novara' and 'Savoia' cavalry regiments and by the brave Blackshirts. The large forces committed by the enemy in the attack against the front held by XXXV Army Corps (C.S.I.R.) demonstrate the importance that the Russian headquarters

---

1   General Messe chose the site of the 'Sforzesca' headquarters for the meeting on purpose, as the Germans had openly and unjustly accused his troops of having fled in the face of the enemy. It was a way to bring justice to the division that had been so unjustly offended.

October 1942: During an official ceremony awarding German decorations to Italian soldiers, General Messe receives an award from a German officer. An L6/40 tank is in the background. Standing beside the tank is a carabiniere with distinctive headgear, and in front of the tank the bersaglieri crewmen likewise are marked by their distinctive plumes adorning their tank helmets. (Vincenzo de Gaetano collection)

had placed on the move intended to distract from the defense of this important sector the forces engaged in the battle for Stalingrad. The tenacious resistance by Italian units employed there and operating on their own not only frustrated the enemy's intentions to break through the front but also rendered vain his prodigious efforts to attract other forces and to lighten the incessant pressure on the Stalingrad front. I thank you in the name of the German Army and especially in the name of all of your German comrades engaged in front of Stalingrad, for your fighting spirit and your tenacity.[2]

A New defensive front

In the meantime, after having completed the various force moves, along with the German head-quarters plans had been made to place the Italian 8th Army between the Hungarian 2nd Army (to the north) and the Romanian 3rd Army (to the south), with the following dispositions of the corps (from left to right):

- Alpine Army Corps[3], with the 'Tridentina', 'Julia' and 'Cuneense' divisions
- II Corps, with the 'Cosseria' and 'Ravenna' divisions

---

2   Marshal Giovanni Messe, *La guerra al fronte Russo*, p. 237.
3   Initially the Alpine Army Corps was to subordinate to Army Group A to be used in the Caucasus. Later, because of the lack of transportation assets that were to have been made available by the

- XXXV Corps, with 298.Infanterie-Division and the 'Pasubio'
- XXIX.Armee-Korps, with the 'Torino', 62.Infanterie-Division and the 'Sforzesca'

In the second echelon were the 294.Infanterie-Division, located behind the Alpine Army Corps, the 3rd 'Celere', behind II Corps and 22.Panzer-Division behind XXIX.Armee-Korps. Available to 8th Army was the 'Vicenza' infantry division, formed for rear area security duties and lacking an artillery regiment.

On 1 November, following continuing disagreements with General Gariboldi and with German headquarters, General Messe asked to be transferred to other duties, turning command of XXXV Corps to General Francesco Zingales. Messe left for Tunisia to assume command of the Italo-German forces there. Before leaving the Don front, Messe addressed the troops of the old CSIR with the following Order of the Day:

> As of today, I turn over the command of the XXXV Army Corps (C.S.I.R.) to His Excellency General Francesco Zingales. I assure you that I feel a profound pain in leaving the courageous men of the old C.S.I.R. and those who, coming after the very hard winter campaign, held with honor their place in the ranks of the XXXV Army Corps ...What we have done together, my valiant boys, is not a page that will fade or be cancelled ... Commemorating the tough tests that led your arms to be victorious from the borders of Hungary to the banks of the Don, all of you, the old hands and the new, will find yourselves side by side...My valiant ones! The homeland owes you much. When you return you can always say with pride: I was with the old C.S.I.R. and the XXXV Corps![4]

Germans and to stem the Soviet offensive along the Don, around mid-August 1942 the corps was transferred to subordination of the Italian 8th Army.

4 Marshal Giovanni Messe, *La guerra al fronte russo*, pp. 241-242.

12

Second Defensive Battle of the Don

The Axis strategic situation on the Eastern Front in autumn 1942 appeared to be essentially static. After the rapid advances of the preceding months, the forces of Army Group B were bleeding themselves along the Don and in the area of Stalingrad and those of Army Group A were engaged in tough fighting in the Tuapse region on the River Terek. The situation of the 6th Army at Stalingrad under General Friedrich Paulus was especially critical. Likewise, the situation of the forces deployed along the course of the Don north and south of the city was worrisome in view of the winter season, not only because of the lack of reliability of the Italian, Romanian and Hungarian armies deployed in these positions, but also because of the presence of many Soviet bridgeheads on the western bank of the river, from which the Soviets would be able to mount counterattacks. Already in August, during the so-called first defensive battle of the Don, the Italian forces had been forced to cede important positions on the right bank of the Don to the Soviets, at Serafimovich and Verhniy Mamon, while other bridgeheads had been taken by the Soviets at Kletskaya and Kremenskaya. After the difficult fighting in August, the Italian forces were shifted further north to the sector of the middle and upper Don, in September leaving the defense of the Serafimovich and Kletskaya sectors to the divisions of the Romanian 3rd Army, which had just arrived.

Alpini strongpoint on the Don front, autumn 1942. (USSME)

Soviet plans

While the Soviet 62nd Army under General Vasily Chuikov continued to hold on doggedly on the Volga, putting the German 6th Army to the test, the Soviet high command (the Stavka) was planning a series of counteroffensives, bearing the names of planets (Uranus, Saturn, Mars and Jove) to trap and destroy the Axis forces in the Stalingrad region and in the Caucasus as well as in the central region (Rzhev-Vyazma). The Soviet counteroffensive on the Stalingrad front was designated Uranus: the Southwest and Don fronts were to attack to the north and the next day, the Stalingrad Front was to attack to the south to eliminate the forces of the Romanian 3rd and 4th Armies. The pincer movement was to close at Kalach, surrounding Paulus' forces. Soon after, Operation Saturn would be launched against the Italian 8th Army, having as its final objective the destruction of Army Group B and the isolation of Army Group A in the Caucasus.[1] In the central sector of the front, General Zhukov had planned Operation Mars, with the Western and Kalinin Fronts engaged in eliminating the Rzhev salient, defended by 9.Armee. Later, the Western Front would launch Operation Jove against Heeresgruppe Mitte in the Vyazma area.

Defensive position being held by Blackshirts on the Don front, autumn 1942. (USSSME)

---

1   The operation was later renamed Little Saturn (in Russian Malyi Saturn) because of the stiff resistance put up by the Germans on the Stalingrad front, with the limited objective of destroying the Italian 8th Army and Heeresgruppe Don. In the new scaled-down version of the operation the Soviet offensive remained unchanged in the initial attack phase against Italian positions on the Don and Romanian positions on the Tchir.

The offensive begins

At 7:20 on 19 November 1942, the Soviets began a new offensive on the Don front, moving from their bridgeheads at Serafimovich and Kletskaya, preceded by artillery preparatory fire from 3,500 guns of varying caliber. However, because of dense fog, the Soviet artillery barrage did not produce the planned results and the Red Air Force was also forced to postpone its attacks to late morning. The infantry elements of the 5th Tank Army led by General Romanenko and of the 21st Army under General Chistyakov of the Southwest Front, attacked with tank support. The Romanian forces, after having overcome their initial surprise, reacted well enough, fighting as best they could. After having easily broken through the first defensive line, the Soviet soldiers in fact suffered heavy losses, thanks in part to the fire of the German-Romanian artillery batteries. But the superiority of the Soviet forces that had been fielded ultimately prevailed and both the Romanian 3rd Army led by General Dimitrescu and the Romanian 4th Army under General Constantinescu were completely overrun and on 23 November, the forces of the Don front and Stalingrad made contact at Kalach, closing Paulus' 6.Armee in a pocket.

Employment of the Italian units

On the Italian 8th Army front, not yet involved in the fighting, by order of Army Group B headquarters, the German divisions subordinate to the Italian Army were shifted to the sectors threatened by the Soviet offensive, in particular, 294.Infanterie-Division, 22.Panzer-Division and 62.Infanterie-Division, thus depriving Italian 8th Army of its second-echelon divisions, the only forces which provided a minimum of depth along its 270 kilometer-long front. In addition, some Italian units also took part in the so-called Battle of the Volga. On 22 November, men of the 2nd Reserve Regiment were placed in defense of Karginskaya to bar the road coming from Bokovskaya. During the night, a company of the II/54 of the 'Sforzesca', reinforced with antitank guns, was moved to Chukarin to bar the valley of the Tchornaya.

An Italian artillery battery ready to open fire, autumn 1942. (USSME)

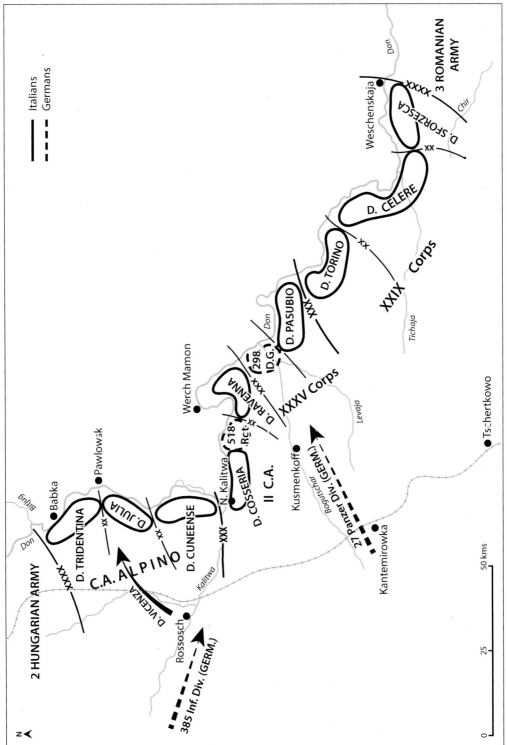

Italian 8th Army line deployments at the beginning of the Second Defensive Battle of the Don, autumn 1942.

A Blackshirt machine gun team in a defensive position in the Verhniy Mamon bend, December 1942.
(USSME)

On 23 November, a reaction group from the 'Sforzesca', led by Geneal Michele Vaccaro,[2] consisting of the headquarters and the 6th Company of the II/54, two companies of the CIV corps machine gun battalion, two 47/32 antitank companies and two 75/32 batteries of the I/201 were trucked into the sector to the right of the Romanian 9th division, which had been forced to withdraw to the right of the River Chir, at the confluence of the Tchiornaya at Bokovskaya. On 24 November, another reaction group arrived that had been sent by the 'Celere', consisting of the LXVII L6/40 tank battalion, the XIII self-propelled 47/32 group and the XLVII Motorcycle Battalion, to protect the right flank of 8th Army. During that same day, the 'Sforzesca' reaction group was engaged against a Soviet column headed from Otbeleize to Verhniy Gruskiy.

During the night of 25 November, the Soviets attacked the positions held by the Romanian 7th division, to the right of the 'Sforzesca', calling Italian artillery into play and at the same time elements of the 54th Infantry were shifted to protect the division's right flank.

Also on the 25th, the Vaccaro group's artillery supported a counterattack by 62.Infanterie-Division, which had just arrived in the sector.

On 28 November, the Italian troops returned to the positions they had occupied earlier.

---

2   Commander of the division's infantry forces.

A Blackshirt light machine gun squad during an attack, December 1942. (USSME)

A Model 35 149/40 gun on the Don front, December 1942. The149/40 was an excellent piece of artillery; all of these guns that were sent to Russia were lost to the Soviets. (USSME)

Italian defensive position with a Breda Model 37 machine gun. (USSME)

Two 47/32 self-propelled guns of the XIII Gruppo 'Cavalleggeri di Alessandria' on the move, December 1942. (from the book *Dalla Russia noi siamo tornati* by Attilio Scolari)

Blackshirts during an attack against an enemy position, December 1942. (USSME)

Trying to take cover

Meantime, because of the presence of strong Soviet forces in the Boguciar sector and of Pavlovsk, 8th Army headquarters tried to bolster the corps front as best it could, transferring the 201st Motorized Artillery Regiment's headquarters and its III 75/32 group, attaching both units to the 'Cosseria' Division. The German headquarters, in that moment worried about reinforcing Army Group Don[3] which was to attack from the southwest, across the Don, along the Kotelnikovo-Stalingrad line in an attempt to restore the continuity of the line between the Don and Stalingrad, but which was short of troops. It was not until the threat from the Boguciar sector loomed that the Germans decided to send in some reserves.

On 9 December, Inf.Rgt.318, commanded by Oberst Erich Mielke, a training unit which replaced the III/90 on the sector's right flank near the 'Ravenna' positions in the Dereskova area, was transferred to the 'Cosseria' division's front. Between 9 and 10 December, also arriving in the II Corps sector was 17.Panzer-Division (consisting of a single tank battalion) which was deployed in the Kusmenkopf-Zapkovo-Krasni area, behind the line of contact between the 'Cosseria' and the 'Ravenna', as well as three German antitank companies which were deployed in the 'Ravenna' sector. The 385.Infanterie-Division was also expected to arrive, moved from the Voronezh front.

Opposite the II Corps sector, where the Soviets had decided to make their main effort, were forces of two different fronts. In particular, the 6th Army of the Voronezh Front was deployed

---

3   Consisting of units gathered under the command of Manstein's 11.Armee, which had been pulled from Army Group Center and rebaptized as 'Army Group Don'. Manstein's forces were to have broken the siege of Stalingrad, but the action failed because of strong resistance by the Soviets.

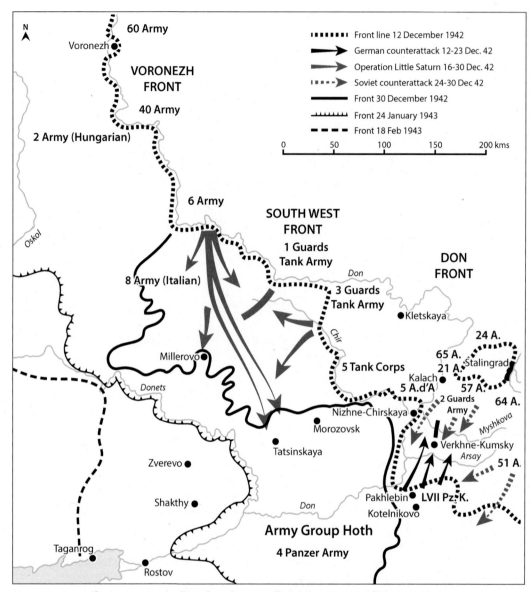

Operations on the Don front between December 1942 and February 1943.

against the 'Cosseria' sector, while units of the 1st Guards Army of the Southwest Front were deployed against the sector held by the 'Ravenna'. The Soviet forces totaled 90 rifle battalions, 25 motorized rifle battalions, 30 tank battalions (with 754 tanks), 2,065 artillery pieces and mortars, 300 antitank guns and 200 multiple rocket launchers. Facing these forces were the two Italian binary divisions (each with two infantry regiments rather than three) 'Cosseria' and 'Ravenna', the '23 Marzo' raggruppamento ('Tagliamento' and 'Montebello'), with 16 Italian infantry battalions, one sapper (XXX), 3 battalions of Inf.Rgt.318, 9 Italian batteries and about 50 panzers.

Italian troops awaiting orders to move to attack, December 1942. (USSME)

Early attacks

According to Soviet historiography, Operation Little Saturn against the Italian 8th Army began on 16 December 1942, when all of the units of the 1st Guards Army and of the 6th Army moved contemporaneously to attack the Italian II Corps. In Italian historiography, however, the same operation, designated as the Second Defensive Battle of the Don, began on 11 December when the first attacks by the Soviets began against the Italian defensive front, made to determine weak points against which the later general offensive would be mounted. These preliminary actions lasted five days, between 11 and 15 December.

At dawn on 11 December, the first attacks against the II Corps front were made near the bend at Verhniy Mamon: at 6:40, after Soviet air attacks against the positions of the 38th Infantry, an attack by two infantry battalions of the 195th Rifle Division followed. At the same time, a battalion of the 128th Rifles attacked Hill 218 and a battalion of the 412th Rifles crossed the Don near the Svinyuka Plain. At 8:30, by request of II Corps headquarters, the Luftwaffe took action to hit the Soviet columns. In the afternoon the Soviets tried to bypass Krasno Orekovo and again attacked the strongpoint of Hill 218.0 near the Svinyuka Plain. The corps commander sent the two 'Valle Scrivia' tactical groups to reinforce the 'Ravenna', to employ one in the Krasno Orekovo sector (I) and the other in the area of Hill 217.6 (II). The 'Leonessa II' tactical group was sent to Svinyuka. The 'Cosseria' positions were not attacked, but its artillery and mortars were committed to repel the enemy attacks.

In this early defensive fighting, Lieutenant Guido Cencetti of the 38th Infantry distinguished himself and was posthumously decorated with the Gold Medal for Military Valor, with the following citation:

> Magnificent figure of a fighter, a volunteer in three wars, full of passion and enthusiasm, bold and energetic arditi [elite assault troops] platoon leader, by word and example he heightened the daring of the infantrymen, hardened their spirit and with his unit, always first among the first, he faced every difficult mission. After the enemy had occupied an important position, he offered to recapture it with his platoon and leading it – heedless of all danger – he rushed into the attack with impetus and ardor. Wounded at the moment in which he was the first to break into the contested trench, he refused all aid and continued, by word and example to urge and push his men to action. Wounded a second time, mortally, he did not cease fighting until he actually died. In the last moments of life, turning his face towards the enemy, he pointed out the next target to his men and, so that he could see the enemy in flight and victory smiling on his platoon, he would not allow himself to be taken from the battlefield. A shining example of an intrepid, heroic soldier, a noble example of devotion to duty pushed to the supreme sacrifice.
>
> Russian front – Don, 11 December 1942.

On the XXXV Corps front, attacks were made against the 'Pasubio' front, near Ogalev, against the I/79 and then spread along the entire front held by the regiment. Thanks to action by the 'Tagliamento' CC.NN. group and the XXX Battalion of the 'Montebello' group, the attacks were repulsed. During the day, the division had received ten 75mm German antitank guns, one 88mm antiaircraft gun and two 20mm antiaircraft guns as reinforcements.

On 12 December, Army Group B headquarters, still unaware that the Soviets had chosen the II Corps sector for their main attack, planned to transfer the 387.Infanterie-Division further to the north, at the juncture point between the Alpine Army Corps and the Hungarian 2nd Army. During the morning, the Soviets attacked with two infantry battalions in the 'Cosseria' division's sector, between Novo Kalitva and Koschiarni, held by the II/89. Another two battalions attacked in the sector between Samodurovka and Dereskova, defended by the II/90. The situation was not restored until that night. On the 'Ravenna' front, attacks continued against the strongpoints of Krasno Orekovo and Hill 218.0. In the afternoon, the 38th Infantry recaptured a strongpoint near Krasno Orekovo, while the 37th Infantry was busy warding off fresh enemy attacks at Svinyuka.

On the XXXV Corps front, the Soviets continued their attacks in the bend of the Ogalev against the length of the 79th Regiment's front. Throughout the day, Soviet attacks alternated with Italian counterattacks, mounted mainly by the 'Tagliamento' group, by the VI CC.NN. Battalion and by two ad-hoc companies. Ogalev was completely levelled during the fighting. Arriving as reinforcement was the 3rd Division 'Celere' reaction group (LXVII Armoured Battalion with 31 L6/40 light tanks, XIII Squadron Group with 19 47/32 self-propelled guns and the XLVII Motorcycle Battalion) as well as all of the XV Sapper Battalion.

Falling while leading his men was Centurione [Captain] Ettore di Pasquale of the VI 'Montebello' truck-borne CC.NN. battalion, posthumously awarded the Gold Cross for Military Valor, with the following citation:

A company commander of great ability and unlimited enthusiasm, he asked for and was allowed to participate in a difficult action. Despite the heavy enemy fire and over ground that was particularly difficult for an attack, he decisively led his company in an assault, directing every move under increasingly violent fire. Wounded, he refused any aid and, still leading his men, personally maneuvered the reserve detachment, leading it right up to the enemy positions and himself fighting hand-to-hand. Wounded a second and a third time by hand grenades, he continued stoically, despite his serious wounds, leading the attack with indomitable spirit, having his men hold him up. With a final supreme effort, at the head of his men, he reached the contested position on the Don, where a fourth wound cut short his heroic resistance. A magnificent example of absolute dedication to duty.

Russian front, 12 December 1942

An Italian soldier in a trench on the Don front, December 1942. (Authors' collection)

On 13 December, along the II Corps front and especially against that of the 'Cosseria', the Soviets attacked Nova Kalitva, engaging the II/89. To deal with them, the III/89 and the 'Cuneense' alpine division's artillery had to rush to their aid. The Soviets made another attack against the eastern part of Samodurovka, held by the I/90 and was driven back. In the late morning, attacks against Hill 192 were resumed but were defeated thanks to the use of reserves from Orobinski. To reinforce the defenses, the Army headquarters granted the use of one battalion from 385.Inf.Div. which had been located in Zapkovo. Towards noon, almost all of Samodurovka fell into Soviet hands; only a few points of resistance continued to fight on. In the afternoon, enemy pressure also increased in the Novo Kalitva area. A counterattack was mounted against Samodurovka which brought the Italian units as far as the right bank of the Don and the Soviets were also thrown off of Hill 192.0. At Dereskova, Inf.Rgt.318 repulsed an attack against the western side of the position. At the end of the day, Grenadier-Regiment 537 entered into action, having been transferred to II Corps, which had already integrated the Italian forces engaged in the sector, namely the II and III/89. The counterattack led to recapture of several strongpoints and to the capture of large quantities of arms and ammunition.

On the 'Ravenna' front, the 'Valle Scrivia I'I tactical group was sent in as a reinforcement in an attempt to restore the situation at Krasno Orekovo, which was still under enemy attack. The follow-on counterattack led to the recapture of two strongpoints that had been lost as well as to the isolation of enemy forces in several balkas. In order to repel any Soviet tank attacks, the transfer of a combat group of the 27.Panzer.Division was requested, which included 16 75mm self-propelled guns, one infantry battalion and two heavy antitank companies, from Pereschepni to Gadyuche.

Alpini of the *Monte Cervino* armed with MAB 38A submachine guns and a Model 91 carbine, before going into action on the Don front, December 1942. (Authors' collection)

On the 'Pasubio' division's front, reinforcement came in the form of a reaction group of the 298. Infanterie-Division to recapture Ogalev. As it had already in part been retaken by the 'Tagliamento' group, then replaced by the XV Sapper Battalion, the division commander decided to keep only a German infantry battalion and its artillery as a reserve.

On 14 December, along the 'Cosseria' division's front, a counterattack was made against Hill 192.0, using the 'Leonessa II' group. It was not possible to have the tanks of 27.Pz.Div. join the action because they were directly subordinate to the Army. However, the Soviets were nonetheless forced to withdraw. At the same time, an attack against III./Inf.Rgt.318 was repulsed on the western side of Dereskova. Around noon, new fighting flared up on Hill 192.0, following an attack by two Soviet battalions. Once again, the 'Leonessa II' tactical group was engaged. Around 14:00, Hill 192.0 again fell into Italian hands, while at Dereskova, several positions held by Inf.Rgt.318 had fallen. From prisoner interrogations it was learned that three Soviet divisions had been in action against the 'Cosseria' but had suffered such heavy losses in the day's attacks that the 127th Rifle Division had to be disbanded. The 'Cosseria' reported the loss of at least a thousand men killed, wounded and missing.

In the 'Ravenna' sector, attacks against Hill 218.0 had resumed at dawn, while arrival of large enemy forces were reported between Verhniy Mamon and the left bank of the Don. In the afternoon, the Soviets attacked the division's left wing in force near Krasno Orekovo, where all of the available reserves were thrown in. The strongpoints were doggedly defended and at 22:00, the 'Ravenna' infantry mounted a counterattack which forced the Soviets to pull back.

On the 'Pasubio' front, at 6:00 the stretch defended by the III/79 was attacked. After about two hours of intense fighting and thanks to supporting fire by artillery and mortars, the attack was driven off. Other attacks were made against the II/79, with the Soviets attempting to push their lines forward.

After four days of continuous attacks against the Italian positions, the Soviets had made an accurate assessment of the situation, identifying the weakest positions in the defensive line. Their actions had focused mainly against the II Corps front, while offensive actions against the 'Pasubio' had been made only as diversions.

New attacks, new dispositions

On 15 December, General Gariboldi requested that new urgent measures be taken by Army Group B, and especially for new reinforcements to lessen the constant enemy pressure. That same day, at 11:30, the 'Cosseria' launched a new counterattack against Hill 192.0, meeting stiff resistance and taking heavy losses. In the afternoon, the German liaison office reported to Italian II Corps headquarters that a battalion of Grenadier-Regiment 539 had been transferred to the 'Cosseria' division to recapture Hill 192.0. In light of the counterattack on the following day, this battalion was resubordinated to 27.Pz.Div. In the meantime, the II/90, the III/90 and the three battalions of the 'Leonessa' group continued to fight around Hill 192.0. In addition, to bolster coordination between the I/90 and the area of Hill 192.0, ad hoc units from the rear area were moved up to the line.

At 20:15, 8th Army headquarters issued the dispositions received from Heeresgruppe B:

- 385.Inf.Div., with all of its units present in the area, came under subordination of II Corps to restore the situation in the 'Cosseria' sector.
- The 'Cosseria' Division, which during the night was to be replaced by 385.Inf.Div., was to have retired its infantry regiments, but was to leave the divisional and reinforcing artillery in place.
- The II Corps commander intended to use the 'Cosseria' troops to support the 'Ravenna'.

Italian troops pulling back to a new position, December 1942. (USSME)

After five days of harsh and exhausting fighting, the Italian 8th Army forces had managed with great sacrifice to substantially hold their positions and General Gariboldi expressed his praise to the combatants: 'To the brave soldiers of II Corps. For five days you have been fighting strenuously and have gloriously earned your motto 'They shall not pass'. Bravo! I am proud of you. We have to hold out tenaciously, with unshakable faith and you will win, earning the admiration and recognition of our homeland'.[4]

The Italians had held up well, but nonetheless the Soviets had been able to achieve their objective during this first phase of the battle, namely, to wear down the Italian forces to the point that they would be less capable during the next phase of the offensive. In five days, the Soviets had mounted a total of twenty-one attacks against the 'Cosseria', 'Ravenna' and 'Pasubio', committing between 26 and 28 infantry battalions.

Operation Little Saturn

At dawn on 16 December, Soviet artillery, with over 2,500 guns of all calibers, opened fire on the Italian II Corps positions. Then the tank and infantry units attacked. The Italian forces, although exhausted by the fighting of the preceding days 'offered fierce resistance and often went on the counter-attack.[5] To effect the breakthrough of the tactical defense, it was necessary from the outset to commit the armoured units. This fact led to the decrease of their combat capability in the later in-depth actions. At the end of the day, the 6th Army forces had advanced four or five kilometers and those of the 1st Guards Army two or three kilometers',[6] respectively against the 'Cosseria' and the 'Ravenna' divisions.[7]

On the II Corps front, throughout the night, the Soviets had made numerous attacks to break through the lines of German Inf.Rgt.318 and the Italian 38th Infantry. In order to ease the pressure, General Zanghieri ordered an attack by a German police battalion, supported by a company of L6/40 light tanks of the LXVII Bersaglieri Battalion. At 6:00, the 'Cosseria' commander, General Gazzale, transferred operational responsibility of the sector to General der Infanterie Karl Eibl, commander of 385.Inf.Div.. The two headquarters had remained at Krasni, to ensure salvaging the Italian units. At 8:00, the situation continued to worsen; Soviet troops had managed to break through the lines of 385.Inf.Div. in several points and Dereskova had been abandoned by the Germans. At the same time, on Hill 192.0, the Italian attack supported by 27.Pz.Div. tanks, was stopped by Soviet artillery and air strikes. Other enemy attacks developed against Samodurovka, where the I/90 was surrounded, while Soviet tanks had already made it to Gorohovka. Around noon, the Soviet attacks spread across all of the right-hand part of the sector, making it impossible to pull out any of the Italian troops. Army headquarters transferred 27.Pz.Div. to II Corps in order to try to maintain contact between the various units.

In the Ravenna sector, beginning with the first light of dawn, Soviet tank units descended from Hill 193.6 and from Ossetrovka. The fire of all of the artillery in the sector was concentrated against them. At the same time, other attacks were made north of Krasno Orekovo, while all of the positions were subjected to massive Soviet artillery fire. To stop the Soviet tanks, Kampfgruppe Maempel was alerted, consisting of self-propelled guns and tank destroyers from 27.Pz.Div., led by Major Rolf Maempel, coming from Pereshchepnoye. At 7:00, two 38th Infantry strongpoints and one of Inf.Rgt.318 were overwhelmed by enemy attacks. At 9:00 the positions on the western side of the bend of Verhniy Mamon were overrun and Soviet armoured units reached the villages of Krasno Orekovo, Gadyucce and Filonovo. In an attempt to salvage the situation, the II Corps commander sent the LXVII armoured battalion and the XIII self-propelled group to reinforce the 'Ravenna'. The first wave of Soviet tanks, consisting of about fifty tanks, was almost completely

---

4   AA.VV.: *Le Operazioni delle Unità Italiane al Fronte Russo (1941-1943)*, page 354.
5   Most historians, both Italian as well as others, mistakenly refer to entire units in flight after the initial shelling.
6   From the Soviet Historical Military magazine, May 1972.
7   AA.VV.: *Le Operazioni delle Unità Italiane al Front Russo (1941-1943)*, page 355.

An Italian 20mm Breda Model 39 anti-aircraft gun on the Don front, December 1942. (USSME)

destroyed by mine fields, artillery fire and by the self-propelled guns of Kampfgruppe Maemel. At 10:30, the 'Ravenna' positions were again under attack by the 195th Rifle Division in the Krasno Orekovo area, where the defensive line had been penetrated and the various strongpoints were surrounded and eliminated one by one by Soviet tank units. On the western side of the bend at Krasno Orekovo, the 41st Guards Division attacked, following the road from Hill 193.6 to Hill 150.2, and to the east, the 44th Guards Division attacked around Hill 218. The Soviet tanks eliminated the strongpoint held by a company of the CII Machine Gun Battalion, which until the very end had inflicted heavy losses on the enemy infantry with the fire from its twelve machine guns.

General Francesco Dupont, commanding the 'Ravenna', decided to stabilize the new line of resistance on the positions at Hill 204.2, Hill 217.6, Hill 196.3 and Svinyuka, striking from the north against the villages of Gadyucce and Filonovo, committing the forces that were withdrawing. But around noon, the situation continued to become more critical, with the 'Ravenna' positions hit by Soviet aircraft and with new tank attacks throughout the sector. General Zanghieri, in agreement with the German liaison officer, proposed shifting the defense along the Zapkovo-Orobinski-Dubovikov-Goly-Hill 179.2-Lufizkaya line in order to cover the Boguciar Valley. In the early afternoon the order was given by Heeeresgruppe B that forbid any withdrawal; the 'Ravenna' division was to hold its positions. At 17:00, the men of the division assumed positions along the line Hill 217.6-Filonovo-Gruscevo balka-Hill 159, where it linked up with 298.Inf.Div., deployed around its artillery pieces and the few German tanks. There were about three thousand men, exhausted after six days of fighting and without enough weapons and ammunition. Further exacerbating the situation were the violent bombardments by enemy multiple rocket launcher batteries and aviation. At 18:00, the Army headquarters informed II Corps headquarters that reinforcements in the form of elements of the 'Julia' alpine division and the 'Monte Cervino' alpine ski battalion would be arriving.

Attacks on XXXV Corps

The attack against the 'Pasubio' positions began at 6:00, without any artillery or rocket launcher preparatory fires, but supported mainly by mortar fire, especially in the Krassnogorodovka-Abrossimova-Monastirschina stretch. In late morning, between 9:00 and 10:00, troops of the Soviet 38th Guards Division breached the positions of the 80th Infantry southeast of Abrossimova, forcing the Italian soldiers to retreat. Abrossimova fell shortly afterwards and the attack continued towards hills 187.9 and 206.3, as well as further to the south, cutting off the Monastirschina Valley. The 1st Antitank Battery of the 1/201, with 75/32 guns, was completely wiped out while attempting to oppose the enemy advance. At the same time, the infantrymen of the II/80 and the gunners of a section of the I/201, through the Artykulny Schlucht Valley, fell back onto the batteries of the III/8, which were also under attack and forced to fire over open sights. Following the withdrawal of the infantrymen, the artillery observers also began to fall back, having to open a path while fighting. On Hill 206.3, the remnants of the III/80 continued to fight doggedly. The strongpoints in the bend of the Ogalev, were still experiencing frontal attacks. At strongpoint Olimpio, all of the defenders were killed by enemy fire. The Blackshirts of the 'Montebello' group counterattacked the enemy forces on Hill 187.9, Hill 178.3 and Hill 175.1 overlooking the Artykulny Schlucht Valley. From Army headquarters came the order to support the 'Pasubio' with Grenadier-Regiment 526 (298.Inf.Div.) and with all of the available forces of XXIX.Armee-Korps. In the afternoon the 298. Inf.Div. reaction group, consisting of a battalion from Gren.Rgt.526 and a 150mm artillery group that was attached to Gren.Rgt.525 already deployed between Hill 201.1 and Hill 156.0, were provided to 'Pasubio' headquarters.

Towards evening, the new 'Pasubio' defensive line was laid out as follows: on the left was the 79th Infantry as far as the southern edge of Krasnohorovka, in the center, from Hill 156.0 to Hill 201.1, were the German units, and on the right, along the line held by the '23 Marzo' Blackshirts were the remaining men of the 80th Infantry and an ad hoc battalion consisting of skiers, carabinieri and headquarters personnel. The front between this last-named battalion and the village of Monastirchina was exposed. At Monastirchina the I/80 was still holding out, with its survivors holed up in the church. In late evening, arriving as reinforcements to XXXV Corps, sent by 8th Army headquarters, were a railway battalion, a bridging battalion and an engineer battalion, all of which were to be used as infantry.

Clashes on 17 December

During the night, the temperature dropped to 30 below zero, making conditions even more difficult for the soldiers who had to fight in the open. On the II Corps front, at 3:00 on 17 December, a new tank attack was made against Samodurovka and Dereskova, making the attempt to establish contact between 358.Inf.Div. and the 'Ravenna' even more difficult. After having reached the Italian artillery positions, Soviet tanks overran the 1st and 3rd batteries of the CXXII 149/13 group of the 2nd Raggruppamento. The new situation and considering the few available forces convinced the II Corps commander not to engage the 'Cosseria' as the link between 385.Inf. Div. and the 'Ravenna'. A little before 9:00, infantry supported by tanks moved from Dubovikov towards Orobinski; facing them were only a few Italian 47mm guns and German 88mm guns. Especially threatened was Krasny, where three division headquarters were located (385.Inf.Div., 'Cosseria' and 27.Pz.Div.). At 9:30, the 'Cosseria' commander was ordered to establish, with the forces still available to him, a defensive front between Ivanovka and Kusmenkov. At 10:15. General Zanghieri informed the Army headquarters that following the fall of Orobinski and Zapkovo as well as the fall of Krasny, a new defensive front could be established along the line Novo Kalitva-Ivanovka-Kusmenkov or along the line Novo Kalitva-Dereskova-Kusmenkov.

Meanwhile, II Corps headquarters moved from Taly to Mitrofanovka. Around 14:00, the Army chief of staff transmitted the orders of the German high command to General Zanghieri: at dusk, 385.Inf.Div. and 298.Inf.Div., with the Italian forces attached to them, were to withdraw to the Novo Kalitva-Zapkovo-Tvyerdoklebovka-Lufizaya-Boguciar line, linking up on the left with the Alpine Army Corps and on the right with the 'Pasubio' division, to form a solid front. On paper, everything seemed simple, but to form a solid front with men that had survived seven days of fighting without a break, with two reduced-strength German divisions and two Italian divisions at the end of their tether, represented a daunting challenge. In any case, at 20:00, the troops took positions along the new line, which began at the Don near Novo Kalitva, with two strongpoints held by the I/89, continued on to Hill 221 (southeast of Koschiarny)-Zapkovo-Sorky-Dolgy-Kusmenkov). Three German battalions were stationed on Hill 190 and at Zapkovo, elements of 27.Pz.Div. were at Sorky, Italian engineer forces and L6/40 tanks at Sorky and Dolgy. Between Dolgy and Kusmenkov was another open gap which was supposed to be occupied by the 'Monte Cervino' battalion.

Throughout the day, on Hill 192.0 the surviving men of the II and III/90, of the 'Leonessa' group and of III/Gren.Rgt.539 had continued to hold out, beating back continuous Soviet attacks. The breakthrough of Soviet tanks at Orobinski had isolated these troops. Therefore, the 385.Inf.Div. commander had ordered their withdrawal after midnight, seeking to break the enemy encirclement.

In the left-hand sector, the survivors of the I/90 pulled back to the support battery, which was left with only one gun, and then to that of the 3rd Battery of the I/108. After more defensive fighting, the men withdrew to Zapkovo, protected by the 3rd Mortar Company of the CV divisional battalion, which unleashed a desperate counterattack.

The divisional artillery positions, attacked by Soviet tanks, defended themselves as best they could. The 2nd Battery of the CXXIII/2 held out until the night but was then overwhelmed by Soviet infantry attacks. The 1st and 2nd 75/18 batteries of the I/108 met the same fate. However, the 2nd and 3rd 105/28 batteries of the IV/108 were able to withdraw while fighting, while the group's 1st Battery also was overrun.

The fall of Hill 217.6, which dominated the villages of Gadyucce and Filonovo, made necessary a further withdrawal by the 'Ravenna' troops to Sovkos Boguciarsky and Pereschepny. Not all of the units of the 'Ravenna' had reached Gadyucce and Filonovo; about a thousand survivors of the 37th Infantry, after having run out of ammunition, continued their march until they reached Pereschepny and the 298.Inf.Div. sector. At 9:30, when General Dupont reported to the corps headquarters, he was ordered to engage the forces present at Pereschepny to support Kampfgruppe Maempel and to establish a linkup position with 385.Inf.Div. at Sovkos Boguciarsky. The remaining personnel of the division were to regroup at Tverdoklebovka to provide support to the two other groups and where the division's tactical headquarters had set itself up. At 10:30 General Manlio Capizzi, the 'Ravenna' infantry commander, arrived in Pereschepny, assuming command of an Italian group which included elements of the 37th infantry, which made contact with 298.Inf.Div.. While awaiting the arrival of the 'Monte Cervino', the division was ordered to establish a defensive position at Kusmenkov, using the available men and equipment to block any enemy penetration in the Boguciar Valley and to the south. At the same time, 298.Inf.Div., which had been subordinated to II Corps, after having been reinforced with the Gruppo Scapizzi,[8] began to withdraw its left wing, to bear against Boguciar. However, instead of the German units deploying along the river, they withdrew further to the rear, along the course of the Levaya, leaving the way to Boguciar and

---

8   The name by which from that moment on the 'Ravenna' soldiers attached to 298.Inf.Div. were known.

Withdrawing Italian troops using mules to carry their heavy weapons, December 1942. (USSME)

the Levaya open to the Soviets and making it possible for the enemy to get around the right wing of the 8th Army, held by the XXXV Corps.

The Soviet attacks against the 'Pasubio' had resumed at dawn against the positions south of Krasnohorovka. Then, after 10:00, the positions held by the III/79 were attacked. An enemy breach on the II/79 front was eliminated by the railway battalion that had arrived the previous night.

Also along the XXIX.Armee-Korps front, the Soviet troops which had crossed the Don during the attack against Monastirschina had extended their action to the south, capturing Hill 162.9, which dominated the entire left wing of the 'Torino' division and in particular the positions of the III/81. The II/81, which had been engaged the previous day at Monastirschina, was thrown into a counterattack, but with no success. In order to restore the situation, the III/82, reinforced with a company from the CIV Machine Gun Battalion, was shifted from the right-hand divisional sector to that on the left.

The 'Celere' situation

Following the defeat of the Romanian 3rd Army at the beginning of the Battle of the Volga, the 'Celere' division, located in the second echelon in the valley of the Boguciar, was called upon to defend a stretch of the front about 50 kilometers long that was occupied by 62.Inf.Div.. The 'Celere', reinforced by the Croat Legion, was thus deployed straddling the lower course of the Tihaya, between the 'Torino' and the 'Sforzesca'. Considering the width of the front to be defended, the division also received the XXVI Mortar Battalion from the 'Torino', a company from the CIV Machine Gun Battalion and the LXXII mixed army group as reinforcements. The mobile elements of the 'Celere', especially the XLVII Motorcycle Battalion, the LXVII Armoured Battalion and the XIII self-propelled group were moved to the XXXV and II Corps sectors.

At 7:00 the division's positions were attacked at the juncture point between the VI and XIII battalions. After about an hour, the attack spread to the positions of VI Battalion, near the confluence of the Tihaya and the Don, where some Soviet forward elements had been able to break through towards Tihovskoy. Other enemy units aimed for Hill 163.3, threatening Mrykin-Konovalov. Meanwhile, the 7th Battery of the II/120 was overrun by the Soviets. At 10:00, the XIX Battalion counterattacked towards the mouth of the Tihaya, but without success. At 13:00, strong Soviet forces went around Tihovskoy from the south, forcing the XIX Battalion to withdraw to the west for about a kilometer and defending Balatschkov. There the 105th divisional engineer company and the German 45th Railway Engineer Battalion arrived. At 15:00, also arriving was the German XVI observation group, consisting of about 200 men, to try to stop the Soviet break-through into the Tihaya Valley. At 16:30, a fresh attack against Hill 163.3 threatened the 3rd Battery of the I/120 and the village of Mrykin, where the headquarters of the 120th Artillery had been surrounded. At the end of the day, the 3rd Bersaglieri sector had not experienced any serious attacks, even though the Soviets, moving from Hill 163.3, were attempting to encircle the regiment's positions from the south. In the 6th Bersaglieri's sector, the Soviets had opened a breach about 12 kilometers wide, which was stemmed in part by counterattacks by Italian and German units. The XIII Battalion was still deployed along the Don, cut off after the Soviet penetration at Biryukov.

The 'Sforzesca' Division had displaced to the extreme right of the Army, in contact with the Romanian 7th Division. Around mid-December, the Romanian lines had been attacked by the Soviets right at the point of contact with the 'Sforzesca'. On 16 December, the Romanian 7th Division was forced to pull back about ten kilometers, leaving the right flank of the 'Sforzesca' exposed. At the end of the day. The Army Group headquarters ordered the withdrawal of the right wing of XXIX.Armee-Korps.

Fighting on 18 December

On the Italian II Corps front, during the night between 17 and 18 December, the remnants of 385. Inf.Div., of the 'Cosseria' and of the 'Ravenna', along with 298.Inf.Div., were to have reconstituted a new defensive front to stem the Soviet offensive. At 4:00 on 18 December, 8th Army headquarters issued a more detailed order regarding the precise tasks to be carried out by the various II Corps units: the line to defend ran from Novo Kalitva to Zapkovo-Tvyerdoklebova-Boguciar. On the left, between Novo Kalitva and Zapkovo was 385.Inf.Div., reinforced by elements of the 'Cosseria'.On the right, from Tvyerdoklebovka to Bouguciar and then on the Don as far as Tereschkova, was 298.Inf.Div., reinforced by elements of the 'Ravenna'. Between Zapkovo and Tvyerdoklebovka, in the gap not occupied by infantry units, was 27.Pz.Div. (minus Kampfgruppe Maemel, which was attached to 298.Inf.Div.) In that space, troops of the 'Julia' alpine division were to arrive. Other reinforcements were expected, such as Kampfgruppe Fegelein, led by SS-Oberführer Hermann Fegelein,[9] which was to take up positions in the valley of the Boguciar to extend the left wing of 298.Inf.Div., and 387.Inf.Div. moved by train to the north of Kantemirovka.

Meanwhile, Soviet tanks had reached Ivanovka, six kilometers south of Novo Kalitva, threatening the withdrawal of the troops, who had to open a way while fighting desperately. Soon after, attacks began against the strongpoint at Taly, initially defended by two Italian battalions and

---

9   Consisting of the headquarters of SS-Kavallerie-Brigade, II/SS-Pol.Inf.Rgt.3 (mot), a battery of heavy howitzers (SFH) equipped with French artillery pieces, elements of II/Pz.Art.Rgt.127 of 27.Pz.Div., elements of Fhr.Flak.Rgt. (mot. Z) equipped with 88mm and 20mm guns and the remnants of Pol. Rgt.15 (Hptm. d. Schp. Sauer) with two Italian tanks.

Italian soldiers in a defensive position with a Breda heavy machine gun, December 1942. (USSME)

a battery. At 7:30, the leading elements of the 'Julia' began to arrive at Mitrofanovka, among them the 'L'Aquila' and 'Tolmezzo' battalions. More attacks followed against the positions at Nova Kalitva, still held by the remnants of the I and II/89, all of which were driven back with heavy losses inflicted on the Soviets. Some elements of the 'Cuneense' alpine division also took part in the defensive combat.

At Kanterimovka, which had been transformed into a logistics center, men and vehicles continued to arrive, completely choking the small town. There were thousands of men coming from various units with which the II Corps commander intended to form several rifle battalions to send to reinforce the 'Ravenna' and 'Cosseria', but heavy weapons, equipment and transport were all lacking, but above all many men lacked even their individual weapons. In the afternoon, SS-Obf. Fegelein arrived at II Corps headquarters to discuss the employment of his combat group with General Zanghieri. A first objective was to make contact, through the valley of the Boguciar, with 298.Inf. Div.. At 16:30, Army headquarters advised that the headquarters of XXIV.Panzerkorps would be installed at Kanterimovka in order to assume control of 298.Inf.Div. and of all of the other German units engaged in the Italian II Corps and Alpine Army Corps sectors. Because of this, II Corps lost control not only of the German units but also of the Italian units that had been sent to reinforce the Germans, even though it still retained operational responsibility in the sector.

In the afternoon, the Soviets resumed their attack against the strongpoint at Taly. At the end of the day, 385.Inf.Div. still held the line from Novo Kalitva to Ivanovka. All of the many attacks against Novo Kalitva were repulsed by fire and counterattacks by the I and II/89, reinforced by the 'Mondovi' alpine battalion and by the 'Cuneense' division. At dusk, a strong enemy column had broken into Zapkovo. The troops that had been surrounded south of Dereskova were finally able to break out and managed to bring their heavy weapons along with them. Losses were, however, quite high.

On the XXXV Corps front, 298.Inf.Div., after having abandoned its positions along the Don and withdrawn to the right bank of the Levaya, between the Don and Radtschenskoye, towards evening clashed with Soviet infantry and Mongolian cavalry units. The entire Levaya Valley was now in Soviet hands. With respect to the situation of the 'Pasubio', since morning the Soviets had attacked the II/79 positions on the Don but were always fended off. A massive attack against Hill 201.1, defended by Gren.Rgt.525 and by the '3 gennaio' raggruppamento was repulsed with heavy losses to the Soviets. In the right-hand sector, held by the 80th Infantry, the attacks were stopped by artillery fire. At Monastrschina, the I/80, still surrounded, continued to hold out.

On the XX.Armee-Korps front, throughout the day the 'Torino' was busy recapturing Hill 162.9, at the point of contact with the 'Pasubio'. With the transfer of the II/82 to the left wing, the situation had further deteriorated, with the Soviets having managed to occupy several positions but a counterattack restored the situation. Troops of the 'Celere' were engaged in repelling a massive attack at the point of contact with the 'Torino'. Other attacks made against the lines of the 3rd Bersaglieri and in the Tihaya Valley had been repulsed. The Soviets brought in fresh forces and at 7:00 renewed their attacks against Biryukov and against the division's right wing. The Soviet objective was to extend their penetration of the Tihaya Valley and to reach Meskov. At 12:00, the 'Sforzesca' reaction group, led by General Vaccaro, moved from Kalinoski with the III/53 and recaptured Hill 154.9. The Soviets counterattacked shortly afterwards, forcing the Italians to defend themselves until late at night.

For the remaining 'Sforzesca' troops who were not engaged in the 'Celere' sector, XXIX.Armee-Korps headquarters issued a withdrawal order for the following night, to occupy new positions between the mouth of the Tihaya and the Tchir Valley, meeting on the left with the Vaccaro group, to which the XIII Bersaglieri Battalion had also been attached.

Fighting on 19 December

On the II Corps front, fighting continued around Taly. If the position fell, Kantemirovka would be threatened, and accordingly General Zanghieri advised Gariboldi to move the units and o reorganize further west, in the Voroshilovgrad area or further north, in the Alpine Army Corps rear area. At 8:00, the alarm was given that Soviet tanks were moving from Taly against Kantemirovka. When they were spotted on the hill that dominated the railway station, it was at first thought that they were German tanks. Any doubt was eliminated within a few minutes when the first rounds began to fall on the village of Kantemirovka, where in addition to many soldiers, there were hundreds of vehicles ready to move with their engines running because of the low temperature. Scenes of panic and terror followed, with men running in all directions to avoid the enemy fire. Many headed for the trucks, some of which left immediately so as to distance themselves as quickly as possible. Groups of vehicles loaded with soldiers and groups of soldiers on foot fled from Kantemirovka, creating a tremendous chaos, heading towards Belovodsk, Starobelsk, Tchertkovo and Millerovo. Weapons, equipment and anything that could slow down movement were abandoned. Complete panic also reigned at the railway station where trains were at a halt, already loaded with soldiers and ready to leave. The few officers on the scene tried to restore order and discipline, but it was not easy. At Belovodsk it was possible to regroup some of the infantrymen of the 38th Infantry, who were posted to defend the logistics base.

A defensive mortar position, December 1942. (USSME)

Meanwhile at Taly the situation became critical; the Soviets continued to attack and men and ammunition were in short supply. In the afternoon, the Army headquarters ordered the 'Ravenna' commander, General Dupont, to leave command of the defense of Taly to the Germans and to return with all of the Italian units.

In late afternoon, the situation on the XXIV.Panzerkorps front was as follows: the 385.Inf. Div. front had been overrun, but the troops had dug in on the line of heights to the west of Novo Kalitva-Hill 176-Hill209. Kampfgruppe Fegelein was digging in along the Dereskova-Atamanski-Schelobok line in an attempt to link 385.Inf.Div. with Taly. XXIV.Panzerkorps intended to hold this line to cover the Rossosch-Millerovo railway line. The 'Cosseria' gathered its men coming from the east behind the 'Cuneense' and as soon as the 90th Infantry returned following its withdrawal from Kantemirovka, was to assume positions in the Pelageyevka area.

On the XXXV Corps front, shortly after noon an attack against Tchertkovo was beaten back by the Italians. During those same hours, 298.Inf.Div. was transferred to XXIV.Panzerkorps and was ordered to pull back to the right bank of the Tihaya, leaving XXXV Corps with only the 'Pasubio' division. At 12:30, General Zingales went to division headquarters to issue the order to withdraw to the south, to the right bank of the Tihaya, between Verchnayakovski and Nasarov. It had not been possible to establish contact with the 'Torino' division on the right flank.

On the XXIX.Armee-Korps front, the troops had been ordered to resist in place. The 'Torino' division was still deployed on the Don, even though it was threatened to be encircled on the right, where a Soviet attack against Surov had been driven back. Other enemy attacks had been made against the divisional rear area, near Kriniza, forcing the III/82 to pull back to Paseka. At Suchoy Donets another Soviet attack was repulsed. In the 'Celere' sector, while the troops were getting ready to counterattack, the Soviets struck first on the right, against the 6th Bersaglieri, and in the area southwest of Mrykin, held by the 3rd Bersaglieri, intending to advance in the Tihaya Valley and move on Meskov. At 10:00, the 3rd Bersaglieri suffered new attacks along the line of the Don, continuing to hold their positions, while the troops defending the Tihaya Valley began to fall back from Birkukov to Melovatyi because of strong enemy pressure. At 14:00, XXIX.Armee-Korps ordered all units to withdraw to the Tihaya, to defend the Meskov-Provalskiy area, between the 'Torino' and the 'Sforzesca'.

New withdrawal orders

Following the deterioration of the situation, at 15:00 Heeresgruppe B headquarters ordered the withdrawal of all of the units engaged south of the Alpine Army /Corps in order to set up a line along the Ticho Shiuravskaya-Meskov-Tchir Valley line. On the Alpine Corps front, replacing the 'Julia' division with the 'Vicenza' was under way. At the same time, Stara Kalitva, held by troops of the 'Cuneense', suffered massive air bombardment. The 'Saluzzo' battalion, deployed on the extreme right of the 'Cuneense', was engaged in a counterattack along with the remnants of the II and III/89 of the 'Cosseria', which were still holding out at Novo Kalitva. Also, on the afternoon of 19 December, the 'Julia' reaction group was used by XXIV.Panzerkorps in the Kriniscnaya-Seleny Yar-Ivanovka area.

In the XXXV Corps sector, in line with new orders, the units began to pull back while enemy armoured units threatened the rear area in the Levaya Valley. The 'Pasubio' first withdrew to the right bank of the Tihaya and then towards evening regrouped in the Arbusov and Alexeyevo Losovskaya area, where they assumed defensive positions to protect the left flank of the other divisions that had to cross the Tihaya.

In the XXIX.Armee-Korps sector, the 'Torino' division had also received orders to deploy along the Tihaya, reaching Meskov in echelons The withdrawal order was also transmitted to the 3rd Bersaglieri Regiment which was deployed on the right and was cut off from 'Celere' headquarters. At 21:30, the order was given to continue the withdrawal to the southwest.

The order to withdraw reached the 'Celere' at 14:00; its units were to move to the Tihaya, between Meskov and Provalsky. At 24:00, because of the continuous threat of Soviet tank attacks to the rear of the division, the order as given not to stop at the Tihaya but to continue to move south, towards Kashiary.

The situation of the 'Sforzesca' was even more dramatic: at 23:00, already overcome on its flanks by advancing Soviet tank units, the order was given to attempt a breakthrough to the south, towards Nizhny Bolischinskoy. Because of a lack of fuel, many artillery pieces had to be left in place and destroyed.

Fighting on 20 December

On the Alpine Army Corps front, in the sector on the right defended by the 'Cuneense', the remnants of the 'Cosseria', elements of II and III/89, now out of ammunition and subordinated to the 'Cuneense', were withdrawn towards Loschtschina and Rossosch and from there, directed to Lisinkova, where they joined the remnants of the 'Cosseria'. To the south of the Alpine Corps, between Nova Kalitva and Taly, on the XXIV.Panzerkorps front, the defensive front was holding and there were no noteworthy actions.

Withdrawal of units was also continuing in the XXXV Corps and XXIX.Armee-Korps sectors. The Soviets had reached Diogtevo, completing the encirclements of those two corps.

After having abandoned their positions on the Don and in view of formation of a new continuous defensive line, the bulk of the troops were divided into two main blocs during the withdrawal; a

Italian troops withdrawing from a Russian village, December 1942. (Authors' collection)

northern bloc, with 298.Inf.Div., the Capizzi group ('Ravenna'), and elements of 'Pasubio' and 'Torino'. A southern bloc, with XXXV Corps headquarters and XXIX.Armee-Korps headquarters, elements of 'Pasubio', of the 'Celere' and of 'Sforzesca'.

The northern bloc made its withdrawal initially passing through Popovka. In particular, 298. Inf.Div. and the Capizzi group moved from the Radtschenskoye-Tereschkova area to Popovka-Makarov. Most of the men of the 'Pasubio', especially the soldiers of the 80th Infantry, reached Popovka and joined the troops of the 'Torino'. The march through Popovka, Osdnyakov and Smirnovski ended at Schepilov. Down to 600 men and four artillery pieces, the division was to assume defensive positions in Schepilov, as it had been surrounded by enemy forces. XXXV Corps headquarters was also alongside the remnants of the 'Pasubio'. The troops of the 'Torino', along with those of 298.Inf.Div. and Kampfgruppe Hufffmann of 27.Pz.Div. (led by Major Heinz Huffmann, commander of Sturmgeschütz-Abteilung 201) reached Popovka during the morning. At 11:00, the town was attacked by Soviet tanks, which were, however, beaten back. The 'Torino' division was ordered to form a rear guard force to cover the withdrawal of the other units, with the withdrawal beginning in the late evening. A great amount of disorder marked the men marching on foot as well as of the vehicles of all sorts.

The southern bloc began its withdrawal from W. Makeievka (21 December) moving towards Kiyevskoye (22 December). The 'Celere' troops spent part of the day of 20 December attempting to make contact with the 3rd Bersaglieri, with the 120th Artillery and with the Croat Legion. It was not until evening that the division headquarters was able to link up with the remnants of the 6th Bersaglieri and of the II/120 Artillery, on the march from Makeievka to Popovka. The 3rd Bersaglieri, along with other reinforcements, found Meskov already occupied by the Soviets. To force them out, the Croat Legion and the XX and XVII bersaglieri battalions were thrown into the fray; one of the important heights changed hands several times. The Croat Legion, led by their commander, Lieutenant colonel Egon Žitnik, hurled themselves like devils against the Soviet positions, with many of them falling. With the onset of night, the attack was called off and the men pulled back to Kalmikov to sleep under cover.

The men of the 'Sforzesca' Division, after having reached the line of the Tchir during the morning, continued to the south, in accordance with orders from XXIX.Armee-Korps. During the march, the Italians were bombed by Soviet aircraft, suffering some losses. Arriving at Popovka at 10:00, a new order was issued forcing the men to return to the Tchir in order to take up defensive positions. Towards evening they were subjected to a Soviet attack which was warded off, but they suffered additional losses. During the night, the Soviets broke through the 62.Inf.Div. lines, reaching Kamenka. There, artillery elements of the 'Sforzesca' drove off the enemy armoured attack, knocking out at least three Soviet tanks.

Fighting on 21 December

With the units subjected to continuous withdrawals under strong enemy pressure, headquarters of Heeresgruppe B decided to move the new defensive line further to the rear, moving it to the River Kalitva-Diogtevo-Verhniy Makeyevka-Verhniy Grekovo line to cover the left flank of Army Group Don. At the same time orders were issued to eliminate the Soviet units that had reached Diogtevo. At that time the forces were deployed as follows:

*   A northern bloc, defended by the Alpine Army corps from Bielogorje to Staro Kalitva and by XXIV.Pz.Korps from Novo Kalitva to Golaya.
*   A central bloc, between Kantemirovka and Diogtevo, held by various units of differing nationality, deployed at Makcevskaya, Tchertkovo, Gartmischevka, Buhaievk and Belovodsk.
*   A southern bloc, between Diogtevo and Verhniy Grekovo, where XXXV Corps headquarters, without its directly subordinate corps units and the XXIX.Armee-Korps units: 'Pasubio' 'Torino', 3rd 'Celere', 'Sforzesca' and 298.Inf.Div., all withdrawing to the Tchertkovo-Diogtevo-Verhniy Makeyevka area.

Following is the situation of the various units. The 298.Inf.Div., along with the Capizzi Group of the 'Ravenna' and the 'Torino', following a night march, reached Posdnyakov at dawn. There were clashes with the Soviets while crossing the Tihaya. At 7:00, at Posdnyakov, the 'Torino' rear guard was attacked from the northwest and from the southeast by two Soviet battalions supported by tanks. At 9:30, with the troops on the right bank of the Tihaya, the Soviets attacked again while enemy tanks tried to completely surround the Italo-German column. In the afternoon, the march continued as far as a hill where the Soviets were well dug in; 298.Inf.Div. troops attacked, supported by Italian soldiers. At the same time, the rear guard of the 'Torino' was again attacked. Towards evening, having gotten past the enemy positions after bitter fighting, the column reached Arbusov.

During the night the 'Pasubio' resumed its march to the south, clashing with Soviet forces at Olchovski. During the fighting, General Adriano Perrod, XXXV Corps artillery commander, was killed. At 7:00 there was another encounter at Tihomirovski, where the Italians overran a retreating Soviet motorized column. Around 8:30, the column reached Verhniy Makayevka, joining the 'Sforzesca' division's column.

The 'Torino' units reached Posdnyakov, forced to march across open fields and thus having to abandon some of their trucks and artillery. As stated previously, around 7:00 two Soviet battalions, one coming from the northwest and one from the southeast, attacked the 'Torino' column. Artillery quickly responded and a counterattack was made by the III/81 Infantry. The Soviets reacted by sending tanks, inflicting heavy losses on the Italians. Not until 9:00 was the march able to resume, then to halt again west of Smirnovskiy, where the presence of a new enemy barrier unleashed a bitter battle that lasted about an hour and a half. While the Italians were fighting

Italian troops during the retreat to the south, December 1942. (Authors' collection)

to open a path, the column's rear guard was attacked. Towards evening, the men finally reached Arbusov. The 'Torino' was left with three artillery pieces and four trucks. All of the heavy weapons and the other vehicles had been lost along the way. Food was also lacking.

Headquarters of the 3rd 'Celere', separated from the rest of the division, reached Voroshilovgrad. At dawn, the remnants of the 3rd Bersaglieri led by Colonel Luigi Longo and a small group of Croat legionnaires dug in at Kalmikov, soon facing attack by strong Soviet infantry forces from the east and the south. The battle morphed into a series of confused and isolated fights, but in the end the entire Italian column was surrounded. Those who were not killed in the fighting were captured by the enemy.

In his conclusions regarding the 17-21 December operational cycle, General De Blasio wrote that the XXIX.Armee-Korps commander had clearly indicated that the 'Celere' was to remain on the Don, even though it was surrounded: 'These orders were carried out to the letter! Not a single man of the 3rd Bersaglieri turned back. Of the Croat Legion: surviving were one officer and one soldier'.[10]

Colonel Luigi Longo, commander of the 3rd Bersaglieri, writing to De Blasio about the happenings of the recent days, wrote: 'The Croat Legion, XXV and XX battalions carried out their duty valorously, but many Croats, beginning with their commander, instead of focusing on their assigned objectives, singly or in groups soon worried themselves with finding a way through the enemy lines with the only aim being to escape from the pocket. This example was followed by some personnel of the regiment but almost no one succeeded in the attempt'.[11]

The 'Sforzesca' was attacked during the night by about fifteen Soviet tanks, six of which were destroyed, while a group of carabinieri was busy dealing with the accompanying infantry.

---

10   The officer was in reality Lt. Zunič, a Dalmatian, who was the Italian liaison officer to the Legion.
11   In Stefano Fabei, *La legione straniera di Mussolini.*

Meanwhile, the infantry regiments had been ordered to regroup at Verhniy Tchirsky to continue to march to the south, crossing the Tchir Valley and that of Yablonovaya. During the withdrawal, the left flank of the 53rd Infantry was attacked by Soviet tanks in the late afternoon. The fighting lasted for about two hours, with heavy losses for both the Italians and the Soviets. Having overcome this first obstacle, the march resumed, but around 23:00 there was a fresh attack by Soviet tanks against the head and flanks of the column, during which the vanguard itself, consisting of the I/53, was cut off. However, the Italians were able to open a breach after having knocked out six enemy tanks. The bulk of the column, consisting of the 54th Infantry, was surrounded. The 6th Bersaglieri, in an attempt to assist the surrounded troops, was attacked and pushed back by enemy tanks. Not until late at night was part of the column able to free itself by opening a route while fighting, reaching Kyevskoye.

Alpini in battle

On 23 December, Heeresgruppe B ordered Armee-Abteilung Fretter-Pico (General der Artillerie Maximilian Fretter-Pico) to assume defense of his right wing in order to shorten the Italian 8th Army's defensive sector. At the same time, the Italian army was ordered to stem the advance of any enemy forces past the Rossosch-Millerovo railway line and to hold the Don front held by the Alpine Army Corps as far as Novo Kalitva and that of XXIV.Panzerkorps from Novo Kalitva to Golaya. Deployed along this stretch of the front, from north to south, were the 'Julia' division, 385.

Monte Cervino alpine ski troops with a Breda Model 30 light machine gun. (Authors' collection)

Inf.Div., SS-Kampfgruppe Fegelein, 27.Pz.Div. and 287.Inf.Div.. Three Italian strongpoints sill held out in the area south of Golaya, at Bugayevka, Gartmischevka and Tchertkovo, which had been cut off but which contributed to slowing down the Soviet advance, covering the left flank of the Fretter-Pico group, which was busy attacking Diogtevo.

To carry out the new orders, the Italian Army headquarters no longer had II Corps, which had been pulled from the front and whose remnants were being reorganized in Voroshilovgrad for the 'Ravenna' division and at Rossosch for the 'Cosseria', as well as the XXXV Corps with the 'Sforzesca', 'Pasubio', 'Torino' and 3rd 'Celere' divisions, all of which were outside the new southern sector boundary and which were withdrawing to the Donets amidst a thousand difficulties. The arrival of 19.Pz.Div. was expected, which was to take up positions on the right of XXIV. Panzerkorps, directly subordinate to Army command.

Since 18 December the 'Julia' division had sent its reaction group to the II Corps sector; the 'L'Aquila' and 'Tolmezzo' battalions, with other reinforcing units, had taken up positions south of Tchyornaya Kalitva, between Novo Meniza and Ivanovka, extending the line of the 'Cuneense' to the south and establishing contact on the right with 385.Inf.Div. The 'Monte Cervino' battalion was also in the same positions, a veteran of the bitter fighting and left with only 200 men.

Seleny Yar crossroads

On 20 December, strong Soviet recon patrols attacked between the crossroads at Seleny Yar and Ivanovka but were pushed back by the alpini of the 'L'Aquila' battalion. The crossroads at Seleny Yar had to be held at all costs because if were to fall in Soviet hands, they would have been able to advance on Rossosch or to fall upon the right flank of the 'Cuneense', the southernmost unit of the Alpine Army Corps. Defense of the crossroads was concentrated on the three heights of hills 205.6, 153.3 and 204.6, where it was possible for the Italian units to dig themselves in properly. Reinforcing this deployment were several batteries of mountain guns and 47/32 guns, in addition to two German batteries equipped with Nebelwerfer rocket launchers. There were also other German units in the nearby sectors, but which had been ordered to pull back to Komarov to protect the headquarters of 385.Inf.Div. in the event that the alpini had lost the positions.

In the morning of 21 December, the Soviets resumed their attack the positions of the 'L'Aquila' battalion with two infantry battalions of the 352nd Division, setting off furious defensive fighting which lasted until late afternoon. All of the attacks were repulsed. In order to face any tank attacks, the German headquarters sent in several tank destroyers.

At dawn on 22 December, a new attack was made using greater forces, three infantry battalions, which focused mainly against Hill 204.6. This time the alpine skiers of the 'Monte Cervino' were committed to the fighting, sent to reinforce the 'L'Aquila' to defend the key crossroads at Seleny Yar; during the fighting the alpine skiers, by individual attacks, knocked out many Soviet T-34 tanks from close range using clusters of hand grenades, Molotov cocktails and antitank mines. But the Soviets, with their infantry and T-34 tanks, finally were able to surround the alpini of the 'Monte Cervino' and 'L'Aquila'. Around noon, thanks to the arrival of several German assault guns, the alpini counterattacked, supported by artillery and rocket launcher batteries. At the same time, the alpini of the 'Monte Cervino' were busy eliminating a small enemy penetration; Lieutenant Carlo Sacchi, commander of the 1st Company of the 'Monte Cervino', with the shout of 'Cervino! Pista!' [Cervino! Make way!] took off his skis and climbed aboard a German Sturmgeschütz III which was already in the midst of the Soviets. All of the alpine troopers followed his lead and soon there were clutches of alpini in white coveralls on each German assault gun, shooting and throwing grenades, scattering the enemy infantry and throwing them off of Hill 204.6. The German self-propelled guns pursued the Soviets as far as Ivanovka. At the end of the fighting, on the vast snowy

A Monte Cervino ski patrol in combat on the Don front, December 1942. (Authors' collection)

plain over which the battle had raged for hours, hundreds and hundreds of Soviet soldiers lay dead, shadows on the white background. A large part of the three Soviet battalions had been eliminated and 157 prisoners were taken, in addition to a large quantity of weapons and equipment. On the Italian side, 40 alpini had fallen (4 officers) and there were many wounded. The 'Monte Cervino' also suffered the loss of Lieutenant Carlo Sacchi, who after having jumped off the assault gun at the end of the attack, was shot in the back by a Soviet soldier and died.

There were many acts of courage and many Gold Medals for Military Valor were awarded posthumously for the hard fighting of those tragic days, among which was that awarded to Enrico Rebeggiani, born in Cheti on 1 August 1916, a reserve lieutenant in the 'L'Aquila' battalion, 9th Alpini Regiment 'Julia', leader of the battalion's arditi [elite] ski platoon: 'Heroic combatant in Albania, although assigned to light duties at a depot because of wounds received in combat, he asked for and was allowed to join his battalion departing for the Russian front. In several days of bloody fighting against an enemy who had a preponderance of men and equipment, he fought uninterruptedly. His courage was a constant example to his alpini, and his valor culminated on 22 December when, leading an elite ski platoon, he occupied by surprise a key position which the enemy had seized from another Italian unit. Counterattacked several times, he held his position with admirable tenacity, even when his platoon was almost wiped out. Although wounded, seeing the enemy withdrawing, he gathered the few survivors together, heedless of the deadly artillery fire, and threw himself in pursuit; wounded a second time he urged his troopers to continue the fight, shouting "Avanti, l'Aquila". Mortally wounded, he consecrated his life to his country'. Russian front, Ivanovka, Hill 204, 19-20-21-22 December 1942.

On 23 December, in light of new attacks against the Seleny Yar crossroads, the Alpine Army Corps headquarters ordered the 'L'Aquila' and 'Monte Cervino' to be replaced by the 'Val Cismon'.

The 'Monte Cervino' was ordered to return to Rossosch. The units were relieved in the night between 24 and 25 December.

New attacks in the Alpine Army Corps sector

In the morning of 22 December, slightly north of the Seleny Yar crossroads, the Soviets attacked the 'Tolmezzo' battalion's positions. After having been forced back, the Soviets returned to attack shortly afterwards with two battalions of the 167th Division. After having suffered more heavy losses, the Soviets ceased their attacks in the afternoon. There were no noteworthy actions on 23 December. On 24 December, fresh enemy attacks were made against the 'Val Cismon' battalion's lines. Support by German assault guns was also needed in this instance in order to deal with a Soviet counterattack, capturing prisoners, arms and equipment. That same morning, the 'Vicenza' battalion, supported by German tanks, was engaged in a counterattack to hit the flank of a large Soviet unit which was readying itself to attack Krinischnaya in the 385.Inf.Div. sector. During the clashes that followed, the Soviets suffered heavy losses and were pushed back.

In the late afternoon, the 'Tolmezzo' suffered a new attack made by two Soviet battalions, right in the middle of a snow squall. This attack was also repulsed thanks to the support of artillery fire by the 'Cuneense'.

At dawn on 26 December, the Soviets attacked the 'Tolmezzo' and 'Val Cismon' positions. In the hours that followed, the major effort was made against the 'Val Cismon', but thanks to an immediate counterattack supported by German tanks, the Soviets were forced back. The XXIV. Panzerkorps commander, General der Artillerie Martin Wandel, expressed his personal admiration for the alpini, characterizing them as 'very aggressive in the attack'. Fighting continued on 27 and 28 December, with continuous attacks and counterattacks, but in the end, all of the contested positions remained in the hands of the alpini.

The Werhmacht bulletin for 29 December 1942 reported that: 'In the defensive fighting in the great bend of the Don, the Italian 'Julia' alpine division distinguished itself in a particular manner'.

At dawn on 30 December, the Soviets resumed their attacks against the 'Tolmezzo' positions, with the support of 25 tanks and artillery fire, along the Novo Kalitva-Komarov road. Having beaten back the first attack thanks to the fire of automatic weapons and artillery, the Soviets returned to attack twice more, taking heavy casualties and were finally forced to withdraw. Other enemy attacks were made further to the south against the 385.Inf.Div. The 'Tolmezzo' battalion and Italian artillery were also engaged in the fighting. In spite of everything, the Soviets were able to capture the position; a counterattack was then mounted by the 'Gemona' battalion, which restored the situation. Fighting dragged on for the entire day.

Other Soviet attacks since early morning had also been directed against the positions of the 'Vicenza' battalion, straddling the Dereskovatka-Seleny Yar road. A few hours after the initial attack, two infantry battalions showed up along with tanks. Four tanks were knocked out at close range. Around noon, German aircraft hit the Soviet columns from above. Soon after, a counterattack was made by the 59th Company of the 'Vicenza' battalion south of the Seleny Yar crossroads, supported by four German self-propelled assault guns and six tanks, thanks to which the Soviets were driven off.

On 31 December enemy attacks resumed in the same sector, again by infantry supported by tanks. After having broken through the Italian lines, the Soviets were quickly thrown back by a counterattack, during which the enemy suffered heavy losses in men and tanks. In the afternoon, another attack was repulsed in the same manner.

13

The Withdrawal Continues

The units of the Italian 8th Army that were withdrawing from the Don front since 19 December had formed two blocs, a southern bloc and a northern bloc, that were following two different routes. The southern bloc had been formed on 22 December at Kiyevskoy, pulling together elements from various units which joined the bulk of the surviving forces of the 'Sforzesca'. Among the more cohesive units that joined the division was he 6th Bersaglieri Regiment. The men coming from II Corps, from XXXV Corps and from the other Italian divisions subordinate to XXIX.Armee-Korps, were used to form an ad hoc regiment designated 'Mazzocchi', led by Colonel Armando Mazzocchi, formerly the commander of the 79th Infantry of the 'Pasubio' division. The new unit was structured with three battalions, designated with the names of the divisions from which their personnel mainly came:

- Battaglione Pasubio, consisting of personnel of the 79th Infantry and other men from the 'Torino', 'Ravenna' and 'Celere' divisions and corps service units.
- Battaglione Celere (minus the 6th Bersaglieri) consisting of personnel coming from the 'Ravenna' and 'Torino' and other corps units and services.
- Battaglione Sforzesca, consisting of all of the personnel on foot from the 'Sforzesca' division who were not part of their regiment or in other smaller units.

At first the battalions were organized with three companies and later with four, dividing them into those men who still had their individual weapons and those who did not. The regiment had only one 75/27 artillery piece that had been salvaged by the 8th Artillery Regiment of the 'Pasubio'.

During that same day, several enemy armoured attacks coming from Nizhny Astachov were repulsed and two Soviet tanks were destroyed.

During the night of 23 December, the 6th Bersaglieri Regiment, reinforced with available artillery, went to relieve a German unit barring the Nagolnaya valley west of Kivskoy, remaining in those positions until the next afternoon and fighting throughout the day. The other units reached Annenskiy, where they found the survivors of the 53rd Infantry and where by order of XXIX. Armee-Korps headquarters, they dug in to face the Soviet forces that had occupied the Nagolnaya Valley. At dawn on 24 December, the men began to march towards Krasnoyarovka, which was occupied by the 6th Bersaglieri at 20:00 after a furious fight that ejected the Soviets. The march ended at dawn on 25 December, resuming on 26 December with a temperature of -38 degrees Celsius [-36 Fahrenheit]. Around noon, several German aircraft mistakenly bombed the column, causing significant losses. Nizhny Petrovskiy was taken at 15:00 after two hours of fighting. In the afternoon of 27 December, a slight shift to the west was made, as far as Nikolayevskiy to find adequate billets for the men to be able to rest, but at 22:00 an order by XXIX.Armee-Korps forced the men to resume their march towards Bolshoi Ternovyi in the Gnilaya Valley. In the early hours of 28 December, while only three kilometers from their objective, a German aircraft dropped a message on the column with a map, warning that Bolshoi Ternovyi had already been

White-clad Italian soldiers in combat using a captured Soviet Degtyarev DP-27 light machine gun.
(Authors' collection)

occupied by the Soviets and that the men were to march to Skassirskaya, which had been occupied by the Germans. More kilometers had to be covered through the cold and snow and with only a few vehicles available. Meanwhile, the head and tail of the column were attacked by Soviet tanks, three of which were knocked out by the few artillery pieces still available. Around midnight of 28 December, the column finally reached the German positions; the survivors were regrouped in the Michailovskiy-Nadeshovska area, where they rested for the entire day of 29 December.

In the morning of 30 December, with the march once again under way, a Soviet tank force attacked some Romanian troops who had joined the Italian column. The Italian soldiers managed to avoid the rout of the Romanians and also destroyed three Soviet tanks. Around 22:00, the column, now consisting only of Italians, reached Yessa Ulov. There, 'Sforzesca' headquarters returned to the regiments their respective banners, which had been collected to avoid having them fall into enemy hands. In addition, General Hans von Obstfelder, the XXIX.Armee-Korps commander, issued a special order of the day to salute the Italian units that were leaving his corps:

After I had the honor of having under my command, since 1 November 1942, the proud 'Sforzesca' Division, it now leaves the ranks of XXIX Army Corps. For all that the division accomplished during this period, I express my profound thanks and my special praise. With tireless work, the division built the positions assigned to it and defended them valorously. During the withdrawal from the enemy imposed by circumstances it carried out the tasks assigned to it in the best manner possible...[1]

---

1   Ufficio Storico dello Stato Maggiore dell'Esercito, *Le operazioni delle unità italiane al fronte russo*, page 700.

On 1 January the column moved Provakskiy. On the 3rd it reached Forchstadt on the Donets. From there, the men were transferred to Rykovo, where they regrouped on 5 January.

Arbusov Basin

As mentioned previously, the forces of the northern bloc, the 'Torino' division, elements of the 'Pasubio', of the Capizzi group and the German 298.Inf.Div., had during the night between 21 and 22 December, reached the Arbusov basin (Arbuzovka), in the center of which lay in a depression the village of the same name. In that basin, which was wide and deep, in a sea of ice and constant snowstorms, the temperature reached 50 degrees below zero [-50 Fahrenheit]. From the previous night, the Soviets had followed the retreating Italo-German columns in order to surround and destroy them and when they moved within the basin, the trap was sprung. The Soviets began to fire on the Italo-German troops who were completely exposed and panic stricken, from all sides. According to some testimonies, the houses had all been occupied by the Germans, who had arrived first.[2]

It seemed impossible to organize an effective defense, but desperate counterattacks were made during the night in order to lessen enemy pressure. In order to escape that meatgrinder and to break the Soviet grip, on the morning of 23 December the German headquarters decided to mount a massive counterattack; the Italian units threw themselves into the assault, bypassing the Germans, breaking through the Soviet lines and opening a large breach. Episodes of courage were not lacking; at 7:00 on 22 December an Italian soldier mounted on a horse and waving the Italian flag, threw himself alone against the Soviet lines, inciting and pulling other groups of men to join in on the attack. The courageous horseman was flamethrower specialist Mario Iacovitti of the Army's 1st Chemical Battalion. The first soldier to follow Iacovitti in the charge was carabiniere Giuseppe Plado Mosca, assigned to the headquarters of the 'Torino' division.[3] The act, the shouts of incitement and the vision of the Italian tricolor flag had the effect of galvanizing the soldiers, who by now had resigned themselves to their sad fate, but fortunately that heroic gesture stirred their souls. Even though weakened and exhausted, the soldiers fixed bayonets and charged into an attack against the enemy, who now certain of victory, was taken completely by surprise by the Italian reaction. It was not to be for Giuseppe Plado Mosca, who was killed during his epic cavalry charge. He was awarded the Gold Cross for Military Valor, posthumously, with the following citation:

> Assigned to the headquarters of a division that was engaged in a difficult and bitter withdrawal, he distinguished himself by his conscious courage. With the troops of the division surrounded and subjected to deadly fire from automatic weapons and artillery, he confirmed his valor by repeatedly taking part in desperate counterattacks. Although exhausted by privation and the freezing weather, in a final desperate burst of energy, he was the first to follow a soldier who, on horseback and waving the tricolor, was charging against the enemy. Spurred on by their magnificent heroism, hundreds of men who, despite being weak in strength, in an overwhelming hand-to-hand assault, managed to break the circle of steel and fire that surrounded them. In reaching the enemy positions, he fell, cut down by a burst of machine gun fire, but his conscious heroism enabled the division's exhausted troops to open break out.
>
> Arbusov Valley (Russia), 22 December 1942.

2   Ufficio Storico dello Stato Maggiore Esercito, *Le operazioni delle unità italiane al fronte russo*, page 409.

3   A. Valori, *La Campagna di Russia*, page 631. This episode of courage s not mentioned in any Russian, German or Anglo-Saxon sources.

Flamethrower operator Mario Iacovitti threw himself into the attack despite having the beginnings of frostbite in his legs. Having miraculously survived the enemy fire, he was captured but thanks to the fact that he had learned to speak Russian, he was able to live through a terrible period of detention in Soviet prison camps, reaching Milan among the first repatriates, given his precarious state of health, once the war had ended, on 26 November 1945. He was awarded the Gold Medal for Military Valor with the following citation:

> A volunteer during the bitter defensive fighting, while the unit he was part of was completely surrounded and pressed by overwhelming enemy forces, worn out by many days of fighting and with his lower limbs suffering from the beginning of frostbite, with a desperate resurgence of energy, he managed to get on a horse and, keeping a tricolor banner on his right, he threw himself against the enemy, by his example gathering a following of hundred men in an attack. Heedless of enemy reaction, he attacked repeatedly. On the fifth charge, having miraculously remained unharmed and after a burst of machine gun fire had felled his horse, he still dragged himself forward on all fours towards an enemy automatic weapon position, which with cold shrewdness and extraordinary courage, he was able to capture by hurling hand grenades. As the desperate fight continued, overwhelmed by a wave of the enemy, he was captured.
>
> Arbusov (Russia), 22 December 1942.

Despite this episode of valor and the courage shown by several groups of Italian and German combatants, the situation in the Arbusov basin became increasingly tragic as the hours passed on 22 December. Around noon, Soviet artillery intensified its fire against the encircled masses causing heavy losses and it became almost impossible, due to lack of medicine and medical supplies, to give aid to the numerous wounded. A Soviet shell hit the 'Torino' command post in full, badly wounding the three regimental commanders: Colonel Di Gennaro died immediately, Colonel Ulisse Rosati, commander of the 52nd Artillery, was mortally wounded in the legs and Colonel Santini was the only survivor despite having sustained serious head wounds.

The first signs of collapse and falling apart began to manifest themselves among the surrounded troops; a group consisting of about 500 Italian soldiers stopped fighting and was captured near the village of Arbusov by Soviet soldiers of the 100th Regiment of the 35th Guards Rifle Division. Other groups, however, continued to fight on doggedly. Also on 23 December, Soviet artillery and rocket launchers continued to hit the Italo-German masses in the Arbusov basin; the 'Torino' commander, General Lerici, ordered the soldiers to burn the regimental banners to avoid having them fall into enemy hands. During the night, orders were issued to break out of the encirclement and the move to the Tchertkovo strongpoint.

To the north of Alekseevo-Lozovskoye, a group of about 6,000 soldiers, mainly Germans and Blackshirts, organized a circular defensive position and fought courageously, repulsing the Soviet attacks and repeatedly attempting to break through the enemy lines. It was the Blackshirts who opened a breach, thanks to the sacrifice of Adjutant Oreste Biagi, who placed himself at the head of his men and was able to break through the enemy lines, dying in the process. He was awarded the Gold Medal for Military valor with the following citation:

> An adjutant with illustrious military virtues, under many circumstances he gave proof of calm, shining personal courage. A platoon leader forged into an instrument of particular aggressiveness in action, he led his unit in an attack against a very strong enemy position. After heavy fighting and having gathered other soldiers who had lost their officers, he quickly reorganized them, leading them personally in an attack, prodding them on and instilling a special impetus to the action. Wounded three times, three times after summary medication and despite his obvious open wounds, he returned to wherever the fight was the most dangerous, urging his

subordinates on by example and by word. With a supreme effort he reached the stubbornly opposing position along with a few survivors, capturing it in a bold rush, finding in this last act of great indomitable ardor a glorious end to his life as a combatant devoted to sacrifice.

Arbusov (Russian front), 23 December 1942.

At 23:00, the Italo-German column resumed its move; only the fittest men could move with it, while the wounded and frostbitten were left in place, later in large part being massacred by Soviet troops. No pity was shown to the dying. At 8:00 Sidorovka was reached and Gussev at 11:00. In the afternoon, after having run into stiff resistance near Mantovo Kalitvenskaya, the column continued on to the south, passing through Poltavka, Ivanovka and Chodokov. The men marched in deep snow, with freezing temperatures and fog. There were many cases of frostbitten soldiers who were abandoned without any hope along the way. Added to these attacks by nature were sudden attacks by Soviet partisans.

In the meantime, in the morning of 24 December 1942, Red Army troops unleashed the final attack against the Italo-German forces remaining in the Arbusov basin. The final battle degenerated into a series of violent and confused separate fights. Once again, some Italo-German groups managed to initially get through the Soviet lines, but were later eliminated by other Soviet troops who had arrived as reinforcements. It was not until 7:00 on 25 December that forces of the 35th Guards Rifle Division were able to break into the village of Arbusov, after a final, furious struggle. According to Soviet records, during that last day of battle, almost 2,00 Italo-German soldiers were killed, while 2,773 were captured.[4]

A German StuG III assault gun with mainly German soldiers aboard, passing by the disordered Axis infantry columns retreating on foot. (Authors' collection)

---

4   G. Scotoni, *L'Aramta rossa e la disfatta italiana*, page 359.

During the fighting in the Arbusov basin, there were many reported instances of a lack of camaraderie between Italian and German soldiers. In particular, official Italian reports point out the violent and brutal behavior of troops of the 298.Infanterie-Division. In addition, the Wehrmacht soldiers attributed the defeat to the lack of combativeness of the Italians. In general, there was little cooperation and there were violent clashes between the men who wanted to occupy the isbas and for use of the transportation assets that were still available. The German soldiers, generally better supplied and having sleds or trucks, in many cases did not provide food and brutally rebuffed requests for aid and assistance by Italian soldiers on foot.[5] However, the Germans played a key role in saving the troops that were surrounded in Arbusov; it was in fact the last remaining armoured vehicles of Gruppe Huffmann (Major Heinz Huffmann), consisting of two assault guns and two tanks, that played a decisive role in the march and the final breakthrough.

Siege of Tchertkovo

At 7:00 on 25 December, near Scheptukovka, the column that had escaped from the battle of annihilation at Arbusov crossed the railway line. At 22:00, the head of the column reached Tchertkovo, where food was distributed and the men were billeted under cover. The influx of those who had escaped the fury of the Soviets continued throughout 26 December. Through the radio of 298. Inf.Div., the Army headquarters was asked to evacuate the most seriously wounded by air or by truck and to deliver medical supplies. On 28 December, an Italian plane dropped food, medicine and ammunition for light weapons. In the afternoon of 29 December, a Savoia-Marchetti SM81 'Pipistrello' tri-motor aircraft delivered General Enrico Pezzi, commander of the 8th Army aviation element, along with medical colonel Federico Bocchetti; it also unloaded food, medicine and supplies and then took off for the rear area after having taken the most seriously wounded aboard. During the return trip the plane disappeared along with its crew.

On 31 December, an Italian hospital was opened in a schoolhouse; more than 1,200 wounded were admitted there. The total number of Italian soldiers present in Tchertkovo at that time was about 7,000 men, of which 3,800 were wounded and frostbitten.[6]

On 1 January 1943, Soviet artillery resumed heavy shelling of the Tchertkovo area. Meanwhile, troops of the 19.Pz.Div., sent to reinforce Tchertkovo, were stalled about 14 kilometers away by strong Soviet units. German aircraft were unable to provide support because of the bad weather. Between 2 and 3 January, there were no actions worthy of note. On 4 January, 298.Inf.Div. attempted to make contact with 19.Pz.Div. but was prevented from doing so by a Soviet counterattack. At the same time the Soviets attacked the Italian positions at Tchertkovo but were pushed back. In the morning of 5 January, a new attack was made directed mainly against the Italian sector but was repulsed. On 7 January, the Soviets tried to break into the town sending patrols ahead, but they were all eliminated. There were also numerous attacks on 9 January, supported by artillery fire and around a dozen tanks, eight of which were destroyed.

Particularly distinguishing themselves in this fighting were the Blackshirts of the 'Montebello' Group, able to put on the line no more than two hundred men still capable of fighting. Nonetheless, on that day of 9 January 1943, the Blackshirts sacrificed themselves to stop a violent Soviet attack, preceded by a strong preparatory bombardment and supported by nine T-343 tanks. When the tanks and the infantry they carried aboard them, who were shouting 'Hurrah Stalin', arrived, the legionnaires replied by singing 'Giovinezza' [the Fascist Party hymn] and taking the infantry riding

---

5   T. Schlemmer, *Invasori, non vittime*, pages 230-231.
6   Ufficio Storico dello Stato Maggiore dell'Esercito, *Le operazioni delle unità italiane al fronte russo*, page 412.

on the tanks under automatic weapons fire before they could set foot on the ground. One T-34 was set afire by Blackshirt Gino Betti, who stopped it with a round from a war booty PTRD antitank rifle, after having waited with great calm until the tank was only ten meters from his position. With every tank that was hit, the legionnaires shouted 'Viva il Duce' and burst out singing 'Giovinezza'. Capomanipolo [Lieutenant] Lamberto Vannuttelli, who had been wounded, was knocked over by a Soviet tank, but still found the strength to sing 'Giovinezza' when the T-34 was hit by his men.

In the counterattacks Capomanipolo Amedeo Cremisi, twice wounded, who, having run out of ammunition, used his carbine like a club against the Soviets who surrounded him. His heroism gained him a posthumous Gold Medal for Military Valor, with the following citation:

> An officer with the highest military qualifications who had distinguished himself in previous actions by his calm disregard for danger and his burning enthusiasm. In a difficult and bitter situation, despite the horrific suffering caused by a third-degree frostbite of his lower limbs, he refused to move back from the line of fire. During a violent enemy attack supported by armoured vehicles, although wounded by a mortar fragment, by word and example he bolstered resistance against the enemy. In a tragic moment, having gathered together the few survivors and by his boundless will having overcome the physical pain of his wounds, he threw himself into a counterattack. Wounded once again and dripping with blood, he still found the strength to throw himself against the enemy using his carbine as a club against the enemy until he finally was killed by a machine gun burst. A shining example of unfettered ardor and supreme dedication to duty.
>
> Tchertkovo (Russia), 9 January 1943.

Italian soldiers in a defensive position, December 1942. (Authors' collection)

The second Gold Medal recipient also fell that same day, Blackshirt Gianfilippo Braccini, who had already been decorated in the field for the fighting of the previous days and who, wounded twice, refused any aid, continuing to fire with his light machine gun and who was hit while moving towards a better position so that he could better aim in order to fire against the attackers.

Black shirt Stefano Migliavacca, with frostbitten feet, responded to his officer who wanted to send him to an aid station that he did not have to be able to march in order to fire with his machine gun; seeing that his protests were in vain, he had his buddies carry him surreptitiously to a very exposed position where he remained for forty-eight hours, despite being freshly wounded by a grenade fragment, all the while keeping the Soviets under fire with his weapon. In two hours of fighting the Blackshirts knocked out eight of nine tanks and wiped out a Soviet battalion, losing two killed (one officer), 11 wounded (2 officers) and 17 frostbitten.[7]

The battle continues

The situation with respect to the wounded continued to become more critical and because of the systematic destruction of houses, adequate lodgings were lacking. Of the roughly 14,000 men in Tchertkovo, the combatants were down to only 2,500 men without ammunition and without food rations. There were no significant actions between 10 and 13 January. On the 14th, the news arrived that 19.Pz.Div. was on the verge of opening a gap in the road to Strelzovka in order to allow the column of trucks bearing the wounded to withdraw, followed by the rest of the besieged troops. At 13:00, however, a new order came, according to which the road to salvation was to be opened by the besieged forces themselves and that the wounded were to be abandoned in place. There were 2,850 wounded Italians of which 1,000 were in no condition to move on their own. There were only two trucks and a few sleds which would enable a maximum of only about a hundred of the wounded to be moved. Thus, at 20:00 on 15 January, the troops that were able to march were organized into columns:

- 'Torino' division: 1,600 men
- 'Pasubio' division: 2,000 men
- XXXV Corps troops and service elements: 1,800 men
- 'Ravenna' and 'Celere' elements: 400 men
- Tchertkovo defense troops: 500 men

At the head of the column was the 298.Inf.Div., which managed to break out of the encirclement, while the Italians remained as a rear guard supported by a few German tanks. At dawn on 16 January, the men reached Losovskaya, while at Beresevo there were clashes with Soviet armoured units. After having avoided Strelzovka because of the presence of enemy forces, at 22:00 the head of the Italian column reached Belovodsk, from where the transfer of the wounded by ambulance to Starobelsk was quickly begun. Other isolated soldiers continued to arrive throughout the night and for most of 17 January.

The situation elsewhere

II Corps headquarters had been ordered to move to Voroshilovgrad to reorganize its units. The move was completed on 21 December. In the meantime, the bulk of the 'Cosseria' division had regrouped at Sofievka: part of the 90th Infantry, the 108th Artillery (minus one group), the engineer and service units. The remnants of the 89th Infantry had gathered at Loschtschina and after having fought until 20 December alongside 385.Inf.Div., on 23 December all of the 'Cosseria' moved to

---

7   P. Romeo di Colleredo Mels, *Le Camicie Nere sul front russo 1941-1943*, pages 73-74.

The mass of retreating soldiers and vehicles on the snow-covered steppe, December 1942.
(Authors' collection)

the area of Lisinovka-Yekaterinovka, near Rossosch, where it remained until 31 December, passing under control of the Alpine Army Corps. Between 1 and 5 January, the units were shifted to the Rovenki-Beloluzkaya area, to protect the right flank of the Alpine Army Corps. From that area, following the deterioration of the XXIV.Panzerkorps situation, the division, which was subordinated to the Army headquarters, was ordered to march to the southwest until it reached Izyum. From there, the men began a long march to the northwest, with frigid temperatures, passing through Kharkov, Ahtyrka, Rommy, Priulki and Neshin until Novo Beliza in the Gomel area, which was reached on 7 March. The division thus rejoined II Corps headquarters and the 'Ravenna'.

Fate of the 'Ravenna

With respect to the men of the 'Ravenna', they had reached Voroshilovgrad between 19 and 21 December, where they were regrouped and reorganized as best as could be and resupplied with arms and equipment. II Corps headquarters which had just arrived in Voroshilovgrad on 23 December was charged to defend the two bridges which provided access to the city. The mission was assigned to the men of the 'Ravenna', who were to challenge any enemy penetration towards the city. On 24 December, the II Corps commander was able to report to 8th Army headquarters that 4,084 men (124 officers) and 33 guns varying in caliber from 20mm to 105mm[8] were committed to defend the bridgehead. That same day, headquarters of Armee-Abteilung Fretter-Pico informed II Corps that it intended to transfer the Italian forces defending the Voroshilovgrad bridges to another sector of the Donets. Despite the doubts expressed by General Zanghieri as to the limited combat capabilities of those units, on 27 December General Fretter-Pico confirmed the move of the 'Ravenna',

---

8   Ufficio Storico dello Stato Maggiore dell'Esercito, *Le operazioni delle unità italiane al fronte russo*, page 417.

which on the evening of 30 December was relieved by the German Schramm group. The Italian division was then subordinated to Armee-Abteilung Fretter-Pico. Between 1 and 6 January, the men of the 'Ravenna' were deployed along the right bank of the Donets, in the stretch between the confluence of the Derkul and the village of Michaylovka, a front of about 45 kilometers. The assigned missions were to hold the positions and to prevent any enemy penetrations. Combat forces consisted of three infantry battalions, a 20mm antiaircraft battery, a 75/27 battery, a 100/17 battery and two 105/28 guns. At the time that the men of the 'Ravenna' were deploying in the new sector, Soviet forces were in the area between Millerovo and the Donets, facing the German 304.Inf.Div. which was withdrawing. Several Soviet advanced elements had however already pushed as far as the northern bank of the river to the point that they threatened the areas west of Kamensk, to the right of the new positions of the 'Ravenna'. Between 6 and 9 January, the division sent many patrols across the river to reinforce the defenses in various villages.

On the morning of 19 January, Soviet artillery began to hit Makarov, Kruschilovka and Ilyevka. In the afternoon, the Italian garrisons at Makarov and Kruschilovka were attacked by partisan bands. At 22:30, Soviet regular units attacked Kruschilovka, held by a rifle company, a mortar company and a section of 75/27 guns. The Italians resisted doggedly, while other forces sent as reinforcements, were in turn attacked and surrounded during their march, but were able to free themselves, stemming the Soviet attack from Kruschilovka towards Ivanovka. At 4:00 on 20 January, the surviving defenders of Kruschilovka mounted a counterattack, managing to break out and make their way to Ivanovka. There, reorganized into a company with two platoons, they were sent to Ilyevka. For the entire day, the Soviets tried to move from Kruschilovka to the south and to the west, but without any success. For the next day, an attack was planned using Grenadier-Regiment 573 (304.Inf.Div.) and the III/38, moving from the Ivanovka-Davido Nicholskiy line towards Kruschilovka. While the Italo-German forces were preparing for action, at 20:00 on 20 January the Soviets attacked Davido Nicholoskiy but were forced back by a counterattack made by the Italo-German forces. Soon after midnight, Soviet and partisan forces attacked the Italian company stationed at Makarov, completely overrunning it after a furious battle. Only a few survivors were able to withdraw to Ilyevka. Because of this new breach which threatened the encirclement of the other forces deployed along the river, the attack against Kruschilovka was cancelled.

At dawn on 22 January, the Soviets attacked the village of Ilyevka from east, north and west with two infantry battalions reinforced by partisans. The position was surrounded and furious defensive fighting followed with heavy losses to the defending Italians, among whom was the commander of the II/38, Lieutenant Colonel Renato Lupo, who was posthumously awarded the Gold Medal for Military Valor, with the following citation:

> Commander of a battalion which he molded with his enthusiasm and his faith and which he had led in previous actions, for three days of bitter and epic fighting made even harder by the cold and by torment, he stopped the offensive impetus of overwhelming enemy forces which, in repeated attacks, tried to submerge the men defending a wide and key sector on the Donets. Then in difficult circumstances assuming the defense in a village attacked by forces superior in numbers and equipment, he held the position infusing his men with an iron will to resist and a high spirit of sacrifice. With the battalion surrounded and reduced to a handful of men, he gathered the survivors and at their head boldly threw himself into a counterattack using hand grenades and the bayonet. Seriously wounded, prostrate and bleeding, but not down in spirit, he continued to incite his infantrymen to fight and who, galvanized by his words and example, were able to prevail over the more numerous adversary. Conscious of his imminent end, which in fact occurred on the battlefield, he expressed his feelings of faith and high patriotism. Decorated for military valor, a great luminous figure of a hero, a synthesis of duty, of daring and of sacrifice.
>
> Russian front (Donets) (19-22 January 1943)

A Savoia-Marchetti SM-81 Pipistrello on the Eastern Front, December 1942.This type of aircraft was used
bring supplies to Italian troops in Tcherkovo. (Authors' collection)

Italian troops retreating across the ice-covered steppe. (USSME)

At 8:00, all that was left were one company, miscellaneous scattered survivors, some artillerymen and part of the III divisional mortar battalion, busy trying to slow down the enemy forces that were advancing towards Novo Svetlova and Voroshilovgrad. Soon after, a Soviet battalion and about a hundred partisans attacked the village of Ivanovka but were driven off by the accurate responding fire of the defenders. The German corps headquarters sent armoured forces that arrived at Ivanovka at 13:30 and from there moved to Kruschilovka, followed by the foot soldiers of the 'Ravenna' who recaptured the position that same evening.

On 23 January, the German armour continued its attack against Makarov and Ilyevka, supported by a truck-borne Italian unit that recaptured Ilyevka, while other Italians also recaptured Makarov. That evening the 8th Army commander General Gariboldi, sent a very brief telegram to the division: 'Brava Ravenna!'.

On 24 January 1943, the surviving men of the 'Ravenna' were regrouped in the Samsonov-Kranodonskiy area to be later moved in phases to the Rovenki area between 27 and 29 January. On 30 January, the 'Ravenna' was again subordinated to Italian II Corps.

14

Retreat of the Alpine Army Corps

Since the second week of January 1943, the Soviets had concentrated many forces against the Italian 8th Army's right wing and against the Hungarian 2nd Army in order to effect a new pincer movement, known in Russian historiography as Operation Ostrogozsk-Rossosch.[1] The operation was launched by the Voronezh Front between 13 and 27 January 1943, with the following objectives: surround and annihilate the forces deployed in the Ostrogozsk-Rossosch area and reach the line Repievka-Alekseievka-Valuyki-Urazovo and to assume control of the Svoboda-Katerimovka railway line. For the offensive, the Soviets committed three groups of forces: in the north, the 40th Army (five divisions, a rifle brigade and an armoured corps), in the center, the XVIII Rifle Corps (three divisions and a rifle brigade, two armoured brigades and an armoured regiment), in the south, the 3rd Tank Army (XXII and XV tank corps, VII cavalry corps, three rifle divisions and one brigade).

In particular, the 40th Army was to attack the Storozevoye area, first to the west and then to the southwest. The XVIII Rifle Corps was to attack from the Schtiuchye area towards Karpenkovo against the Hungarian VII Corps which was deployed along the left flank of the Italian Alpine Army Corps. The 3rd Tank Army was to attack from the area north of Kantemirovka towards Alekseievka, making contact with the 40th Army and trapping the Italian, Hungarian and German forces in a pocket. To that end, the VIII Cavalry Corps, engaged on the left flank of the 3rd Tank Army, was to occupy the area between Valuyki and Urazovo to cut the Kastornoye-Kupyansk railway line and had been reinforced with a tank brigade, three rifle ski brigades, an antitank regiment, a mortar regiment, an antiaircraft regiment and a multiple rocket launcher battalion.

Situation of the Axis forces

The Italian 8th Army was deployed in the action sector of the southern branch of the pincer movement and considering the vastness of the front to defend as well as the few forces available to XXIV. Pz.Korps which were fated to be directly attacked by the Soviet offensive, the situation appeared to be specially critical. The Italian Alpine Army Corps, with few reserves available, was strung out along the course of the Don, while XXIV.Pz.Korps and 19.Pz.Div. were also engaged in holding a very widespread front, with the men split up into holding various positions. Heeresgruppe B headquarters issued a warning about an imminent attack against the Hungarian 2nd Army along the line of the Svoboda-Rossosch railway. Therefore, reinforcement of the antitank defenses in the Alpine Army Corps sector was ordered, transferring all of the weapons possible from other sectors of the Army.[2] The German headquarters were unaware that the main effort of the new Soviet

---

1   In Italian historiography the second defensive battle of the Don includes all of the fighting by the 8th Army on the Eastern front from 11 December 1942 until 31 January 1943.

2   Of the 18 50mm antitank guns, only six were transferred.

offensive would not involve the Alpine Army Corps, but rather that of XXIV.Pz.Korps, consisting of three divisions, the 'Julia', 385.Inf.Div., 387.Inf.Div. and the 27.Pz.Div. (essentially with no tanks left), which had already been heavily engaged in the earlier fighting.

The attack begins

On 13 January, the forces to the north of the Voronezh Front attacked in the Storozevoye area, rolling over everyone and everything, especially in the Hungarian sector. The fire from numerous Soviet artillery batteries hit hard against the defenses at Storozevoye and Suche, causing the rapid collapse of the Hungarian army. Shortly after, Soviet tank columns penetrated deeply towards Ostrogozsk and Alekseevka, surrounding and wiping out the Hungarian divisions that were already in flight. Thrown into a counterattack was Gruppe Cramer (the Gen.Kdo. z.b.V. Cramer, led by General der Panzertruppen Hans Cramer), consisting of the Hungarian 1st Armoured Division and the German 26.Infanterie-Division, but to no avail; the Soviet advance continued to be unstoppable.

On 14 January, the offensive extended further to the south and in the Italian 8th Army sector the Soviets hit the southernmost part of the XXIV.Pz.Korps right wing, aiming to the west and northwest towards Kamenka and the upper valley of the Bielaya. Additionally, the Soviet XVIII Rifle Corps, busy overrunning the Hungarian VII Corps, from the Sctiuchie area was on the verge of threatening the left wing of the Italian 8th Army as well, defended by the Alpine Army Corps. Army headquarters quickly informed Army Group B of the possibility of pulling the left wing of XXIV.Pz.Korps back towards the Krinitshnaya Valley so as to shorten the defensive front and save 385.Inf.Div. and to make available part of Gruppe Cramer and of 320.Inf.Div. to contain the enemy attacks. Heeresgruppe B headquarters authorized the Italian proposals, except for the use of Gruppe Cramer, which was already committed to the north. Accordingly, orders were issued to restore the defensive front on the Don as far as Novo Kalitva, continuing on through Krinitshnaya-Mitrofanovka-Kulikovka-Bondarevo-Novo Markova. At the same time, General Gariboldi requested that Army Group B see to the withdrawal of the Alpine Army Corps in a timely fashion in order to avoid it being cut off.

Alpine artillery position with a 75/13 Model 1915 gun on the Don front, January 1943. (Authors' collection)

Also on 14 January, on the Alpine Army Corps front, the Soviets attacked the positions held by the 'Vestone' alpine battalion, in the 'Vicenza' division's sector, with two battalions.

On 15 January, the Soviets attacked with large, armoured forces, wiping out the remnants of XXIV.Pz.Korps and after having overrun 387.Inf.Div. as well, reached Michailovka, Shilono, Novo Belaya and Beloluzkaya. Because of the collapse of the XXIV.Pz.Korps right wing in the Mitrofanovka area, 385.Inf.Div. and the 'Julia' were forced to fall back to the west to cover Rossosch. At that time the 'Julia' was deployed in the Krinitschnaya area. In the meantime, strong Soviet armoured forces had reached as far as Olichovatka and Rossosch.

Battle for Rossosch

An element of a Soviet 3rd Army tank brigade, consisting of about twenty tanks with infantry aboard, broke into Rossosch at dawn. The city hosted the headquarters of the Alpine Army Corps, which had sent its antitank guns to the front line and thus was not able to mount an effective defense on the outskirts of the town. Furious fighting erupted in the streets, which saw officers and alpini of the various headquarters and service units, as well as the 'Monte Cervino' ski battalion, supported by two German self-propelled guns engaged. Due also to support by a squadron of Stukas about a dozen enemy tanks were destroyed, about forty prisoners were taken and the infantry accompanying the tanks eliminated. At 16:00, the last of the Soviet survivors abandoned Rossosch.

Following is the testimony of Second Lieutenant Carlo Vicentini or the 'Monte Cervino' headquarters platoon:

> Rossosch was a bedlam. Dozens of Soviet tanks, the huge T-34s, ran rampant through the snow-covered streets firing and machine gunning. They were running in every direction and were on top of you unexpectedly at every street corner They fired on stone houses, sheds and any motor vehicle, overrunning with infantile fury the signposts which were at every crossroads in the rear. The sounds of their guns, made even colder and metallic by the bitter cold, were counter-punctuated by rifle fire, by our machine guns, by the bursting of mines, by the straining engines of vehicles in flight. Making this concert even a little more spasmodic, every once in a while the Stukas would show up with the whine of their engines and the blasts from their bombs. All of this lasted three hours. At dawn the tanks had broken into the city without any warning and, firing wildly with all of their weapons, had rudely awakened the Italians and the Russian population. All of the Alpine Army Corps headquarters personnel, the accountants, the warehouse men, the commissariat people and the carabinieri, the work shop and motor pool mechanics, the engineers and the bakers who, being more than 30 kilometers from the front, slept safely and certain that they would never see a Red Army soldier, now found themselves outside their billets, taking over.[3]

The alpini of the 'Monte Cervino' faced the enemy tanks at close range, using mines as their main weapon. In several cases, the alpini attacked the tanks by climbing on their hulls, seeking to open the turret hatch so that they could throw grenades into the tank. In one of these actions senior corporal Angelo Mabellini died, having already knocked out a tank with a mine, while another unidentified alpino, to be certain that the tank could not avoid the device that he intended to place

---

3   Carlo Vicentini, *Non soli vivi*, p. 17.

under the track, placed it only a few moments before it passed by and naturally he went up in the air along with the tank.[4]

Withdrawal request

Following the retreat of the Hungarian 2nd Army, 8th Army headquarters again requested authorization to pull its defensive front back. But the German headquarters was unmovable: the Alpine Army Corps was to remain on the Don. In the meantime, the Soviet penetration between Michailovka and Kamenka continued to cause worry, as there were no forces available to plug the breach. To the north were the Alpine Army Corps and the few remnants of XXIV.Pz.Korps, while to the south were 19.Pz.Div., the remnants of 27.Pz.Div. and a few men of 320.Inf.Div.. Some Soviet tank units had already pushed north, behind the Alpine Army Corps, while their infantry units had followed behind them, pushing to the northwest, towards Valuyki.

Alpini of the Julia in a rare moment of rest on the Don front, January 1943. (Authors' collection)

---

4   .L.E. Longo, *I Reparti speciali italiani nella Second Guerra Mondiale 1940-1943*, pp. 242-243

On 16 January, north of the breach, strong enemy pressure forced XXIV.Pz.Korps to fall back to the Tchornaya Kalitva-Rossosch-Olichovatka line. During the withdrawal, the 'Julia' was attacked, sustaining heavy losses, especially by the 'Tolmezzo' and 'Val Cismon' battalions. South of the breach, the remnants of 27.Pz.Div. continued to hold out along the Novo Belinskaya-Donzokava-Tischov line. Similarly, 19.Pz.Div. held the positions it had occupied, where the forces from the Tchertkovo garrison also arrived. That same day, the small Italian garrison near the Gartimischevka airfield, after having been surrounded, was evacuated by transport aircraft. Meanwhile, the Soviet forces that had overrun the front of the Hungarian 2nd Army had advanced more than fifty kilometers towards Ostrogozsk. Army Group B headquarters continued to issue senseless orders, such as the one ordering XXIV.Pz.Korps to counterattack towards Rovenki to halt the Soviet advance. After having once more requested to withdraw its forces from the Don front, 8th Army headquarters decided to quickly move the Alpine Army Corps headquarters from Rossosch to Podgornoye, leaving the defense of the city to the men who were already there. Orders were also issued to concentrate the trucks and depots at Podgornoye for a follow-on move to Karpenkovo and Nikolayevka. In the meantime, the 'Edolo' battalion of the 'Tridentina' division was busy repelling repeated Soviet attacks.

Also on 16 January, the Soviets again attacked Rossosch with infantry and tanks. Much of the city was lost, while several groups of alpini continued to hold out on the outskirts.

The order is given

In the night between 16 and 17 January, two Soviet regiments attacked the 'Tridentina' division's positions but were forced back by the 'Vestone', 'Morbegno' and 'Edolo' battalions. The Soviet attacks continued to the west. The Hungarian units began to abandon their positions on the Don and it was only then that the Army Group authorized the withdrawal of the Alpine Army corps; at 11:00 on 17 January, the corps headquarters issued the withdrawal order to its divisions, which was to be a phased move through three successive lines:

- Yevdakovo-Rossosch railway;
- Olchovatka Valley;
- Aydar-Nilolayevja Valley[5]

That same day, the Alpine Army Corps headquarters had been informed that the Soviets had already occupied Postoyalyi, thus blocking the withdrawal from Podgornoye because since the 15th, the Rossosch-Olchovatka road had already been cut. Actions by Soviet armoured and motorized units behind the Alpine Army Corps forced it to open a way to the west on its own. Meanwhile, Heeresgruppe B headquarters had transferred to the Alpine Corps what remained of XXIV.Pz.Korps, which was left with 4 tanks, 2 self-propelled guns, 5 artillery pieces and a rocket launcher battery. The 385 and 387.Inf.Div. had been practically wiped out during the tough fighting of the previous months and their few survivors had joined the withdrawing Italian columns.

Slowing down the movements of the four Italian divisions were about 10,000 stragglers from German and Hungarian units with many sleds and assorted vehicles who were interested only in escaping and not in taking part in any fighting.

---

5   Ufficio Storico dello Sato Maggiore dell'Esercito, *Le operazioni delle unità italiane al front russo*, p. 434.

The retreat begins

At dusk, there was no more contact with Soviet units along the Alpine Army Corps front, while the divisions began to form up in columns for the retreat. The 'Tridentina' division, led by General Luigi Reverberi,[6] formed three columns which began to march to Podgornoye, reaching the first phase line during the night. The Army Corps headquarters, still at Podgornoye, joined the 'Tridentina', transferring part of the corps troops and service units to its subordination.

The 'Vicenza' division formed into two columns during the withdrawal towards the railway line. The northern column headed to Podgornoye, where the 'Morbegno' and 'Vestone" battalions returned to subordination of the 'Tridentina'. The 'Vicenza' saw the return of its two battalions that had been subordinated to the 'Tridentina' in late December. The southern column headed towards Popovka. Also, at Podgornoye the Corps headquarters ordered that about 3,000 soldiers from the corps service units should join the retreat with the 'Vicenza'.

The 'Cuneense' division also formed two columns, withdrawing towards Popovka, protected by the 'Saluzzo' battalion which had been left behind as a rear guard after having been deployed at the extreme southern end of the corps, staying in close contact with the Soviet forward elements. As soon as the withdrawal began, division headquarters lost contact with the Army Corps.

The 'Julia' division, commanded by General Umberto Ricagno,[7] after having been engaged the preceding day in extending its defensive front by 25 kilometers in order to replace the German units that had been moved to other sectors, had withdrawn to the northern bank of the Tchornaya Kalitva. However, the division still maintained a bridgehead on the southern bank near Novo Melniza, held by the 'Tolmezzo' battalion. The alpini of this battalion were kept busy repulsing furious attacks and then found themselves surrounded. Opening a way out with a bayonet charge, the 'Tolmezzo' managed to rejoin its division. At dusk, the 'Julia' resumed the retreat, forming two columns heading towards Popovka-Lesnitschianskiy.

---

6   Luigi Reverberi was born in 1892 in Cavriago (Reggio Emilia). In 1913 he was in Libya as a second lieutenant. He took part in the Great War with the 7th Alpine Regiment, earning three Silver Medals, a war Cross and the Military Order of Savoy in 1918. In 1939, he was nominated as chief of staff of the Autotransportable Army Corps. In July 1939 he was promoted to brigadier general and in February 1941 he was sent to Albania with XXVI Corps headquarters. Assuming command of the 'Tridentina', in 1942 he was posted to Russia with the ARMIR.

7   Umberto Ricagno was born on 14 March 1890 in Sezzadio in Alessandria Province. After having joined the Regio Esercito he attended the Royal Military Academy of Infantry and Cavalry in Modena as a cadet officer, graduating as a second lieutenant in the infantry, alpine corps, in 1910. He took part in the Italo-Turkish war, fighting with the 'Fenestrelle' alpine battalion of the 3rd Alpine Regiment and was awarded a Bronze Medal for Military Valor and a War Cross for Military Valor. Later, he participated in the First World War as a captain commanding the 27th Company, distinguishing himself in 1915 on Monte Nero and was decorated with a second Bronze Medal for Military Valor, then was in action on the Vrsic and on Monte Rosso. In 1917 he was promoted to major and was assigned to the general staff. He continued to serve as an officer on the general staff until 1920, then took command of the 'Vestone' alpine battalion of the 6th Alpine Regiment. Promoted to lieutenant colonel in 1926, he was assigned to the general staff and taught at the Army War School from 1928 to 1931. From 1932 to 1934 he was posted to Albania as chief of staff of the Albanian 'Koova' division. Promoted to colonel, he first took command of the 5th and later of the 1st Alpine Regiment. Chief of staff of the 7th 'Leonessa' infantry division and then of the 4th 'Cuneense' alpine division, in 1940 he became a brigadier general and chief of staff of the High Troop Command in Albania, a function which he carried out from his base in Bari. From March to April 1941, he took part in operations on the Yugoslav front with XIV Corps. On 19 August 1941 he took command of the 3rd 'Julia' alpine division, at the head of which in July 1942 he departed for the campaign in Russia as part of the ARMIR..

Monte Cervino alpini in combat, January 1943. (Authors' collection)

On 18 January, the Soviets continued to encircle the Axis forces with strong forces that reached Rossosch, Olchovatka and the roads that led to the road fork at Postoyalyi. Other enemy units were also spotted in the Opyt area.

The 'Tridentina' division continued its march with only two columns, also moving at dusk. The 'Vicenza' division moved from the Pogordnoye-Popovka area towards Samoylenkov. During the preceding night, between 17 and 18 January, the men of the 'Cuneense' had abandoned the positions on the Don in an orderly fashion. Only in the Annovka area were they attacked by Soviet regular forces and partisans. The 'Julia' division had been resubordinated to the Alpine Army Corps, but with strength reduced after the hard fighting of the previous months. The 'Tolmezzo' battalion, after having lost its 12th Company during the fighting at Meshonki, was reinforced by three hundred men of the VIII reserve battalion which had reached Rossosch on 13 January. On 18 January, the 'Julia' was at Popovka and Sotniskaya, while its headquarters were at Podgornoye. During the night, on the outskirts of Popovka the 9th Alpini were busy warding off a Soviet attack.

The march continues

On 19 January, the columns continued their retreat, moving slowly because of the terrible weather conditions. The men of the 'Tridentina' were engaged against Soviet forces: the 6th Alpini column, with the 'Bergamo' and 'Vicenza' groups, the II Mixed Engineer Battalion and divisional services were also engaged in protecting the right flank of the Corps, and while moving towards Postoyalyi, found that it had already been occupied by the Soviets. To oust the enemy, the 'Verona' battalion was thrown into an attack, which however did not succeed in capturing the position due to the presence of Soviet tanks. The alpini of the 'Verona' were thus forced to pull back to Repyevka. While moving towards Skororyb, the 5th Alpini, with the 'Val Camonica' group, was attacked by a Soviet motorized column. During the clashes that followed, the alpini were able to capture the village and knock out several enemy tanks. Some prisoners were also captured, as were various kinds of equipment. While the alpini of the 'Verona' were fighting at Postoyalyi, the rest of the column reached Opyt, southeast of Repyevka. From there, the 'Val Chiese' battalion was sent to reinforce the 'Verona', which was dug in at Repyevka. The Alpine Army Corps headquarters and XXIV.Pz.Korps headquarters, many men of the 'Julia' and about a thousand stragglers from the Hungarian 23rd Division reached Opyt. The following morning, more Hungarian stragglers and the remnants of XXIV.Pz.Korps which had been assigned to the 'Tridentina' also arrived. Finding himself with his right flank exposed and with the 'Tridentina' having moved ahead of the movement of the other divisions, General Nasci decided to stop for the entire day before resuming the attack in the Postoyalyi area the following day. The men took advantage of the break to reinforce the Opyt defenses and to reorganize the stragglers, forming them into ad hoc units. The 6th Alpini and some Germans were concentrated at Reyevka.

During the morning the 'Vicenza' division was engaged in occupying Samoylenkov, which was seized after a brief fight. In the afternoon the Army Corps headquarters issued the order to continue on to Lesnitschianskiy, to take part the following day in an action against Postoyalyi with the 'Tridentina'.

The 'Cuneense' division had not been able to make contact with the Army Corps headquarters. In a discussion with the commander of Kampfgruppe Rheingold at Popovka, General Battisti, the 'Cuneense' commander, was informed that the Popovka-Kulasscevka-Shelyakino-Valuyky road was in Soviet hands. Battisti then decided to march to Valuyky, following an alternate route. After having destroyed the vehicles that had run out of gas, the men of the 'Cuneense' resumed their march divided into two echelons, with the III/27 as a rear guard. Around 19:00, Soviet soldiers wearing white camouflage smocks and initially mistaken for Germans by the alpini, attacked and inflicted heavy casualties on the rear guard. The 14th Company of the 'Borgo San Dalmazzo' battalion and the 72nd Battery of the 'Val Po' group were attacked and almost destroyed. The 21st Company of the 'Saluzzo' battalion then joined the action, sacrificing itself in bitter fighting and almost being massacred on the spot, allowing the rest of the column to disengage and continue on to Novo Postoyalyi.

After an exhausting march the 'Julia' division arrived in the Novo Postoyalovka-Soloviev-Kopanki area, which was already occupied by a large Soviet force, engaging in hard fighting which lasted the entire day.

On 20 January, the Corps headquarters ordered the 'Vicenza' to move to Kharkovka so that it could then move to the west of the Olchovatka Valley and repeated the order to the other divisions as well. At the same time, the XXIV.Pz.Korps commander was given the mission to regroup all of the scattered German units in the Skororyb area in order to use them in defense of that sector and to cover the retreat. Around 7:00, the Soviets attacked Opyt, where the Alpine Army corps headquarters was still in place. The few personnel present there were completely overrun and many vehicles and all means of communication were lost. Only one German radio station mounted on a half-track escaped destruction. What was left of the Alpine Army Corps headquarters moved to Novo Kharkovka.

Having noticed that the Soviet attacks were not coming from the east but set up continuous obstacles to get past, General Nasci decided to organize a strong vanguard force. In the meantime, since the early morning hours the 'Tridentina' division was busy pushing back Soviet attacks coming from the north, in the Opyt area. The 'Vestone' battalion was especially involved in this defensive fighting. At dawn, the column with the services and stragglers came under fire of the Soviets who

A retreating motorized column, January 1943. (Authors' collection)

during the night had made an encircling maneuver. The situation was resolved by a desperate counterattack by the II divisional engineer battalion, which however suffered the loss of two-thirds of its men. The 6th Alpini was engaged in tough hand-to-hand fighting to capture the village of Postoyalyi. The march continued on towards Novo Kharkovka, thus bypassing the first Soviet encirclement. General Luigi Reverberi assumed command of the vanguard, consisting of the 6th Alpini (minus the 'Verona' battalion), reinforced by the 'Bergamo' and 'Vicenza' artillery groups and by German artillery, rocket launchers and tanks. After having reached Novo Kharkovka around 17:00, it was again necessary to fight to wrest the position from the enemy, repulsing several successive counterattacks. The 'Verona' battalion, engaged in protecting the exposed right flank, threw back a Soviet attack and continued its march at the tail end of the divisional column. Meanwhile, the 5th Alpini and other units reached Novo Kharkovka, getting past the second Soviet roadblock.

During the night between 19 and 20 January, the vanguard of the 'Vicenza' division attacked Lesnischyanskiy, held by Soviet infantry supported by tanks. Thanks to a circling maneuver by the 'Pieve di Teco' battalion which had in the meantime joined the column, the Soviets were forced to retreat, suffering the loss of three tanks. The division's march continued towards Postoyalyi, supporting the movement of the 'Tridentina'.

Battle of Novo Postoyalovka

Still on 20 January, the men of the 'Cuneense' reached Novo Postoyalovka around 2:00, finding he men of the 'Julia' already there, fighting in an attempt to open up a breach. Colonel Luigi Manfredi, commander of the 1st Alpine Regiment, sent the 'Ceva' battalion ahead, supported by the 'Mondovì' group, to attack the center of the village; the alpini immediately came under enemy fire, suffering heavy losses, while the 'Mondovì' batteries, after having sought in vain to deal with the Soviet tanks, ended up being massacred under the tracks of the T-34s. The Soviets asked for the Italians to surrender, but Generale Battisti refused o surrender, deciding to try everything possible to escape the enemy's grip. Accordingly, around noon, he ordered Colonel Luigi Scrimin, commander of the 2nd Alpini Regiment, to attack with his 'Borgo San Dalmazzo' and 'Saluzzo' battalions; the alpini dove into the snow on the completely white hills, the 'Saluzzo' on the right and the 'Borgo' on the left. The action seemed to be headed to success, but from a ridge rising between two small villages, the Soviets unleashed a hurricane of artillery fire, then attacking with

Italian and German troops retreating, January 1943. (Authors' collection)

an enormous mass of infantry supported by many tanks. The 21st Company of the 'Saluzzo' was completely wiped out by the Soviet artillery fire, with the ground beginning to be covered by many Italian bodies. However, with the force born of desperation, the alpini managed to knock out several Soviet tanks, but others took their place and it was all in vain. At the end of the furious battle, of the two battalions only 120 alpini had survived, led by a few officers; losses amounted to about 1,600 men. Among those killed was the 'Ceva' battalion commander, Lieutenant Colonel Giuseppe Avenanti. Attacks by the alpine troops continued all day but were always driven back by Soviet artillery and machine gun fire from positions among the houses of Novo Postoyalovka and by incursions by Soviet T-34 tanks.

General Battisti, who was still decided to escape the encirclement, tried to head west with the remaining men, intending to join up with the 'Tridentina'. He placed the remnants of the 'Mondovì' battalion as a rear guard, led by Major Mario Trovato. The Siberian troops again loosed a furious attack against the column's rear guard, consisting of the 'Mondovì' and of a battery of the 'Val Po', wiping it out completely.

The Soviet attacks persisted and the remnants of the 2nd Alpine Regiment, thanks to the sacrifice by a company of the 'Dronero' battalion, were able to disengage and head north, towards Postoyalyi. The toll of losses for the 'Cuneense' was tragic; four alpine battalions, one infantry battalion, a 75mm artillery group and a 105mm battery destroyed. By the evening of 20 January, General Battisti had lost the 'Dronero' battalion, the 'Pinerolo' artillery group, the engineer battalion and the rest of the battalions. The march resumed with about 2,000 alpini of the 'Cuneense' and another thousand or so men from disbanded units. In three days of retreat the 'Cuneense' had lost about 13,000 alpini.

General Emilio Battisti, in the report 'La Divisione Alpina Cuneense al fronte russo', wrote that: 'On 20 January, to break through the enemy barrier…four alpine battalions were committed, which were almost completely destroyed'.

General Emilio Faldella, in his 'Storia delle truppe alpine', describes the battle of Novo Postoyalovka as follows 'that bloody, separate battle that lasted, almost uninterruptedly, for more than thirty hours and in which shined through the superhuman and unlucky valor of the battalions and groups of the 'Julia' and of the 'Cuneense' , which emerged just a little less than completely destroyed … the hardest, longest and most cruel among the many battles fought by the alpini, both on the line as well as during the course of the retreat'.

The men of the 'Julia' were also busy the entire day of 20 January in attempting to force a passage through the enemy lines at Postoyalovka. Towards evening the division headquarters, the 8th

Alpini and Germans while retreating, January 1943. (Authors' collection)

Alpini and the 'Conegliano' group managed to disengage from the fighting and joined the attempt to circle to the north which had been made by the 'Cuneense' towards Postoyalyi. The 9th Alpini along with the 'Udine' and 'Val Piave' groups, from Kopanki, where they had been stopped by the enemy all day long, headed towards Samoylenkov.

The losses are counted

The sacrifice of the men of the 'Julia'and of the 'Cuneense' in the Novo Postoyalovka area contributed greatly to saving the northern column of the Army Corps, which was already under attack on its front and on its right flank, but which avoided being attacked from the south as well. At the end of the day of 20 January, most of the Alpine Army Corps forces were at a minimum in terms of operational capability: the battalions of the 'Julia' were down to less than 150 men each, supported by just a few guns of the 'Conegliano' group with almost no ammunition left. The 'Cuneense' was left with three very battered battalions and with no artillery. The 'Vicenza' division, despite having been reinforced with the 'Pieve di Teco' battalion, was in dire condition. Only the 'Tridentina' was somewhat better condition, as it reinforced with (a few) German armoured vehicles. Thus, on 21 January, General Nasci chose the 'Tridentina' as the vanguard of the entire corps, which was to follow the route Krazkovka-Shelyakino-Ladomirovka-Schiabskoye-Nikolayevka-Valuyky.[8] The other divisions were to follow the same route. The men of the 'Tridentina' moved from Nova Kharkovka towards Lymarevka and Shelyakino, with the intention of marching rapidly so as not to give the Soviets enough time to prepare new obstacles. It was also decided to move mainly at night in order to escape enemy observation, to avoid the main roads and population centers and to keep the combat units segregated from the mass of stragglers. The vanguard captured Lymarevka

---

8   Nikolayevka is a village south of Varvarovka, not to be confused with the other locality later reached by the 'Tridentina'.

at 8:00, wresting it from Soviet regular and partisan forces who had already been pushed back from Novo Kharkova the preceding day. Because of a sudden snowstorm and the freezing temperatures, it was decided to let the column rest in Lymarevka; some of the men had to stay in the open because of the lack of a sufficient number of houses. A sort of field hospital was set up to assist those who were not able to march. Meanwhile, the 'Vicenza' division that was following in the wake of the 'Tridentina' had not been able to make radio contact with the 'Cuneense' and the 'Julia'. Soon after, the commanders of the two divisions arrived and were able to get their orders directly from General Nasci.

Marching in the snow

At dawn, the surviving men of the 'Cuneense', after having marched through the night, reached Postoyalyi. At 12:00, the 1st Alpini captured the village with the support of a German unit. The march continued on towards Novo Kharkova, which was reached towards evening and where the men stopped for the night.

The men of the 'Julia' division had moved from Samoylenkov with the 8th Alpini and the 'Conegliano' group to Novo Kharkova and after having passed through it, continued on to the west. The division headquarters and the 9th Alpini with the 'Udine' and 'Val Piave' groups reached Lesnishanskiy. From there, the headquarters continued on to Novo Kharkova, while the men stopped to rest a bit and to eat their rations. But just at that moment, the Soviets attacked with infantry and tanks; in a matter of a few minutes, the alpini were almost completely wiped out and only a few men managed to escape the slaughter.

During the night, Heeresgruppe B headquarters sent a radio message to XXIV.Pz.Korps to indicate Nikitovka as the assembly area for the Alpine Army Corps, thus modifying the planned route. This was because the shortest way to Nikitovka passed through Varvarovka. However, because there was not enough time to issue new march orders to all of the units, General Nasci decided to move to Shelyakino, skirting Varvarovka from the south. Around 10:00, the vanguard of the 'Tridentina', consisting of the 6th Alpini, got close to the village of Shelyakino, coming under enemy fire. The 'Vestone' and 'Val Chiese' alpine battalions and the German tanks, supported by the 'Bergamo' and 'Vicenza' groups, attacked the village. In the meantime, the 'Edolo' battalion of the 5th Alpini made a flanking move on the left. The Soviets brought fresh tank units into the area to try to force back the Italo-German attack. The alpine units held fast after they had managed to immobilize a good portion of the enemy tanks and to reduce the Soviet artillery to silence, then went on to root out the Red Army soldiers out of the houses, one by one. With the alpini of the 'Edolo' joining the action, the Soviets abandoned the village after having taken heavy losses. At dusk, the column continued on to Ladomirovka, which it reached during the night. During the march, the column's flank was attacked by other Soviet armoured forces and to avoid being overrun, the column detoured to Varvarovka where the 'Morbegno' battalion, after having clashed with other enemy units coming from the north, was engaged in a bitter battle, sacrificing itself to enable to rest of the column to distance itself by deviating to the west.

The 'Vicenza' division had also resumed its march during the night, along with three German self-propelled guns, with little ammunition. When the men reached Shelyakino, they found the village again occupied by the Soviets who had returned to the position after having been thrown out by the alpini of the 'Tridentina'. A new attack was mounted by the remnants of the II/277, but in vain. Then the entire column was committed with the support of the German SP guns allowing the alpini to break into the village, knocking out numerous Soviet tanks and eliminating enemy defensive positions. In turn, other Soviet forces attacked the column's rear guard, eliminating the

General Reverberi, in the center, having a discussion with his officers during the retreat. (Authors' collection)

division headquarters and a good part of the CLVI divisional machine gun battalion. In any case, the attack by the 'Vicenza' contributed to easing the pressure on the men of the 'Tridentina'.

At dawn, the remnants of the 'Cuneense' resumed their march towards Lymarevka, which they reached around noon. The 1st Alpini had in the meantime joined the column but was attacked by three Soviet tanks. Having repulsed the attack, the regiment also reached Lymarevka. The remaining men continued on towards Novo Dmitrovka, which was already occupied by the enemy. An attack by the 'Dronero' battalion and by the IV mixed engineer battalion ejected the Soviets. During the retreat the division had continued to leave behind hundreds of alpini who had frozen to death. Towards evening, General Battisti, considering the seriousness of the situation, authorized everyone to leave the column to try to take their chances on their own. Turning to his officers he said: '…shall we continue to march all together or shall we try to escape from this pocket in small groups?'. Naturally, the response was 'All together!'. Shortly before dawn the next day the division regrouped at Novo Dmitrovka to continue on, divided into two echelons, marching for the entire day towards Garbusovo and Rybazin.

The retreat by the 'Julia' plodded on amongst a thousand difficulties. During the morning, the remnants of the 8th Alpini were caught up and surrounded by the Soviets in the Novo Georgevskiy area. With no capability to react, they were all captured. During the day, the division headquarters reached the Shelyakino area where it was also surrounded and attacked. In the fighting that followed, most of the alpini were killed or captured. General Ricagno, along with four officers and about fifty alpini, managed to escape capture, joining the 'Cuneense' column the next day.

At dawn on 23 January, 8th Army headquarters informed the Alpine Army Corps headquarters by radio that Nikitovka had been occupied by the Soviets, so the column of alpini halted at Romakova to reorganize and to prepare for more fighting.

Also at dawn, the men of the 'Tridentina' resumed their march in order to try to take advantage of the previous day's success. Near Nikolayevka, about nine kilometers west of Shyabskoye, there was a clash with a partisan formation which was supported by some artillery pieces; the alpini, supported by German tanks, eliminated them with no problem. The march then resumed towards Kovalev.

The men of the 'Vicenza', still without contact with higher headquarters, moved towards Varvarovka in order to be able to halt and to establish contact with the 278th Infantry. While the division's commander, General Etelvoldo Pascolini, was busy trying to reorganize the column, violent mortar fire coupled with a Soviet air attack hit them, creating panic and confusion. After having managed with great effort to restore order, a Soviet armoured formation attacked the column after having overrun and eliminated the remnants of the 278th Infantry. When the furious Soviet armoured attacks were over, what was left of the division, namely, the headquarters, two carabinieri sections, some infantrymen of the 277th, the remnants of the CLVI machine gun battalion, headquarters of the horse artillery regiment and about a thousand stragglers who had been pulled together in ad hoc formations, dug in around and inside a farm near Varvarovka. When night fell, the men moved towards Bolshe Lipyagi.

The retreat continues

Also on 24 January, the Alpine Army Corps continued to receive no news about its various subordinate divisions, except for the 'Tridentina'. The lack of maps of the area made the situation even more difficult. During those hours, General Nasci informed 8th Army headquarters that because of the heavy losses of men and equipment, the Alpine Corps was no longer operational as a combat unit.

After a night march, the vanguard of the 'Tridentina' division reached Malakiyeva at 10:00, coming under Soviet artillery fire, a sign that the position was in enemy hands. Preparations were made to attack; the artillery was put in position while the 'Vestone' and 'Val Chiese' battalions attacked, supported by German tanks. Around noon, the village was taken; the corpses of about 600 Soviet soldiers lay on the ground. The march continued on to Romankovo, which was reached at 16:00. Meanwhile, the 'Verona' battalion returned to its parent 6th Regiment. The men were famished, it had been days since they had a hot meal. To stave off hunger, the soldiers and pack animals ate frozen snow!

The 'Vicenza' division continued to march and in the morning halted at an unnamed village.

Weather not fit for man nor beast: Italian soldiers retreating in a snowstorm. The dog in the foreground is looking at the camera. (Authors' collection)

After having passed through Garbusovo, the men of the 'Cuneense' division, its headquarters and the 2nd Alpini reached Rybalzin around 8:00, stopping for a pause. The 1st Alpini, after having reached Garbusovo at dawn, was attacked by Soviet tanks, suffering new heavy losses. Reaching Rybalzin, the alpini found themselves in the midst of a snowstorm and were forced to halt in the village for the entire night.

On 25 January, an aircraft sent by Army headquarters landed near the Italian column in order to inform General Nasci that the new rally point was the road fork 16 kilometers southeast of Novi Oskol. In order to continue on it would also be necessary to capture the village of Nikolayevka which was held in strength by the Soviets.

At dawn, the 'Tridentina' division resumed its march to Nikitovka, which was captured after a brief clash with Soviet regular and partisan forces. Other villages were passed through where the alpini were supplied with food by Russian civilians. The division's vanguard, consisting of the 'Verona' and 'Vestone' battalions, the 255th Company of the 'Val Chiese', a battery from the 'Bergamo' group and the German tanks, continued on for a couple of hours, reaching Arnautovo. Division headquarters issued order for the following day, mainly for the attack against Nikolayevka, initially by the vanguard and then by the rest of the column.

The 'Vicenza' division resumed its march towards Bolshe Lipyagi, which it reached during the night. The 'Pieve di Teco' battalion, in the vanguard, after coming under enemy mortar fire, attacked and seized the village, in the process also freeing about a hundred Italian soldiers who had been captured by the Soviets.

The men of the 'Cuneense' continued their march to Malakiyeva. The 'Dronero' battalion, in the lead, to open a way for the column, was engaged in a fight near the village of Shukovo, from which heavy machine gun fire had emanated. Supported by the 'Mondovi', and by a group of artillerymen, the alpini of the 'Dronero' attacked with fixed bayonets, putting the Soviets to flight and

Alpine troops making use of a sled during the retreat, January 1943. (Authors' collection)

freeing about 200 Italian prisoners. The divisional column, however, split in two: the headquarters and 2nd Alpini reached Malakiyeva around midnight, while the 1st Alpini remained in the village of Solonzy.

26 January was a decisive day for the retreat of the Alpine Army Corps. The vanguard of the 'Tridentina', on the western edge of Nikitovka, was attacked at 2:00 by Soviet regular and partisan forces. After about two hours of close and bitter firefights, the enemy was forced back. Also, near Arnautovo strong Soviet forces attacked the column that had just begun to march, in an attempt to cut off the vanguard consisting of the 'Tirano' battalion and 'Val Camonica' group. In the fighting that followed, the Soviets brought in fresh forces, but the quick reaction of the 5th Alpini was able to upset the attackers and reopen the road for the rest of the column.

Battle of Nikolayevka

Meanwhile, the 6th Alpini, having reached close to Nikolayevka, launched its attack against the village which was heavily defended by the Soviets. The enemy soldiers were well dug in among the houses of the village, which rose on a small hill, protected by a railway embankment which surrounded the entire village, offering protection to the enemy. The Soviet forces that barred the way of the alpine units were assessed to be about a division. Even though exhausted by the earlier fighting and by the cold and hunger and despite the massive barrage fire unleashed by the Soviets, the order to attack came around 9:30. The initial attack was made by the remaining alpini of the 'Verona' and 'Val Chiese', of the 'Vestone' and the II Mixed Engineer Battalion of the 'Tridentina', supported fire of the 'Bergamo' artillery group and three German self-propelled guns. After bitter and furious fighting, the alpini were able to get across several points of the railway embankment on the eastern edge of Nikolayevka, climb the hill and at 11:00 reach the first houses of the village, where they quickly set up machine guns. Losses, however, were very high because of the violent Soviet fire. Despite everything, the alpini fought doggedly. Furious attacks and counterattacks followed, house to house. The railway station was captured, while a platoon of the 'Val Chiese' managed to get as far as the church, in whose belfry was a Soviet machine gun that was slaughtering the alpini. The Soviets reacted by bringing in fresh forces and intensifying their barrage fire; the alpini were forced to pull back to less exposed positions, mainly digging in along the railway embankment.

The bulk of the column arrived around noon, along with the remnants of the 'Edolo'. 'Morbegno' and 'Tirano' battalions, the 'Vicenza' and 'Val Camonica' artillery groups and other surviving elements of the 'Julia' with the 'L'Aquila' battalion. These providential reinforcements were quickly thrown into the heart of the battle and the attack was resumed. But the Soviets did not stand idly by, continuing to put up stiff resistance and intensifying their barrage fire, binging in their airpower, whose attacks led to scenes of panic and terror in the masses in the column, which consisted of sleds, horses, vehicles and many, many soldiers of various nationalities. There was no lack of acts of personal heroism by officers, NCOs and soldiers, moved even to the ultimate sacrifice of their lives, but the Soviets continued to hold their positions with fierce determination, barring the road to possible salvation of the alpini. The situation became increasingly critical and with the approach of dusk, the temperature began to drop making everyone worry about freezing and death. It was at that very moment, when it seemed that there was nothing that could be done to break out of the encirclement, that General Reverberi, the 'Tridentina' commander, climbed aboard a German self-propelled gun and despite being under enemy fire, with a shout of 'Tridentina avanti!' [Forward Tridentina] incited his alpini to go on the attack once again. His shout echoed like thunder, rousing the feelings of the enormous mass of stragglers who, like an avalanche, and following the example of those who were still fit to fight, threw themselves yelling towards the railroad underpass and

German half-tracks and assault guns retreating along with alpine troops, January 1943. (Authors' collection)

escarpment, overwhelming the Soviet lines. The alpini again managed to break into Nikolayevka, ensuring that the great multitude of stragglers following them had a place to shelter for the night.

For this action, the commander of the 'Tridentina', General Luigi Reverberi, was awarded the Gold Medal for Military Valor, with the following citation:

> As commander of the 'Tridentina' he prepared, forged and wisely led his regiments in Russia with his mind and by example, and who earned him in recognition the Gold Medal for Military Valor by their common heroism. In the tragic retreat from the Don, after thirteen victorious combat actions, at Nikolayevka the enemy who was significantly superior in men and equipment and strongly holding an advantageous position, decided not to let the Italians pass and resisted against many of our bloody attempts. Sensing that this was a question of life or death for everyone, in the critical moment the Commander made the decisive gesture. At the head of a handful of stalwarts, he climbed aboard a tank and threw himself in lion-like fashion into the fury of the enraged enemy reaction, against the obstacle, by word and example inciting the column which, electrified by his heroic example, followed him enthusiastically in a wave crowning the day's success with a shining victory and the happy conclusion of the move. Shining example of a generous and conscientious leader, and of heroic valor as a soldier.

Caught by the speed of the action, the Soviets were forced to withdraw and abandon their dead, wounded, arms and equipment on the field. The alpini also suffered heavy losses and after the battle thousands of dead were left on the field.

Amongst the dead was General Giulio Martinat,[9] chief of staff of the Alpine Army Corps, who followed his alpini in the attack with the cry of 'Avanti che siete Alpini!' [Forward, you are Alpini]. According to another account, after having attended a meeting of officers, Martinat saw the alpini of the 'Edolo' passing by and his decision was immediate: 'I began with the 'Edolo' and I want to finish with the 'Edolo'. After having picked up a carbine, he began to shout 'Forward alpini, forward, Italy is over there, forward!'.

Alpino Valentino Petrelli was a witness to his death: I think it was afternoon, early afternoon. I was about fifteen meters from Martinat, no more than that. We were running, even he was running, and we scattered when the Katyushas began to fire. I remember that we were behind a tracked vehicle, and General Reverberi was on top of it shouting and waving his arms. About two hundred meters from us was a Russian who was firing on us with a small mortar. He was hidden in the snow, you could hardly see him. He fired at a very fast rate and he was killing us like dogs. We rushed forward, enraged, yelling, we pulled him out of his hole, one of killed him with a single shot to the head. Later a round exploded near the general and a splinter opened up his chest. He fell and then got up and shouted twice "Forward, you are alpini!' Then he fell again. I can still see him before my eyes. Other alpini said that they heard him murmur: 'I was born in the 'Edolo' and I want to die in the 'Edolo'. In the end, the hill was covered with dead and wounded…'[10]

General Martinat was posthumously awarded the Gold Medal for Military Valor:

> Chief of staff of an army corps, a soldier of exceptional courage and undisputed valor, veteran of four campaigns, decorated multiple times, of high quality of mind and heart, having seen an alpine company which was going into the line to decide the bitter battle under way, giving in to his instinctive enthusiasm as a soldier and combatant, he put himself in the lead imbuing everyone with his words and burning ardor and becoming an irresistible personal example. Standing up in a position exposed to heavy fire, while he was firing with his carbine against

---

9   Giulio Martinat was born on Maniglia di Perrero on 24 February 1891. After having volunteered for a reserve officer's course, in 1910 he left for the Italo-Turkish war as a sergeant assigned to the 'Edolo' battalion of the 5th Alpine Regiment, distinguishing himself in combat at Derna. Awarded a Bronze Medal for Military Valor, he was promoted to reserve second lieutenant. Returning to Italy and taken into permanent active duty, he was transferred to the 'Pinerolo' battalion of the 3rd Alpine Regiment, in which he served in the Great War, distinguishing himself in the fighting at Monte Mrzli, earning a second Bronze Medal for Military Valor and promotion to first lieutenant (July 1915) and then to captain (in early 1916), ending the war assigned to the 1st Machine Gun Regiment. At the end of the war, he was assigned to the 6th Alpine Regiment, 'Monte Baldo' battalion, during the operation by the Italian occupation corps in Upper Silesia at Teschen. Returning to Italy, he earned a law degree at the University of Naples in spring of 1921. In 1923 he was assigned to the Reserve Officers Cadet School in Verona. Between 1924 and 1927, he served with the Italian Military Mission in Ecuador as a machine gun and automatic weapons instructor, and upon returning to Italy attending the 57th Advanced War Institute Course. Promoted to major, he was posted as a staff officer in Trieste (1930-1931), later assuming command of the 'Pinerolo' battalion. Promoted to lieutenant colonel (1934), he served with the general staff in Alessandria and the next year as chief of staff of the 'Julia' alpine division. In late 1935 he was assigned as chief of staff of the IV CCNN division 'Tevere' which had been mobilized for the war in Ethiopia, on the Somali front, where he was awarded the Silver Medal for Military Valor. Returning to Italy he returned to his post as chief of staff of the 'Julia' until 1937 when, promoted to colonel, he took command of the 11th Alpine Regiment in Brunico. In September 1939 he again became chief of staff, first at the 5th Alpine Division 'Pusteria', then at XVI and IV Corps. In 1940 he left for Albania as chief of staff of the Alpine Army Corps, earning his second Silver Medal for Military Valor and the Knight's Cross of the Military Order of Savoy. On 17 July 1942 he left, still as chief of staff of the Alpine Army Corps, for the Russian front, where he was promoted to brigadier general in November.

10   Arrigo Petacco, *L'armata scomparsa*, pp. 151-152.

enemy soldiers at close range, a bullet cut short his bold action and took his life, but victory had been assured and the enemy was in flight. A shining example of high fighting virtues and of supreme dedication to his country.

Niolayevka (Russia), 26 January 1943.

On 3 April 1943, the Germans bestowed the Knight's Cross, posthumously, to General Martinat.

Flight to safety

With the Soviet barrier at Nikolayevka eliminated, considering the disastrous state of the various units, which were left with few weapons and little ammunition and fearing new Soviet attacks, General Nasci ordered the retreat to continue after a brief pause, in order to get past the gorge at Uspenskaya. The 'Vicenza' division's column resumed the march at dawn, with the objective of reaching Valuyky, but found that all of the villages in the area were in Soviet hands. It was thus necessary to fight to eliminate the continuous enemy barriers which slowed down the march significantly. In addition, the column was attacked repeatedly by Soviet aircraft. Around noon, the column came under fire from Soviet rocket launcher batteries, with no capability to return fire, as repeated attacks were also made by the partisans. Around 15:00, the column, which by now was reduced to about three thousand men, was blocked frontally by heavy machine gun fire, while Soviet cavalry units attacked the left flank. The alpini of the 'Pieve di Teco' were able to take up positions to defend themselves from the attack, but the shortage of ammunition enabled them to stem the attack only temporarily. Soon after, other Cossack cavalry units, supported by tanks and artillery, attacked the tail of the column, completing its encirclement. The Soviets called upon the alpini to surrender, requesting an answer within thirty minutes. With no hope of being able to escape from the Soviet grip, with no ammunition left, General Pascolini, the division commander, decided to surrender. While Pascolini was taken as a Soviet prisoner, the other officers who had accompanied him returned to their units to tell them that surrender had been accepted, but in the meantime the Soviets had captured the entire column.

The two echelons of the 'Cuneense' had also resumed their march and in the afternoon, after having been attacked by Soviet aircraft, joined together to form a single column. Arriving near a village, they found it in Soviet hands. The column then skirted the village but was spotted by the enemy and attacked by squadrons of Cossack cavalry reinforced with machine guns on sleds and an artillery battery. The Soviets requested a surrender, but General Battisti refused. Meanwhile, the 'Dronero' battalion was able to deploy for combat, forcing the Soviets to withdraw. The march resumed, but the 1st Alpini lost contact with division headquarters.

On 27 January, during its march to the west, headquarters of the Alpine Army Corps was overtaken by the men of the 'Tridentina' and the rest of the column, which was about 30 kilometers long. Soviet aviation continued to hit the column. The ever-deeper snow hindered the already painful march of the men, causing abandonment of the last few artillery pieces and the horses and mules to die of exhaustion. Along the way, officers and men who stopped in the isbas for a moment of rest were often captured. After having reorganized the men as best as possible during the nighttime halt, the 'Tridentina' headquarters ordered the march to resume, moving the 5th Alpini, the 'Bergamo' and 'Vicenza' groups and the last remaining German tank and two German artillery pieces into the vanguard. After having covered more than forty kilometers under attack by Soviet aircraft and having lost still more men from exhaustion along the way, the column reached Uspenskaya and Lutovinovo after nightfall.

Meanwhile, after having gotten close to Valuyky, the 'Cuneense was attacked again, first by devastating artillery fire and then overrun by a Cossack cavalry corps. At first the alpini mistook

The great black tide of retreating Axis troops. January 1943. (Authors' collection)

An Italian column marching in the snow and cold, January 1943. An abandoned truck and equipment lie by the side of the road. (Authors' collection)

From the left; Lieutenant Colonel Policarpo Chierici, commander of the Val Chiese, Lieutenant Danilo Bajetti, Colonel Paolo Signorini, commander of the 6th Alpine Regiment and General Luigi Reverberi at Nikolayevka on 26 January 1943. (Tridentina Alpine Brigade historical archives)

the enemy for Hungarian cavalry moving towards them. When they realized their mistake, it was too late; the Soviets surrounded them and there was a desperate battle. General Battisti was at the head of the vanguard when, crossing the railway line, the Cossack cavalry made its final charge; fighting was hand-to-hand, as there was ammunition left. The last surviving officers of the 'Cuneense' were captured; General Battisti, along with the commanders of the 1st and 2nd Alpini, colonels Manfredi and Scrimin. But groups of alpini continued to fight on stubbornly, refusing to surrender, In the afternoon, the last elements of the 'Borgo San Dalmazzo' and of the 'Saluzzo' also surrendered. Only the 'Mondovì' battalion still refused to surrender, prolonging its agony until evening when, out of ammunition, it was finally forced to lay down its arms.[11]

On 28 January, the men of the Alpine Army Corps headquarters were attacked since early morning by Soviet infantry and tanks. It was thus necessary to change the direction of march, heading towards Slonovka. With temperatures between -35 to -40 degrees Celsius [-31 to -40 Fahrenheit], the men continued to move forward, taking the wounded and frostbitten along with them on the few sleds that remained.

---

11   Of all of the 'Cuneense', only 791 alpini were able to escape from the pocket and later join up with the 'Tridentina'. Other groups, for an overall force of 809 alpini and 409 mules, were able to save themselves by venturing out onto the steppe with no fixed direction. The most amazing route was that which was followed by Lieutenant Meinero: without any means of orientation and moving in a direction opposite that of the Alpine Corps, led his men to safety reaching the city of Odessa after a journey of 1,600 kilometers. Another group, however, fared badly: disoriented, it marched for days and days in the frozen steppe, only to find itself on the banks of the Don in the midst of the Russians. From Arrigo Petacco *L'armata scomparsa*, p. 142.

On 29 July the column reached Bessarab, now down to only about 20,000 Italians, among which were about 2,000 wounded and 5,000 suffering from frostbite. The number of Germans and Hungarians who were following along had dwindled to about 15-16,000 men.

On 30 January the column reached Bolsche Troitzkoye, where there were mobile German outposts and where the foreign troops were separated from the Italians. The worst seemed to be over, especially when the first trucks arrived to evacuate the most seriously wounded.

On 31 January, the vanguard of the Alpine Army Corps reached Shebekino, parading in front of General Gariboldi. The men were put up in adequate billets for several days, for a much-needed period of rest while awaiting the arrival of all of the other men of the column, which was completed on 3 February. The wounded were loaded aboard Italian trucks and moved to Kharkov. That same day, after having handed over responsibility for its sector to Armee-Abteilung Lanz[12], Italian 8th Army headquarters concluded its operational activity on the Russian front.

The situation elsewhere

At the end of January 1943, after the return of the remnants of the 'Torino' division with other elements attached to it and those of the Alpine Army Corps, what was left of the Italian 8th Army were located as follows:

- A northern bloc, with the remnants of the Alpine Army Corps, consisting mainly of the 'Tridentina' division and Corps units and quartermaster units, with about 16,000 men and 2,500 mules.[13]
- A central bloc, with the remnants of the 'Cosseria' division, the horse raggruppamento, alpini reserves and quartermaster units, with about 9,000 men, 2,500 horses and mules and 130 vehicles.
- A southern bloc, with the remnants of the 'Sforzesca', 'Ravenna', 'Pasubio', 'Torino', 3rd 'Celere' and part of the 'Cosseria' divisions, II Corps and XXXV Corps troops and services and quartermaster units, with about 65,000 men, 300 mules and 1,500 trucks, scattered over a wide area from the Donets mineral basin to Dniepropetrovsk.

Naturally, the men were to be moved in the shortest time possible still further to the west, in the area around Gomel for later repatriation and the move had to be carried out by train for the northern and central blocs and on foot for the southern bloc. However, following the continuation of the Soviet offensive on the Oskol River, there were no trains available so 8th Army headquarters ordered the immediate move of all blocs by foot.

---

12   Led by General der Gebirgstruppen Hubert Lanz, it was created on 1 February 1943 in the Heeresgruppe B sector on the Don River by the Stab des Deutschen Generalstabes beim italienischen Armee-Oberkommando 8 (Chief of German Staff at Italian 8th army).
13   Ufficio Storico dello Stato Maggiore dell'Esercito, *Le operazioni delle unità italiane al fronte russo*, p. 470.

Alpini and Germans attacking at Nikolayevka, January 1943. (Tridentina Alpine Brigade historical archives)

The Carloni Column

While the northern bloc was moving from the Dniepropetrovsk area, the last echelon which was completely motorized, consisting of various units connected with the 6th Bersaglieri Regiment,[14] known as the Carloni column, led by Colonel Mario Carloni, ran out of gas in Pavlograd on 8 February. On 10 February, after the fall of Lozoaya to the Soviets and the approach of other enemy forces near Pavlograd, the Italian unit was subordinated to the German headquarters at Dniepropetrovsk and Carloni was assigned to command the Italian and German forces in Pavlograd, with the mission to defend the city and the approaches to it. Between 10 and 20 February, the Italians of the Carloni column were engaged in repelling attacks by Soviet motorized and armoured forces in addition to having to defend themselves from partisan attacks in Pavlograd itself. Following are the words of Colonel Carloni.[15]

'The commander of the garrison handed over about two hundred German soldiers with few automatic weapons and no antitank weapons; the aviation commander showed me the defensive organization at the airfield with about four hundred combat troops…The engineer head of the agricultural section provided me with about twenty Germans and about two thousand laborers for the defensive works. The manager of the food warehouse had food for twenty days for two thousand men. The Italian transportation battalion had about two hundred fifty men, equipped with few automatic weapons. All told, I thus had about two thousand Italian combatants and six hundred Germans, with six 75mm guns and four antitank guns and about two thousand laborers for the necessary construction improvements…The forces were modest for an effective and long fight, if one thinks that the city's perimeter, with a sprawling industrial zone, was about ten kilometers with many approaches that could be easily used by enemy tanks. The heterogeneous nature of these forces, the shortage of artillery and of antitank guns made the effectiveness even more fleeting. Nevertheless, we quickly got to work…on the 9th, I issued orders for the deployment and organization of the

---

14 Headquarters and headquarters company of the 6th Bersaglieri, an ad hoc battalion of the 6th Bersaglieri, the Cosentino ad hoc bersaglieri battalion, II group of the 17th Artillery Regiment of the 'Sforzesca' division and XIX antiaircraft artillery group.

15 Mario Carloni, *La campagna di Russia*, p. 138.

Long columns snaking their way across snowy ground towards safety. (Authors' collection)

A group of survivors following the retreating column in the cold and snow, January 1943.
(Authors' collection)

perimeter and interior defenses. I also arranged for long-range reconnaissance patrols, to be carried out on the 10th, towards Losovaya and Grishino...'

Carloni's bersaglieri were also busy coping with a revolt by the Ukrainian auxiliaries in German service. Following is Colonel Carloni's testimony[16]:

On the 12th, a bersaglieri patrol, coming from a recon at Yurievka, was attacked by fire from soldiers of the Ukrainian gendarmerie working for the Germans, waiting in ambush in houses in the village of Verbky, a few kilometers north of Pavlograd...This behavior of the Ukrainian gendarmes at Verbky, which was added to other similar episodes that had been reported to me as having occurred in other places, induced me to devote close attention to the behavior of the Ukrainian gendarmerie in this city as well. The police captain assured me again that he vouched completely for his men, all chosen and faithful and of whom you could be absolutely sure. We got the answer the following day when unexpectedly, from a factory located on the northeast side of the city, a patrol of German soldiers was hit by intense fire and suffered one killed and three wounded. This episode coincided with the report of the presence of many tank patrols around the city and Russian motorized patrols that had infiltrated the suburbs. Evidently it was an action that had been secretly agreed to between troops and local personnel to attack the troops defending the city from the front and the rear. I ordered Lieutenant Colonel Marini to immediately eliminate the source of the revolt constituted by the factory, in which many well-armed men were holed up, almost all of whom belonged to the city's Ukrainian police. After a short but intense action by Italian and German troops, to which the insurgents put up a violent reaction, the factory was occupied and everything returned to normal ...'

In the days that followed, there were new attacks by Soviet regular forces, all forced back thanks in part to the use of German tanks. When Soviet pressure became very heavy, between 18 and 19 February the Italians began to abandon Pavlograd and withdrew in phases towards Novo Moskovsk, then to regroup at Dniepropetrovsk. The fighting at Pavlograd represented the last operational employment of Italian troops on the Eastern Front.

Repatriation begins and counting the losses

In early March, the remnants of the Italian 8th Army were regrouped in the Gomel-Klinzy-Shlobin area. As soon as the units of the Alpine Army Corps reached the Gomel area, the move by train to Italy began. Departures lasted from 6 to 15 March. Meanwhile, the Italian Supreme Command in agreement with the Germans had planned to maintain the II Corps on the Eastern Front, with the 'Ravenna' and 'Cosseria divisions, transferring to them all of the men still fit to fight. But the idea was quickly abandoned and arrangements were made to be repatriated to Italy, which happened in April 1943. Departures from Gomel ended on 22 May 1943.

In March the first men from Russia returned to Italy, that is, the survivors of XXXV Corps and of the Alpine Army Corps, all told some 65,000 men. What remained of the Alpine Corps returned to Italy aboard fourteen trains; eight months earlier eight hundred trains had been needed to move them to Russia. During the month of April, 40,000 II Corps survivors were repatriated. The last to return, on 22 May, were the 9,500 soldiers of the quartermaster corps. Returning to Italy were 114,500 of the 229,005 men of the Italian army who had gone to Russia. The Italian

---

16   Mario Carloni, *La campagna di Russia*, pp. 143-144.

Survivors of the long retreat smiling for combat photographers, January 1943. (Authors' collection)

The faces of the survivors of the retreat reflect their happiness after their ordeal, January 1943.
(Authors' collection)

armed forces in Russia lost a total of 89,938 men killed and missing and another 43,282 wounded or suffering from frostbite.

The fate of the prisoners who survived the so-called march of the 'davai' (move, or forward in Russian) was tragic; during the march, the prisoners who lacked the strength to carry on were finished off with a shot to the back of the neck. The Blackshirt Militiamen were amongst those who suffered the highest losses because in case of capture, its members were usually shot on the spot. Of the Italian prisoners of war interned in England, India and other parts of the British Empire, 98.4 percent returned, of those held prisoner in the United States 99.8 percent returned, and of those interned in Germany after 1943 94.4 percent returned to Italy. From the USSR, however, only 14 percent returned. These data are reported officially in a chart titled 'Italian Prisoners in the Second World War', presented in the report of the Italian delegation to the UN Commission for Prisoners of War. Of about 70,000 Italian soldiers captured by the Red Army after the defeat of the ARMIR, 10,087 were repatriated, or only 14 percent.[17] remaining 86 percent died in Soviet prison camps.

The disastrous military defeat suffered by the Axis forces on the Eastern Front had significant repercussions on the Italian homefront. Upon their return to Italy, Mussolini addressed the veterans of the Russian front with the following proclamation:

> Officers, NCOs and Soldiers of the 8th Army! During the difficult fight carried on alongside the German and allied armies on the Russian front, you gave innumerable, decisive proofs of your tenacity and of your valor. Against preponderant enemy forces, you fought to the greatest possible limit and consecrated the banners of your divisions with blood. From the 'Julia', which for many days broke the first waves of the Bolshevik attack, to the 'Tridentina' which, surrounded, opened a gap through eleven successive battles, to the 'Cuneense' which held fast until the end, according to the traditions of the Italian alpini, all of the divisions deserve to be placed in the nation's order of the day. Thus, you labored mightily until the ultimate sacrifice, you combatants of the 'Ravenna', of the 'Cosseria', of the 'Pasubio', of the 'Vicenza', of the 'Sforzesca', of the 'Celere' and of the 'Torino', whose resistance at Cherkovo is a page of glory and you Blackshirts of the '23 marzo' and '3 gennaio' raggruppamenti, who emulated your comrades from the other units. Privation, suffering, endless marches put your physical and moral resistance to an exceptional test. Only with a high sense of duty and with the ever-present image of the homeland could they be overcome. No less serious were the losses which the battle against Bolshevism imposed on us, but it was and is a case of defending the age-old European civilization against the Muscovite barbarism …

---

17 P. Romeo di Colleredo, *Croce di Ghiaccio. CSIR e ARMIR in Russia,1941-1943*, p. 79.

Appendix I

CSIR Order of Battle 1 August 1941

Comander: Lieutenant General Giovanni Messe
Chief of Staff: Colonel Giulio Piacenza
Artillery commander: Brigadier General Francesco Dupont
Engineer commander: Colonel Mario Tirelli

Army Corps units:

Headquarters
    193rd, 194th and 684th Royal Carabinieri
        Motorized Sections
    32nd Topographic Section
    33rd Topographic Section for Artillery
    3rd Photographic Section
    8th Military Post Office
    Army Corps Headquarters Motor Pool
    13th Road Movement Detachment
    Highway Militia Motorcycle Company

Directly subordinate units, consisting of:
    CIV Corps Machine Gun Battalion
    II Antitank Battalion (47/32)
    1st Bersaglieri Motorcycle Company

Artillery:
    30th Corps Artillery Raggruppamento
    (Colonel. Lorenzo Matiotti)

Engineers:
    IV Engineer Battalion
    I and IX Engineer Bridge Battalion
    VIII Engineer Communications Battalion

Chemical Corps
    63ª Legione CC.NN. d'Assalto 'Tagliamento': Console Niccolò Nicchiarelli

General Giovanni Messe, CSIR commander.
Messe is considered by many historians to have
been the best Italian general of the Second World
War. (Authors' collection)

9th Autotransportable Infantry Division 'Pasubio': Major General Vittorio Giovanelli

Headquarters and Headquarters Company

Headquarters, with:
  25th Royal Carabinieri Motorized Section
  26th Royal Carabinieri Motorized Section
  9th Infantry Division Headquarters Motor Pool
  91st Fuel Depot
  9th Road Assistance Detachment
  8th Road Movement Detachment
  I Photographic Group
  83rd Military post office

79th and 80th Infantry Regiment 'Roma', each with:
  Headquarters and Headquarters Company
  Mortar Company (81 mm)
  Support Gun Company (65/17)
  I, II and III Infantry Battalions

8th Artillery Regiment 'Pasubio', with:
  Headquarters and Headquarters Battery
  I Motorized Group (100/17)
  II and III Motorized Group (75/27)
  85th and 309th Light Antiaircraft Battery (20/65)
  V Mortar battalion (81mm)
  IX Mortar battalion (81mm)
  9th Antitank Company (47/32)
  141st Antitank Company (47/32)
  30th Engineer Company
  9th Engineer Signal Company
  95th Searchlight Section
  5th Medical Section
  825th Field Hospital
  826th Field Hospital
  836th Field Hospital
  874th Field Hospital
  25th Surgical Detachment
  11th Commissariat Section
  26th Bakery Squad with mobile ovens

52nd Autotransportable Infantry Division 'Torino': Major General Luigi Manzi

Headquarters and Headquarters Company

Headquarters with:

56th Royal Carabinieri Motorized Section
66th Royal Carabinieri Motorized Section
52nd Infantry Division Headquarters Motor Pool
52nd Fuel Depot
52nd Road Assistance Detachment
5th Road Movement Detachment
II Photographic Group
152nd Military Post Office

81st and 82nd Infantry Regiment 'Torino', each with:
Headquarters and Headquarters Company
Mortar Company (81mm)
Support Gun Battery (65/17)
I, II and III Infantry Battalions

52nd Artillery Regiment 'Torino' with:
Headquarters and Headquarters Battery
I Motorized Group (100/17)
II and III Motorized Groups (75/27)
352nd and 361st Light antiaircraft battery (20/65)
XXVI Mortar Battalion (81 mm)
LII Mortar Battalion (81 mm)
52nd Antitank Company (47/32)
171st Antitank Company (47/32)
57th Engineer Company
52nd Engineer Signal Company
69th Searchlight Section
52nd Medical Section
89th Field Hospital
90th Field Hospital
117th Field Hospital
578th Field Hospital
52nd Surgical Detachment
52nd Commissariat Section
65th Bakery Squad with mobile ovens

3rd Celere Division 'Principe Amedeo Duca d'Aosta': Brigadier General Mario Marazzani

Headquarters, with:

Headquarters and Headquarters Company
355th Royal Carabinieri Mobile Section
356th Royal Carabinieri Mobile Section
3rd Motor Pool for Celere Division Headquarters
3rd Road Movement Detachment
III Photographic Group
40th Military Post Office

3rd Bersaglieri Regiment, with:
    Headquarters and Headquarters Company
    Mortar Company (81mm)
    2nd Bersaglieri Motorcycle Company
    3rd Bersaglieri Motorcycle Company
    XVIII, XX and XXV Truck-borne Bersaglieri Battalions
    129th Light Motor Pool

'Savoia Cavalleria' and 'Lancieri di Novara' Regiments, each with:
    I and II Squadron Groups
    5th Machine Gun Squadron

3rd Artillery Regiment of Mobile Artillery with:
    Headquarters and Headquarters Battery
    I, II and III Horse Artillery Group (75/27)
    93rd and 102nd Light Antiaircraft Battery (20/65)
    III Light Tank Squadron Group 'San Giorgio' (L3/35)
    XXVI Mortar battalion (81 mm)
    LII Mortar battalion (81 mm)
    105th Engineer Company
    103rd Engineer Signal Company
    73rd Medical Section
    46th Field Hospital
    47th Field Hospital
    148th Field Hospital
    159th Field Hospital
    20th Surgical Detachment
    93rd Commissariat Section
    59th Bakery Squad with mobile ovens
    213th Mixed Motor Pool

Aviation Headquarters of the Italian Expeditionary Corps in Russia: Colonel Carlo Drago

LXI Army Observation Group or 61st Independent Air Observation Group (32 Ca.311) commanded by Giordano Chiereghini with:
    34th Observation Squadron led by Captain Cesare Bonino
    119th Observation Squadron led by Captain Giovanni Disegna
    128th Observation Squadron led by Captain Igino Mendini replaced on17 August by Lorenzo
        Tomaj

XXII Fighter Group or 22nd Independent Fighter Group (51 M.C.200) commanded by Major Giovanni Borzoni with:
    359th Fighter Squadron led by Captain Vittorio Minguzzi
    362nd Fighter Squadron led by Captain Germano La Ferla
    369th Fighter Squadron led by Captain Giorgio Jannicelli
    371st Fighter Squadron led by Captain Enrico Meille
    Six sections of light antiaircraft guns (Breda 20/65 Mod. 1935)
    Motor Pool

Appendix II

Italian 8th Army Order of Battle

Army commander: General Italo Gariboldi
Chief of staff: General Bruno Malaguti
Artillery commander: General Mario
    Balotta
Engineer commander: General Arnaldo
    Forgiero
Chemical detachment commander:
    Lieutenant Colonel Cesiro Mischi
Aviation commander: Air Brigadier General
    Enrico Pezzi
21st Independent Fighter Group: Major
    Ettore Foschini
Quartemaster General: Brigadier General
    Carlo Biglino
German liaison officer: General der
    Infanterie Kurt von Tippelskirch (27
    August 1942 – 1 February 1943)
Chief of staff at liaison office: Oberst Walter
    Nagel (18 September 1942–5 January
    1943), then Generalmajor Hans Speidel
    (5 January 1943–5 February 1943)
Barbò horse raggruppamento: Brigadier
    General Guglielmo Barbò di
    Casalmorano
    3rd Cavalry Regiment 'Savoia
        Cavalleria': Colonel Alessandro
        Bettoni Cazzago
    5th Cavalry Regiment 'Lancieri di
        Novara': Colonel Carlo Pagliano
    3rd Horse Artillery Regiment
9th Amy Artillery Raggruppamento
    201st Motorized Artillery Regiment: Colonel Enrico Altaville
    4th Anti-aircraft Artillery Raggruppamento: Colonel Giuseppe di Martino
    31st, 40th, 42nd and 65th Anti-aircraft batteries

Alpine Army Corps: Lieutenant General Gabriele Nasci
Chief of staff: Colonel Giulio Martinat
Artillery commander: Brigadier General Carlo Filippi

General Italo Gariboldi speaking with bersaglieri in the front lines, summer 1942. Gariboldi was well liked by the troops who referred to him as 'Papa Gariboldi'. (USSME)

Engineer commander: Brigadier General Cesare Tamassia
2nd Alpine Division 'Tridentina': General Luigi Reverberi
    5th Alpini Regiment: Colonel Giuseppe Adami
    6th Alpini Regiment: Colonel Paolo Signorini
    2nd Alpini Artillery Regiment: Colonel Federico Moro
3rd Alpine Division 'Julia': General Umberto Ricagno
    8th Alpini Regiment: Colonel Armando Cimolino
    9th Alpini Regiment: Colonel Fausto Lavizzari
    3rd Alpini Artillery Regiment: Colonel Pietro Gay
4ª Alpine Division 'Cuneense': General Emilio Battisti
    1st Alpini Regiment: Colonel Luigi Manfredi
    2nd Alpini Regiment: Colonel Luigi Scrimin
    4th Alpine Artillery Regiment: Colonel Enrico Orlandi
11th Army Corps Artillery Raggruppamento: Colonel Giovanni Giua
Alpini Ski Battalion 'Monte Cervino'
XXXII 149/40 Cannon Group of the 9th Army Corps Artillery Raggruppamento
XXIV 149/28 Cannon Group of the 9th Army Corps Artillery Raggruppamento
612th artillery Regiment (German)

II Army Corps: Lieutenant General Giovanni Zanghieri
Chief of staff: Colonel Ugo Almici
Artillery commander: Brigadier General Italo Giglio
Engineer commander: Brigadier General Balilla Rima
5th Infantry Division 'Cosseria': Major General Enrico Gazzale
    89th Infantry Regiment: Colonel Paolino Maggio
    90th Infantry Regiment: Lieutenant Colonel Giacomo Lapenna
    108th Artillery Regiment: Colonel Ernesto Drommi
    318th Grenadier Regiment: Oberst Erich Mielke (of the 213th Security Division)
3rd Infantry Division 'Ravenna': Brigadier General Francesco Dupont
    37th Infantry Regiment: Colonel Giovanni Naldoni
    38th Infantry Regiment: Colonel Mario Bianchi
    121st Artillery Regiment: Colonel Giacomo Manfredi
2nd Army Corps Artillery Raggruppamento: Lieutenant Colonel Liberato Mascagna
52nd and 5th Anti-aircraft Batteries
'23 marzo'CC.NN. Raggruppamento: Major Generale Luigi Martinesi
    'Leonessa' Group of Battalions: Colonel Graziano Sardu
    'Valle Scrivia' Group of Battalions: Colonel Mario Bertoni
III Group of the 201st Motorized Artillery Regiment
XXXI 149/40 Cannon Group of the 9th Army Artillery Raggruppamento
101st Engineer Company

XXXV Army Corps (ex CSIR): Lieutenant General Giovanni Messe, then Francesco Zingales
Chief of staff: Colonel Gaetano Vargas
Artillery commander: Brigadier General Paolo Perrod
Engineer commander: Brigadier General Mario Tirelli
298th Infantry Division (German): Generalmajor Arnold Szelinski
    525th, 526th and 527th Grenadier Regiments
    298th Artillery Regiment
9th Infantry Division 'Pasubio': Major General Guido Boselli

79th Infantry Regiment: Colonel Armando Mazzocchi
80th Infantry Regiment: Lieutenant General G.B. Casassa
8th Motorized Artillery Regiment: Colonel Alfredo Reginella
30th Army Corps Artillery Raggruppamento: Colonel Lorenzo Matiotti
95th and 97th Anti-aircraft Batteries
'3 gennaio' CC.NN. Raggruppamento: Major General Filippo Diamanti
    'Montebello' Group of Battalions: Colonel Italo Vianini
    'Tagliamento' Group of Battalions: Colonel Domenico Mittica
III Group of the 201st Motorized Artillery Regiment
XXXIV 149/40 Cannon Group of the 9th Army Artillery Raggruppamento
L 149/28 Cannon Group of the 9th Army Artillery Raggruppamento

XXIX Army Corps (German): General der Infanterie Hans von Obstfelder
Chief of staff: Oberst Albrecht Ritter von Quirnheim
52nd Infantry Division 'Torino': Major General Roberto Lerici
    81st Infantry Regiment: Colonel Biagio Santini
    82nd Infantry Regiment: Colonel Evaristo Fioravanti
    52nd Artillery Regiment: Colonel Giuseppe Ghiringhelli
3rd Fast Division 'Principe Amedeo Duca d'Aosta': Major General Ettore de Blasio
    3rd Bersaglieri Regiment: Colonel Ercole Felici
    6th Bersaglieri Regiment: Colonel Mario Carloni
    120th Motorized Artillery Regiment: Lieutenant General Ugo de Simone
    XLVII Bersaglieri Motorcycle Battalion and LXVII Bersaglieri Armoured Battalion
    XIII 'Cavalleggeri di Alessandria' Group
    Croat Legion: Lieutenant Colonel Egon Žitnik
2nd Infantry Division 'Sforzesca': General Carlo Pellegrini
    53rd Infantry Regiment: Colonel Massimo Contini
    54th Infantry Regiment: Colonel Mario Viale
    17th Artillery Regiment: Colonel Achille Tirindelli
LXXIII 210/22 Howitzer Group of the 9° Army Artillery Raggruppamento
156th Infantry Division 'Vicenza': Brigadier General Etelvoldo Pascolini
    277th Infantry Regiment: Colonel Giulio Cesare Salvi
    278th Infantry Regiment: Colonel Gaetano Romeres

21° Independent Fighter Group
356th Squadron
361st Squadron
382nd Squadron
386th Squadron

71st Independent Air Observation Group (71st Flight Group)
    38th Squadron
    116th Squadron

Appendix III

Italian Air Corps in Russia 1941-1943

Organization

C.S.I.R. Aviation Headquarters
Pilot Colonel Carlo Drago

Fighter Organization
22nd Independent Fighter Group (MC 200 – Ca 133, SM.81):
Pilot Major Giovanni Borzoni
359th Squadron: Pilot Captain Vittorio Minguzzi
362nd Squadron: Pilot Captain Germano La Ferla
369th Squadron: Pilot Captain Giorgio Iannicelli
371st Squadron: Pilot Captain Enrico Meille

Aerial Observation
61st Independent Air Observation Group (Ca 311):
Pilot Lieutenant-Colonel Bruno G. Ghierini
34th Squadron: Pilot Captain Cesare Bonino
119th Squadron: Pilot Captain Giovanni Disegna
128th Squadron: Pilot Captain Igino Mendini

Transport Section
245th Transport Squadron (SM.81): Pilot Captain Ernesto Caprioglio
246th Transport Squadron (SM.81): Pilot Captain Nicola Fattibene

Since the C.S.I.R. was first organized, it was decided to send an air component to the Eastern Front as well which was designated Corpo Aereo Italiano in Russia (CAI, Italian Air Corps in Russia). In August 1941, an air element consisting of about 85 aircraft, including fighters, bombers, reconnaissance and transport aircraft was transferred and stationed at several airfields west of the Dnieper. The C.S.I.R. aviation command was officially constituted on 29 July at Tudora, along the border of the USSR and Romania. On 12 August the 22d Fighter Group consisting of 51 Macchi MC.200 (359th, 362nd, 369th and 371st Squadrons) arrived from Italy. The interceptors were accompanied two Savoia Marchetti SM.81 trimotor transport and logistic support planes and by three smaller Caproni Ca.133 trimotor transport planes.

In September 1941, with the arrival of eight more SM.81 transports, the 245th Squadron was constituted at Krivoy Rog. This unit provided a link with Bucharest, which was the terminus for the militarized S.A.S. (special transport units) aircraft arriving from Italy.

Italian pilots at an airfield in Russia, summer 1942. (USSME)

The previous month, on 3 August, the 61st Air Observation Group arrived at Tudora, with 32 twin-engine Caproni Ca.311 aircraft (34th, 119th and 128th Squadrons) and a large Savioa Marchetti SM.82 tri-motor and support aircraft.

The formation of the CSIR Air Corps was completed with the assignment of all of the ground technical and service units that were indispensable for the proper operational readiness of the flying units. In particular, six sections of 20mm Breda anti-aircraft cannons were assigned to defend the airfields, along with the associated personnel and a motor pool with about 300 vehicles of all types.

Initially the CSIR Air Corps consisted of about 1,900 men: 140 officers, 180 NCOs and 1,500 other ranks (specialists and airmen), plus 90 specialized workers.

In combat

After having reorganized the units, overhauled and refueled the aircraft, the first echelon of the CAI was moved to the front where, on 11 August, the Italian troops of the 'Pasubio' division had experienced their baptism of fire in the first clashes with the Soviets.

On 27 August, the Macchi MC.200 planes of the 22nd Gruppo began their operational cycle by attacking several squadrons of Polikarpov I-16 fighters that were escorting Tupolev SB-2 Katyusha medium bombers. These were aircraft well known to the Italian pilots, who had often encountered them in Spain. During the engagement the Italian pilots downed six bombers and two enemy fighters, suffering no losses.

In late August, following the breakthrough of the enemy front and the rapid eastward advance of the German, Romanian and Italian forces, the entire CAI moved from Tudora to Krivoy Rog, where in September eight Savoia Marchetti SM.81s arrived from Italy which, added to the two trimotors already present at the Russian field, formed the 245th Transport Squadron.

On 22 September, after the bitter fighting suffered by the Italian units in the Petrikovka area, the city of Stalino, one of the most important urban centers in the Donets industrial basin, was captured. This success forced the 22nd Group and a reconnaissance squadron equipped with twin-engine Capronis to shift eastward again as far as Zaporozhe, on the left bank of the Dnieper.

On 25 November 1941 he 246th Squadron arrived from Italy with another six SM.81s in reinforcement and which was sent as far as Stalino to provide adequate support to the fighter units as well as to the front lines of the CSIR. Soon after, considering the progressive increase in distance and the continuous expansion of the front, a third transport squadron arrived from Italy, the 247th, which was based at Otopeni in Romania with the mission of covering the intermediate stretches.

The arrival of the autumn season, characterized by rain, snow and a rapid drop in temperature, down to -30 C [-22 Fahrenheit], created problems not only for the CSIR troops, which were totally unprepared from the equipment standpoint to fight in these extreme conditions, but also for the personnel and equipment of the CAI engaged, in October and November, in continuous and feverish work to clear the snow from the airstrips and to clean and repair the motors and weapons that had been frozen or damaged by ice and by the not infrequent incursions by Soviet bombers.

On the ground front, late in the day on 2 November, men of the 80th Infantry of the 'Pasubio', led by Colonel Chiarimonti, after four days were able to occupy the villages of Gorlovka and Nikitovka, but were soon after stalled by a violent Soviet counterattack and surrounded. Thanks to rapid action by the 371st Squadron which in one day carried out about half a dozen successful strafings against the Soviet 74th Division, the enemy infantry was forced to break off their attacks, allowing the men of the 'Pasubio' to hold out and reorganize. The Italian aircraft continued to attack the Soviets and to resupply Chiarimonti's men throughout the siege of Nikitovka.

On 5 November the new 246th Transport Squadron arrived in Stalino, joined four days later by the 371st Fighter Squadron, reinforced in late December by a second Macchi MC. 200 fighter squadron. In early December, on the eve of the great Soviet winter counteroffensive, the Italian Expeditionary Corps still found the strength, despite the heavy losses it had sustained, to advance to the east, seizing new positions. But on the eve of Christmas the feared new Soviet counteroffensive was unleashed, which forced the German divisions of Heeesgruppe Süd, to which the CSIR was subordinate, to withdraw from the area of Rostov, which had been recaptured by the Soviets.

The Soviet move, made by many divisions supported by cavalry troops, also forced the Italians to withdraw to more secure positions. The withdrawal was effected with air support provided by the ever-present Macchi MC.200s which, once again, made repeated attacks against the many Soviet infantry columns with the Breda Safat 12.7mm machine guns and with 50 kilogram wing-mounted bombs, as well as engaging in many air actions against enemy fighters and medium bombers. At the end of December, the Italian fighters were able to claim downing 12 Soviet aircraft for the loss of only one Macchi.

Following quite a long period of partial inactivity between December 1941 and January 1942, when atmospheric conditions were horrible, the temperature dropped to minus thirty degrees, snow blocked the landing strips and the lack of fuel forced almost all of the Italian units to reduce their activity, on 4 February the fighter squadrons began to take off again for new and arduous interdiction, escort and attack missions. On 5 February, several dozen Macchi MC.200s of the 22nd Group attacked the Soviet airfield at Krasny Liman, destroying at least 15 fighters and medium bombers without incurring any losses.

Following this brilliant action, the MC.200s resumed their attacks, carrying out many strafings and bombings against enemy airfields in March and April, hitting the fields at Leninskiy Bomdardir and Luskova.

Between February and September 1942, the 22nd Group inflicted the loss of 47 enemy aircraft in air combat and on the ground against the loss of 10 MC.202s. Meanwhile, the Caproni Ca.311 reconnaissance and light bombers were also committed to offensive action against the enemy rear area and against motorized columns and Soviet troop concentrations.

Italian pilots and aircraft at an airfield in Russia, 1941. (USSME)

Eastern Front Air Command

In the spring of 1942, aware of the now excessive extent of the front and the scarce size of the air units supporting the CSIR, the Regia Aeronautica command decided, in view of the arrival in Russia of additional Italian divisions and in preparation for the announced major German summer offensive, to reinforce the organization of the expeditionary force with delivery from Italy of new aircraft, fuel and supplies and, naturally, with substantial numbers of pilots and specialists. Accordingly, the Comando Aeronautica Fronte Orientale (CAFO, Eastern Front Air Command) was established.

In June 1942, the CSIR was disbanded and with the arrival of new divisions the Italian 8th Army in Russia (ARMIR) was constituted. During the same period, the 22nd Fighter Group, worn out by months of activity, was replaced by the 21st Gruppo (with Macchi MC.200 aircraft), consisting of the 356th, 382nd, 361st and 386th Squadrons, while the 71st Air Observation Squadron with Caproni Ca.311 aircraft (formed by the 38th and 116th Squadrons) replaced the 61st. Later, to offset the losses and to face ever-increasing commitments, the CAI was reinforced, although not in a satisfactory manner because of the difficult situation in the Mediterranean, where the Regia Aeronautica was constantly engaged. Between August and December 1942, the 71st Gruppo received 12 Fiat BR.20M 'Cicogna' heavy twin-engine bomber and reconnaissance aircraft, while the 21st Fighter Group was issued with some more modern aircraft, namely, the Macchi MC.202 'Folgore'. Meanwhile, the ARMIR reached the middle Don, taking up defensive positions between the Hungarian 2nd Army and the Romanian 3rd Army.

In August, during the first defensive battle of the Don, which was mounted by the Soviets against the ARMIR lines, all of the CAI was engaged in the battle to support the ground troops. On 6 August the Fiat BR.20Ms of the 38th Squadron of the 71st Air Observation Group carried

Pilots of the 21st Fighter Group ready for a combat mission, summer 1942. (USSME)

out their first bombing mission east of the course of the Don, hitting Soviet artillery and infantry concentrations. Participating in similar sorties were MC.200s (fitted with two wing-mounted 50-kilogram bombs) and the small Caproni twin-engine recon aircraft. Despite its small size, the CAI did what it could, and it due to the courage and spirit of sacrifice of its pilots and specialists that the Italian ground divisions were able to contain and push back all of the Soviet attacks, even though sustaining heavy losses.

With the arrival of autumn and after two months of intense activity, the operational conditions of the Italian air units deteriorated even further, especially the fighter units. In September 1942, thanks to the arrival of 12 new Macchi MC.202 fighters, the 21st Fighter Group was able to initiate a series of low-level attacks against Soviet positions east of the Don.

Between mid-October and mid-November, all of the Macchi MC.200, MC.202 and Fiat BR.20Ms continued to carry out low-level attacks to hit the enemy motorized columns and troop concentrations, with good results.

During the Soviet offensive that followed, in the so-called second defensive battle of the Don, because of harsh weather conditions and frigid temperatures, the Italian aircraft could do precious little to try to slow down the unstoppable Soviet advance. With temperatures of 40-45 degrees below zero, with ice that froze the landing gears and the weapons on board, the Macchis, Fiat BR.20s and the Caproni Ca.311s took off anyway from the snow-covered fields harassed by Soviet fighter-bombers to try to support the withdrawal of Italian troops.

The Macchi MC.200 fighters, which had an open cockpit and whose pilots therefore had to deal with frightful temperatures while in flight, strafed and bombed the Soviet columns, supported by a handful of the more modern MC.202 which also had to deal with enemy fighters. The Soviets threw hundreds of fighters and bombers into the fray. Despite the enemy's clear superiority, the fighters of the 21st Gruppo managed to do their best, while the surviving Fiat BR.20s and Capronis, sought in isolated actions to bomb the Soviet armoured formations. The few SM.81 trimotor transports were engaged in providing a minimum of logistic support to the Italian troops, a task that was accomplished at the cost of heavy losses.

The transport group of the CAI played an important role in Russia. Between 18 and 21 December 1941, the SM.81s had distinguished themselves by having been able to evacuate the airfield at Kantemirova, surrounded by Soviet armoured troops, saving pilots, specialists and more than 70 seriously wounded.

Between late 1942 and early 1943, concurrent with the major Soviet winter offensive called Little Saturn, the slow but robust Savoia-Marchetti trimotors continued to supply food, medicine and ammunition to the Italian front lines, losing at least six aircraft, three of which were downed by Soviet anti-aircraft fire, and the rest of the aircraft being damaged.

The commander of the CAI in Russia, General Enrico Pezzi, disappeared aboard one of the SM.81s during a hazardous resupply mission for a large Italo-German force that had been cut off.

On 29 December 1942, at Tcherkovo, 7,000 Italians and 4,000 Germans were surrounded after an attack by Soviet armoured forces. Pezzi, a veteran pilot in Ethiopia, Spain and North Africa, didn't think twice about taking part personally in the relief mission. Before departing General Pezzi said that he would return at 14:30 with all of the crew members, plus any wounded from the garrison. At 11:25 his SM.81 took off from Voroshilovgrad, with medical lieutenant Federico Bocchetti and pilot and specialists Romano Romanò, Giovanni Busacchi, Luigi Tomasi, Antonio Arcidiacono, Salvatore Caruso and Alcibiade Bonazza. The plane, full of food and medicine, was able to reach Tcherkovo, after which it took off with a number of wounded in an attempt to reach the rear area, but it did not make it. General Pezzi's SM.81 disappeared, probably shot down by Soviet fighters.

Following is the citation for the posthumous gold Medal for Military Valor for General Enrico Pezzi:

> A veteran of four wars where he always knew how to wrest from the sky a strip of blue to decorate his chest. In Russia with his boldness, he sculpted the example of calm while facing danger, in gold letters the outline of Italian wings. In a sublime risky offering to save Italian soldiers who were closed in a ring of fire, he immolated his young life with a smile of the brave in the skies of heroes'. Russian front 29-12-1942.

Following a long and laborious operational cycle, in early 1943 the last of the SM.81 transport planes were gradually transferred to fields that were less exposed to the final Soviet offensive. When Stalino, one of the major rear-area bases was abandoned, the 245th and 246th Squadrons were concentrated, along with other surviving units of the CAI, at the airfield in Odessa where they remained until March 1943, even though in reality the last SM.81s of the 246th Squadron did not return to Italy until the month of May.

The last combat action of any note carried out by the CAI in Russia to place on 17 January 1943 when a mixed formation of 25 MC.200s and MC.202s of the 21st Gruppo, which now had left only 30 MC.200 and 9 MC.202, attacked a strong Soviet armoured and motorized column that threatened the Italian retreat, inflicting heavy casualties on the enemy.

1. Order of Battle of Regia Aeronautica units on the Eastern Front 1941

CSIR Aviation Command: Pilot Colonel Carlo Drago

Fighter
22nd Independent Fighter Group (Macchi 200/Ca.133): Pilot Major Giovanni Borzoni
359th Squadron (SM.81): Pilot Captain Vittorio Minguzzi
362nd Squadron: Pilot Captain Germano La Ferla
369th Squadron: Piot Captain Giorgio Iannicelli
371st Squadron: Pilot Captain Enrico Meille

Air Observation
61st Independent Air Observation Grouop (Caproni 311): Pliot Lieutenant Colonel Bruno G. Ghierini
34th Squadron: Pilot Captain Cesare Bonino
119th Squadron: Pilot Captain Giovanni Disegna
128th Squadron: Pilot Captain Igino Mendini

Transport Squadron
245th Squadron T.M. (SM.81): Piot Captain Ernesto Caprioglio
246th Squadron T.M. (SM.81): Pilot Captain Nicola Fattibene

The CSIR aviation element was completed with the assignment of all of the technical services, the commissariat, medical services, the Aircraft and Engine Repair Team and all mobile shops and equipment necessary for the complete functioning of three airfields. These were provided with six sections of 20mm anti-aircraft guns and a motor pool with 300 vehicles of all types. Initially the CSIR Air Corps consisted of about 1,900 men: 140 officers, 180 NCOs and 1,500 other ranks (specialists and airmen), plus 90 specialized workers.

2. Order of Battle of Regia Aeronautica units on the Eastern Front 1942

CSIR Aviation Command: Pilot Colonel Carlo Drago – Gen. B.A. Enrico Pezzi

Fighters
22nd Independent Fighter Group (Macchi 200): Pilot Major Giuseppe d'Agostinis
359th Squadron: Plot Captain Vittorio Minguzzi
362nd Squadron: Pilot Captain Germano La Ferla
369th Squadron: Pilot Captain Giovanni Cervellin
371st Squadron: Pilot Captain Enrico Meille

Note: With the gradual phase-in of the 21st Independent Fighter Group (4 May 1942) and the replacement of the 22nd Fighter Group, the situation was as follows:

21st Gruppo Autonomo C.t. (Macchi 200/Macchi 202) – Pilot Major Ettore Foschini
356th Squadron: Pilot Captain Virginio Teucci
361st Squadron: Pilot Captain Francis Leoncini
382nd Squadron: Pilot Captain Enrico Candio
386th Squadron: Pilot Captain Bruno Mondini

Air Observation
61st Independent Air Observation Group. (Caproni 311): Pilot Lieutenant Colonel Giordano Ghierighini
34th Squadron: Pilot Captain Cesare Bonino
119th Squadron: Pilot Captain Giovanni Disegna
128th Squadron: Pilot Captain Lorenzo Tomai

Note: With the phase-in of the 71st Independent Air Observation Group (May 1942) and the replacement of the 61st Air Observation Group, the situation was as follows:

71st Independent Air Observation Group (Caproni 311/Fiat BR.20M): Pilot Colonel Achille Fanelli
38th Squadron
116th Squadron

TransportSection
245th Squadron T.M.: Pilot Captain Enrico Caprioglio
246th Squadron T.M.: Pilot Captain Ettore Valenti
247th Squadron T.M.

3. Order of Battle of Regia Aeronautica units on the Eastern front 1943

ARMIR Aviation Command (CAFO) – Air Brigadier General Ugo Rampelli

Fighters
21st Independent Fighter Group (Macchi 200/Macchi 202): Pilot Major Ettore Foschgini
356th Squadriglia: Pilot Captain Aldo Li Greci
361st Squadron: Pilot Captain Francis Leoncini
382nd Squadron: Pilot Captain Enrico Candio
386th Squadron: Pilot Captain Bruno Mondini

Air Observation
71st Independent Air Observation Group (Caproni 311): Pilot Lieutenant Colonel Alberto Scottu
38th Squadron (Caproni 312)
116th Squadron (Fiat BR.20M)

Transport Section
245th Squadron T.M. (SM.81)
246th Squadron T.M. (SM.81)
247th Squadron T.M. (SM.81)

Appendix IV

Regia Marina on the Eastern Front

In addition to the ground forces of the CSIR and of the ARMIR, a small naval component was also committed to the Eastern Front, sent by the Regia Marina to operate on the Black Sea to be engaged in the siege of Sevastopol and to challenge the presence of Soviet cruisers and submarines. The unit was designated the 101st MAS Flotilla and placed under command of Commander Francesco Mimbelli, a valorous officer who had been awarded ten medals for military valor (one Gold, three Silver, five Bronze and a War Cross), as well as having been awarded the German Iron Cross First and Second Class. It was formed in March 1942 with personnel coming from the X Flottiglia MAS, which had already gained fame in the Mediterranean and at Gibraltar. Because of Turkish neutrality, it was not possible to sail the ships through the Dardanelles Straits, so that the CB class pocket submarines, the five torpedo boats and five explosive motorboats were transferred by air as far as the Black Sea coast, making their bases in the Crimean ports of Yalta and Feodosia in May 1942. The Italian motor torpedo boats and submarines were soon engaged in operations against the Soviet fortress of Sevastopol, which was being besieged by Romanian and German troops, attacking supply traffic headed for the fortress. In addition to sinking merchant ships, during the siege of the city, on 19 June 1942, the Soviet submarine Equoka was also sunk.

An Italian motor torpedo boat in action on the Black Sea. (Authors' collection)

Lieutenant Commander Salvatore Todaro also took part in operations against the city, a future captain of the submarine Cefalo and Gold Medal of Honor awardee, distinguishing himself by his boldness and skill in leading the motor torpedo boats under his command, earning a Silver Medal for Military Valor with the following citation:

'A wise and passionate organizer of assault craft he offered himself to lead them in the waters of a very strongly defended Soviet fortress. An example to everyone of boldness and fearlessness he was always first in the riskiest and most difficult missions. He attacked an enemy patrol boat at very close range and then knew very ably how to escape its reaction. Having spotted small boats full of enemy soldiers with all types of automatic weapons in full daylight, he attacked them, machine gunning them at close range. He persisted in the action until he ran out of ammunition, even though his second pilot had been badly wounded and his craft was hit by many enemy rounds. Waters of Sevastopol, June 1942'.

On the Sea of Azov

After the capture of the city on 4 July 1942, the 101st MAS Flotilla was moved to the Sea of Azov to protect German naval traffic, and later to continue with patrol missions along the coastline controlled by the Soviets. During their service on the Sea of Azov, the Italian MTBs inflicted heavy losses on Soviet naval forces: in the night between 2 and 3 August 1942, MAS 548 commanded by Lieutenant Emilio Legnani, during a security and escort mission protecting German ships which were transferring a group of soldiers to the front line, he found himself facing a large Soviet naval formation that was searching for the Italo-German ships. Despite a contrary wind and rough seas, the Italian crew deftly handled the small craft between enemy cannon and small arms fire; when within range, Lieutenant Legnani fired his two torpedoes which scored a direct hit on the largest ship, the cruiser Molotov, seriously damaging it. After the torpedo launch, MAS 568 was chased by the destroyer Kharkov, which Legnani shook off by dropping ten antisubmarine depth charges, which damaged the bow of the Soviet ship which was forced to break off its pursuit.

For that action, Lieutenant Legnani was decorated by Victor Emmanuel III with the Gold Medal for Military Valor which was awarded to him by the King on the Altar of the Country on 10 June 1943 with the following citation:

'A motor torpedo boat commander, operating in far-off waters, he gave proof in bold combat missions of perfect preparation, of calm daring and deep expertise in the employment of the powerful war machine entrusted to him. Assigned to carry out a difficult ambush mission, he went forth decisively to intercept a Soviet naval formation consisting of a cruiser and a destroyer, courageously and boldly facing the well-aimed fire that was repeatedly directed against the small craft. Despite unfavorable light conditions and the hammering of enemy fire, he decisively headed for the enemy and, at close range, fired two torpedoes at the first and larger target which, upon exploding, covered the enemy ship in a sheet of flame and which sank in a few minutes. Having completed the heroic act which renewed with unsurpassed energy the glorious traditions of our MAS [MTBs], he disengaged from the furious reaction of the enemy escort vessel and from the persistent air attacks, returning to his base without any losses. He thus demonstrated how the spirit which animates Italian sailors knows how to defeat the enemy in any trial and daring to triumph against all odds'.

Black Sea, 3 August 1942.

The lack of fuel and the unfavorable turn of military operations in the winter of 1942-1943 had strong repercussions on the activity of the Italian naval craft. On 20 May 1943, the surviving MAS were turned over to the German Kriegsmarine and the crews sent back to Italy. The submarines, however, continued to operate with Italian crews from the base at Sevastopol until August 1943. Following the 8 September 1943 Italian armistice, some of the crews joined the Italian Social Republic and others were interned by the Germans, while the craft, now in a terrible state of maintenance, were taken over by the Romanians, later to fall into Soviet hands at Costanza in 1944. During its operational period, the flotilla sank three transport ships and Soviet submarines and, importantly, damaged the cruiser Molotov and the destroyer Kharkov. Losses amounted to one CB pocket submarine and two MAS torpedo boats, with two sailors killed and ten wounded.

MAS on Lake Ladoga

Another small Italian naval unit that operated between 15 August and 22 October 1942 on the shores of Lake Ladoga, supporting German and Finnish troops engaged in the siege of Leningrad was the 12th MAS Flotilla. The unit, led by Lieutenant Commander Bianchini and consisting of about a hundred men (17 officers, 19 NCOS and 63 other ranks) was integrated into the Laivasto Osasto K, literally, Naval Detachment K. This force grouped together the Finnish, German and Italian naval forces located on Lake Ladoga. Four motor torpedo boats (MAS 526, 527, 528 and 529) were moved overland by train from the city of La Spezia to Innsbruck, then continuing to Stettin. There they were embarked to cross the Baltic Sea and to be towed as far as Lake Ladoga. Operational in late July 1942, the unit was engaged in opposing Soviet naval traffic, which represented the only way to resupply besieged Leningrad. August saw the first successes for the Italian crews: in the night between 15 and 15 August, after having dropped off several Finnish intelligence personnel on the Soviet-occupied coast, MAS 527 and 528 ran into a group of three Bira-class gunboats. After having been spotted, enemy fire was directed against the small Italian torpedo boats. Maneuvering handily, MAS 527 under Lieutenant Junior Grade Renato Bechi closed to a distance of 350 meters, opening fire with its on-board weapons and riddling the bridge of the Soviet ship Finding himself in an optimal position, two torpedoes were launched against one of the three gunboats, sinking it a few moments later.

For this action, Bechi was awarded the Silver Medal for Military Valor, with the following citation: 'Commander of a MAS in a wartime mission, spotting a formation of three enemy gunboats, he steered decisively to attack and, although hampered by bad weather and having been targeted by violent enemy fire which repeatedly hit his craft on the bridge, he loosed his torpedoes at short range, hitting and sinking one of the three enemy ships. With able maneuvering and skill, he was able to disengage and return his MAS to its base with no crew losses, demonstrating throughout the action his calm courage and highly aggressive spirit. In an allied country, on our navy's fourth front, he reaffirmed superbly with this brilliant action the traditional virtues of courage and boldness of the MAS'. Lake Ladoga, 15 August 1942.

But this was not the only Italian success; several days later, another Soviet convoy was intercepted on Lake Ladoga. This time entering action was MAS 528 commanded by Lieutenant Junior Grade Aldo Benvenuto; it was 27 August when, during a night patrol searching for supply convoys bound for Leningrad, several tugs towing a large barge were spotted. Despite having been spotted in the calm waters of the lake lit by moonlight, the Italian crews of the two boats wanted to take their chances, coming under fire from the machine guns on the Soviet vessels. At a distance of more than five miles, MAS 528 fired a single torpedo, which after about ten seconds, hit the large barge which was carrying fuel and ammunition. It exploded with a mighty roar and disintegrated completely.

Aldo Benvenuto was also awarded the Silver Medal for Military Valor, with the following citation: 'Commander of a MAS in a nighttime ambush along enemy coastal routes, seeing a large enemy transport, he maneuvered skillfully and boldly to get himself into a favorable attack position.

An Italian CB-class mini submarine in port on the Black Sea. Behind it is a German
motor torpedo boat. (Authors' collection)

Although being taken under heavy fire, he fired his torpedo at close range hitting and sinking the enemy vessel'. Lake Ladoga, 28 August 1942.

With the approach of the autumn season and then of winter, the activity of the 12th MAS Flotilla scaled back dramatically. The last sorties were attempted in September 1942; on 1 September there was a proper air-naval battle which witnessed Soviet and Italian surface units and German Luftwaffe aircraft engaged. In the early morning, MAS 529 was carrying out patrol activity along the lake's coast; after a few hours it was spotted by two Russian patrol boats which immediately opened fire. Thus, a rapid exchange of fire broke out; the 45mm guns on the Soviet vessels were met by 20mm cannon fire from the Italian torpedo boat. Meanwhile, moving rapidly, all three craft avoided being hit. The MAS reached an optimal position to fire its torpedo, which however missed its target; only the arrival of the German planes broke off the naval battle, while the Soviet patrol boat Purga was sunk by German bombs. Finally, on 29 September, MAS 529, commanded by Commander Bianchini, attempted a new attack against a convoy of tugs and supply barges which were sailing close to his position. Although close to each other, Bianchini made a wide circling maneuver, initially disengaging himself from enemy fire and then getting into a torpedo launch position His torpedo missed the target, forcing the MAS to return because of the high volume of fire that had been directed against the Italian crew.

In winter 1942, having turned over the assault craft to the Finnish navy, the flotilla was disbanded and the crews, in their entirety, returned to Italy.

Appendix V

After-action Report by General Reverberi on the Russian Campaign

---

Headquarters 2nd Alpine Division 'Tridentina'

Report
of the actions carried out by the 'Tridentina' Division on the Russian front
The division's operational cycle consisted of three periods:

1st period: mid-August- 9 October (move to the assembly area of Novo Gorlovka – occupying defensive positions in the Gorbatovo sector on the middle Don);

2nd period: 10 October – 16 January (move to the Podgornoye sector and defensive deployment on the Don);

3rd period: 17 January – 30 January (withdrawal under enemy pressure and breaking out of the enemy encirclement).

First Period (mid-August – 9 October 1942)

Month of August

On 16 August, the division having begun movement on foot for Rostov, headed for the Caucasus, after several halts (because of the collapse of a stretch of the front along the Don held by CSIR troops), it was rerouted to Voroshilovgrad to contain the enemy on the Yagodny-Bolshoi front.

From Voroshilovgrad (given the urgent situation created by the threatening gap) the battalions of the 5th Alpini with only the mules of the combat echelon were moved by truck (towards Millerovo – Varinovskaya) while the rest of the division was headed to the front on foot. From the Millerovo area the 'Vestone' and 'Val Chiese' battalions of the 6th Alpini were also moved by truck.

From 27 to 30 August the regiments (after several resubordinations to other divisions) were deployed subordinate to the 'Celere' and the 'Sforzesca', with:

> 5th Alpini on the left;
> 6th Alpini (minus the 'Verona' battalion which had not yet arrived) on the right of the Yagodny – Hill 228 – Hill 176.8 – Bolshoi – Hill 188 front.

Month of September

On 1 September the CSIR headquarters ordered that the battallions 'Vestone' and 'Val Chiese' respectively attack the enemy positions of Stop No. 4 – Hill 209.6 – Hill 236 – and Kotowski – Hill 195 in order to shrink the dangerous salient that the Russians had created when the sector was held by the 'Sforzesca'.

German armoured forces were to contribute to the attack with a simultaneous action on the right.

The 5th Alpini (on the left) were to be ready to follow up on the success. With dash and magnificent daring, the two battalions overran enemy resistance and reached the assigned objectives within a few hours. The 'Vestone' fell upon the medium caliber artillery positions and captured guns and crews.

The failed intervention by German armoured forces does not allow the positions reached to be held, and the headquarters orders the alpine battalions to pull back to their departure points.

Despite this decision, which turned over to the enemy the positions which had so gloriously and bloodily captured, the action gave immediate and profitable fruit because the high offensive spirit shown by our alpini and the losses inflicted by them profoundly shook the enemy's morale and forced him to pass from a confident offensive to a clear defensive posture, thus rendering the wedge that it had previously made useless. The brilliant action by the battalions of the 6th Alpini aroused the marvel and unconditioned admiration of their comrades of the CSIR and of the nearby allied troops.

On 9 September the division is deployed in accordance with its commander's orders along a front about 25 kilometers long between Hill 228 and Bolshoi, an area completely of steppe and lacking any tactical foothold. A defensive position and strongpoints were built at a feverish pace. Alpini, gunners and engineers compete in terms of skill, training and ingenious field works. The II Engineer Battalion stands out in particular for its expertise.

The work is especially hard and exhausting because:

Of the onerous duty on the line and patrol duty;
Of the need to do most of the work at night because of the lack of natural cover and because of the terrain which has no defiles;
Of the absence of materials of all kinds;
Of the considerable distances from supply bases;
Of the unsuitable transportation assets;
Of the climate.

Despite the fact that the division was busy in setting up the aforementioned defensive position:

Cuts short all enemy attempts to attack out positions with bold actions;
Keeps the enemy under constant nerve-wracking tension with successful raids;
Is able to hand over to the Romanian troops (since 9 October when they replace the division) an almost completed defensive position, earning admiration for the impressive and rational work that had been done.

Second Period (10 October 1942 – 16 January 1943)

Month of October

With the replacement of the 'Tridentina' by a Romanian division (8-10 October) the division moves on foot to the Podgornoye sector. The troops brilliantly cover about 400 kilometers in phases. The particular difficulties due to mud and the early cold were overcome by the tenacity and high spirit of the troops who crossing the entire front of the ARMIR elicited the admiration and congratulations of Italian and allied headquarters.

Month of November

On 6 November the division assumes responsibility of the sector on the Don (until now held by the Hungarian 23rd Division) from the area of Karabut to that of Bassavka along a front of about 28 kilometers. For various reasons the sector had been organized in a very embryonic fashion by the Hungarians and in a manner that absolutely did not lend itself to winter quarters,

The battalions and groups in this sector also worked hard with strong will and patience making superhuman efforts to create a defensive system that would be proof against enemy attacks and the rigors of the Russian winter.

In evaluating the effort required and the extent of the work accomplished it should be considered that the alpini, artillerymen and engineers had to build everything, from shelters to positions to observation posts to command posts to barbed wire entanglements to antitank ditches and minefields.

If the environmental conditions and climate are considered and if it is borne in mind that while the defensive system was being built, patrols were carried out almost daily to determine enemy deployments and intentions, whose every offensive thrust was always rebuffed, one has an idea of the effort which all men of the division have to make.

Month of December

It is characterized by bold and brilliant coups de main whose aim is to determine the enemy's intentions more in depth and to upset his offensive plans, whose actions give the precise sensation that he wishes to initiate some action in this sector in concert with what he is doing in other sectors further to the south.

Month of January (from day 1 to day 17)

Increased air activity and the resumption of actions by fire, especially artillery, now make an imminent attack certain.

On 15,16 and 17 January, enemy forces estimated at about two regiments, supported by numerous batteries and mortars of all calibers and Katyushas unleash violent attacks in the area where the 'Tridentina' and the 'Vicenza' meet. The behavior of the battalions under fire is superb, which hold their positions despite not light losses. On 15 January the 'Vestone' throws back seven attacks and counts about 200 enemy corpses in front of its lines. On 15, 156 and 17 January the 'Edolo' breaks the enemy's savage fury without losing a meter of ground, counterattacks and puts the enemy to flight, capturing much equipment and nipping in the bud a tank attack that was about to be made. Our losses were painful, but the results achieved were obvious in preventing the enemy from breaching the Alpine Corps front and striking into the heart of his rear area, cutting the Podgornoye-Rossosch rail and road lines.

Third Period (17 – 30 January 1943)

But even all of the valor of our Alpini was not enough to bring the joy of holding our positions at the price of so much blood. Events in other sectors forced the higher authorities to order the withdrawal of the 'Tridentina' to Podgornoye. The withdrawal was made in three columns protected by a strong rear guard. All of the impedimenta were abandoned, and all of the transport assets were loaded with ammunition, food and medical supplies. Despite the pain of having to abandon a line that had been made with such passion and held at the cost of sacrifice, troop morale is intact, nor do the particularly harsh weather conditions dampen their spirits.

The other divisions of the Alpine Army Corps ('Vicenza'-'Cuneense'-'Julia') were to withdraw to the left of the 'Tridentina', and to the right the Hungarian 23rd Division.

Day 18

On the night before the 18th the division deploys to defend Podgornoye: front facing east.

Meanwhile, events become pressing. Headquarters of the Alpine Army Corps (which reached Podgornoye with the rest of the Corps troops and services, which are made available to the 'Tridentina'), becoming aware that the enemy, moving on the flanks, is trying to get behind our troops, urges a resumption of movement. As a result, arrangements are made for the division, at night, to move west in two columns:

On the left: 5th Alpini and 'Val Camonica' group

On the right: 6th Alpini – engineer battalion – 'Vicenza' and 'Bergamo' groups – divisional services.

Day 19

The 5th Alpini, which is headed to Skororib, soon makes contact with the enemy who, having occupied the town, moves against out columns with motorized troops. Violent fighting soon erupts; it is necessary to reach the town which is in a dominant position.

The dash and valor of the alpini of the 5th supported ably by the 'Val Camonica', overcome the Russian resistance. The town is occupied and a good number of Russian soldiers are captured, as well as arms and ammunition; the first tanks are knocked out.

The 6th Alpini, headed for Repyevka above Postoyalyi, finding this latter location occupied by the enemy, attacks it with the 'Verona' battalion. The fighting which began favorably for the 'Verona' (not being able to be supported by the other battalions who had stayed behind for a number of reasons) then took an unfavorable turn and went in favor of the enemy when substantial armoured forces joined them. The 'Verona' is forced to pull back to Repyevka and manages to hold off – although at the cost of bloody losses – the enemy's pressure.

The bulk of the column reaches Opyt and the 'Val Chiese' is sent to support the 'Verona' (which is ensconced in Repyevka).

During the night, arriving at Opyt (southeast of Repyevka) were the headquarters of the 'Tridentina', the headquarters of the Alpine Army corps, headquarters of the German XXIV Armee Korps, many alpini and about a thousand Hungarian stragglers. A Hungarian colonel who was among the stragglers, reported that the Hungarian division which was to withdraw to our right had been cut up and that its remnants sought to escape the enemy's grip.

In the early morning hours of the 19th another thousand Hungarian stragglers, around a thousand Germans (the remnants of XIV Corps) with many sleds, assault guns, a rocket launcher battery and a medium caliber artillery group all made their way to Opyt.

The German tanks, rocket launchers and artillery (under Major Fischer) were subordinated to the 'Tridentina'.

The situation began to become clearer, but unfortunately it looked very serious. In fact:

Of the German corps (which was to operate on the left of the Alpine Army Corps) only remnants remained, most of which, passing through the Alpine Army Corps, had met up with the 'Tridentina';

The Hungarian corps, which was to withdraw on our right, was in rapid retreat exposing the right wing of the 'Tridentina';

Russian units of unknown size, but undoubtedly large, faced our division.

Given that the other divisions were delayed with respect to the movement of the 'Tridentina', the Alpine Army Corps commander ordered out division to halt on the 19th in the positions we had reached and to resume the attack on the 20th, with the Postoyalyi area as its objective. Based on the orders and in consideration:

Of the serious events that left no doubt as to the encirclement of the division;

Of the enormous logjam caused by the columns of escaping men, especially of the allies, who seriously hindered any movement;

Measures were taken to:

Reorganize the tide of stragglers which was flooding the town of Opyt as much as possible;

Reinforce the defense of Opyt, to safeguard the area from any enemy attacks and to protect the departure of all of the men gathered there on the next day;

Send all of the men of the 6th Alpini (minus the 54th Company of the 'Vestone') to Repyevka so that the regiment could have its three battalions for the next day's attack;

Send as reinforcements to the 6th Alpini the German units subordinate to the 'Tridentina';

Reorganize the Hungarian stragglers into ad hoc battalions;

Gather together all of the impedimenta (sleds, mules, etc.).

Orders were issued for the attack:

The 6th Alpini were to seize Postoyalyi and quickly move to Novo Karkovka;

The 5th Alpini were to support the action of the 6th Alpini with a flanking action on the left and then follow it with a forward movement.

Day 20

At 0200 the enemy attacked the Opyt area from the north but was forced back by the heroic alpini of the 54th Company of the 'Vestone' who fought like lions.

This attack made it certain that the right of the division was completely exposed. Plans were made for the departure of the services, the headquarters, the straggler columns and the impedimenta to leave at dawn. As soon as movement began, intense mortar, artillery and automatic weapons fire hit the entire area. During the night the enemy, taking advantage of darkness, made a wide movement attempting an encirclement.

All of the available men were committed to stopping the enemy effort which, if it had succeeded, would have destroyed and captured the headquarters and cut the division in two by wedging itself between the operating columns of the 5th and 6th Alpini.

The men, including the division headquarters, accomplished wonders of valor, but did not succeed in their attempt. The only thing left at hand was the II Engineer Battalion which, by order of the division commander, counterattacked with decisive results against an enemy flank, halts him, throws him back and thus eliminates the serious and immediate threat.

The counterattack, carried out with irresistible boldness, cost bloody losses to the heroic engineers (more than 60 percent of the force), but their sacrifice allows most of the headquarters and of the units gathered in Opyt to leave. At Postoyalyi meanwhile, the 6th Alpini, supported by the 'Bergamo' and 'Vicenza' groups and by German units, after hours of violent combat during which there is bloody hand-to-hand fighting, is able to sweep away the enemy and to occupy the town. The courageous behavior of the 6th Alpini, according to prisoners, amazes the enemy.

Following a brief pause the regiment continues on to Novo Karkovka.

The 5th Alpini and the 'Val Camonica' have, by their action, contributed significantly to the success of the 6th.

Thus around 1300 this day which is full of developments, which for us for many hours created an almost desperate situation, the first enemy ring was broken and the Russian attempt to split the 'Tridentina' was shattered. The unshakeable tenacity of all of the alpini, artillerymen and engineers and their strong desire to open a path at any cost had triumphed. Here the traditional values of the mountain troops were reconfirmed and surpassed. There were innumerable acts of legendary heroism, considering that on this longest of days there were various fights that took place:

Against overwhelming forces supported by many tanks;
In adverse weather conditions, with the men tired by long marches almost without any breaks;
With communications effected only by runners, as radio and telephone communications had been cut;
With the obstacles created by the columns of enormous masses of impedimenta and services.

The headquarters of the Alpine Army Corps, having reached Postoyalyi around 1400, now convinced that enemy attacks would be made along the direction of march rather than to the rear as they wished to bar our advance ordered the 6th Alpini (minus the 'Verona' battalion), reinforced by German assault guns, by the 'Bergamo' and 'Vicenza' groups, the Fischer Group and by the rocket launcher battery, to constitute a strong vanguard to break through any obstacles and to open the way for the rest of the column. Given the importance of the mission it places the division commander himself in command who sets Novo Kharkovka as its objective.

On the left (in line with orders issued the previous evening) the 'Cuneense' was to operate with the mission of also reaching Novo Kharkovka. As a result of these orders the commander of the 'Tridentina', having turned over command of the divisional troops to the commander of the 5th Alpini and given orders so that the 'Verona' battalion, as soon as it had completed its mission of disengaging from the flank, serve as rear guard for all of the divisional troops, resumes the movement.

From Postoyalyi it is indispensable to use the only direction of movement because of the deep snow. With a very quick movement the vanguard reaches Novo Kharkovka at 1700, and finding it occupied by the enemy prepares for an immediate attack.

The enemy that holds the town with a force estimated at two battalions reinforced with tanks, artillery and mortars defends itself furiously but, mainly because of the speed of the attack which does not allow him to deploy his forces as he might wish, has to give ground. The sorties by tanks which are knocked out are useless, so that they have to give up the fight.

The town is finally prepared by us for defense against a possible attack by motorized forces. Meanwhile the rest of the divisional column followed the movement rebuffing ambushes as well as small attacks by partisans who take advantage of the many wooded areas to impede out march.

The 'Verona' battalion, assigned to protect – as has been said – the right flank of the column, although already heavily involved in the morning and the previous day, drives back, after bitter fighting, a Russian column that tries to hit our right flank and in spirited and sharp counterattacks puts them to flight.

General Reverberi departing by train for the Eastern Front. (Authors' collection)

It then takes up as the rear guard of the 'Tridentina'. Thus, on the night of the 21st the second barrier that the enemy had set up along our withdrawal route could be considered to have been broken and overcome.

Day 21

Alpine Army Corps headquarters, having reached Novo Kharkovka on the night of the 21st, orders the move to Lymarevka and Shelyakino to continue. The concept of the enemy action is now clear: interdict the movement with successive barriers along the roads that bar our column's axis of march, using motorized units which he has in great abundance. What kinds of measures could be taken to frustrate the enemy's actions and reach the allied forces which air reconnaissance reported to be west of the Valuiky meridian and this more than 90 linear kilometers further?

Not to concede any pause in the movement at the cost of superhuman efforts in order not to give the enemy forces time to organize themselves in positions and to disorient the enemy headquarters with rapid in-depth actions;

To move mostly in the night hours in order to leave the enemy uncertain as to the route of the withdrawal and to at least escape massed tank and air attacks;

Avoid (as much as possible) movement along roads and through towns;

Try to impede the enormous mass of other Italian and allied divisions that were moving towards the 'Tridentina' from mixing in with the combat units so that unit cohesiveness was not compromised and action was not hampered;

Take advantage, during the brief rest stops, of populated areas to give shelter to the troops who were already beginning to suffer the from the effects of the extremely cold temperatures (-30 degrees at night).

Simple concepts, but difficult to carry out given the particular circumstances and the execution of which had to be accomplished at all costs with ability and iron will by commanders of all ranks. Each infraction, shilly-shallying or weakness could compromise the desired result: escape capture and destruction.

At 0200 on day 21 movement resumed. The II Engineer Battalion, considering its meager surviving force (about 150 men out of 700) was reorganized into an ad hoc company, placed at the disposition of the 6th Alpini.

After a march made under exceptionally bad weather conditions, the vanguard entered Lymarevka around 0800, after having completely wiped out several regular and partisan formations which, thrown out of Novo Kharkovka, sought to bar the way on the hills in front of the town. Given the weariness of the troops and the raging of a furious storm, a pause became indispensable.

21 January was a particularly harsh day because of the cold. The enormous column was not able to find sufficient shelter and suffered atrociously from the cold and left not a few men hit by freezing and frostbite along the way. Meanwhile, transport for the sick and wounded became increasingly needed and the medical supplies continued to dwindle. For as much that these considerations were of extreme seriousness for the consequences which they could have, the lack of fuel made it necessary to abandon the small trucks that until that time had been part of the move. All of the gasoline had to be used for vehicles to tow the artillery. Most of the trucks were used to carry ammunition and food. It was a tough but unavoidable necessity.

The most generous examples of comradeship were then seen: alpini who took up the loads of their tired companions, alpini who carried stretchers with the sick and wounded, alpini who took the place of mules to pull the sleds.

On that day the generosity of the great Italian heart perhaps wrote its most beautiful pages. Everything that was humanly possible was thought of and put into effect by the soldiers of the

'Tridentina' so that the goal could be reached and so that Victory could be enjoyed by the greatest number of Italians and allies.

Day 22
Objective of the day: Ladomirovka

To reach it, it was necessary to cross through Shelyakino which it was logical to assume was occupied by enemy troops given the importance of the town and of the Rossosch-Alexeyevka road that ran through it. At first light, the vanguard continued its move. The tide of those following in the wake of the 'Tridentina' was increasing greatly. Checkpoints and special detachments are organized to keep order in the movement.

As soon as the vanguard reaches the Shelyakino saddle that dominates the town (around 1000) it is greeted by heavy automatic weapons, artillery and mortar fire. The battalions and the German assault guns deploy and begin to attack the town supported by the 'Bergamo' and 'Vicenza' artillery groups. With the arrival of the lead battalion of the 5th Alpini, the 'Edolo', it is given the mission of flanking the town from the left. Just at that moment a column of Russian tanks breaks out of the southern part of town, where the leading elements of the vanguard have already infiltrated. The moment is delicate, but the steadfastness of the commanders (who were aware of the maneuver under way by the 'Edolo'), the steadiness of the troops who had already victoriously cut off an attack by armoured vehicles, dominate the situation. With some of the tanks immobilized, the artillery met with counterbattery fire and silenced, the defenders rooted out of the houses and the 'Edolo' action coming into play, the battle is won. Hundreds of enemy bodies, many abandoned artillery pieces, very many automatic weapons are left on the ground, marking a formidable enemy defense, the bitterness of the fight and the greatness of the victory.

Everyone competed in skill: alpini and artillerymen. There is no longer any distinction between units: whether from the 5th or the 6th they know that salvation will come from a common effort and they work side by side in boldness and daring. The behavior of the German units was magnificent, who in a perfect display of comradeship, applaud the Italian victory. But even success cannot allow any pauses, because losses have that already thinned the ranks do not allow any pity or respite, we must keep on going forward.

While night falls the vanguard continues on to Ladomirovka, followed by the immense column. Unfortunately, the events of the tiring day are not yet over. Fresh enemy formations (partly armoured) come from the south and attack the column's flank which, in order to not be overrun, part of the column diverts to the north, on the road that leads to Varvarovka. It is in this locality that the 'Morbegno', clashing with other units coming from the north, writes pages of glory by sacrificing itself to let the other units that have detoured to save themselves by taking the western route along which the bulk of the division was marching.

Heroism and generosity were fused in an admirable marriage. During the night when the shadows are deep, the day's objective is reached.

This memorable day closes with breaching the new encirclement laid by an enemy strong in equipment and heavily supported by armoured units that were measured against men that had marched for five days amid innumerable difficulties and untold suffering. Hunger, freezing, losses did not diminish their spirit, the supreme faith and the will of our alpini.

Day 23
Before dawn breaks, the movement resumes and conducted quickly to take advantage of the defeat inflicted upon the enemy the previous day. Although tired, the troops feel the pressing need and with admirable effort of will follow the orders of their commanders. There are no traces of the

enemy until Nikolayevka where a formation of regulars, supported by four medium-caliber guns, want to challenge the movement of the alpini.

But will alone, which until then did not strengthen their efforts which became spasmodic and in a daring assault, more than a true and proper combined action, the alpini, in the wake of the German tanks, fall upon the Russians and in short order defeat them. The vanguard's action was so rapid and violent that the column was not able to hear its sounds. Movement continues in a snow-storm and the advance continues until physical effort is exhausted.

Deep in the night the column halts in the Kovalev area. There is little shelter for the men, but diminishing energy also imposes the law of the steppe which calls for a refuge for men and animals: the alternative is death.

But in the steppe the ever-present vision of the homeland that gives them hope and pushes them wins over the adversities of climate and of their lot.

Day 24

The dawn that breaks between a violently swirling snowstorm finds the column again on the move. It is 1000 when the first enemy attacks come from the town of Malakevka.

Medium caliber artillery hits the vanguard. There is no time to lose because the terribly cold day threatens to cause a catastrophe if the march is stopped. The artillery is deployed in an instant; the German assault guns surrounded by alpini of the 'Vestone' and 'Val Chiese' move directly on the town. To describe the fighting is impossible – it is a series of small actions and individual initia-tives – it is a new brilliant affirmation of cooperation between the arms, a fraternity of combatants.

The results provide a feel for the effort: at 1200 the town is captured, more than 600 enemy corpses are counted, 12 medium caliber guns are out of action, dozens of mortars, machine guns and submachine guns are abandoned by the fleeing enemy. The march continues to Romankovo with a temperature of -40 and in a snowstorm which has become very violent. The soldiers are running out of food.

Alpini and mules stave off pangs of hunger and thirst by eating snow; but their spirits remain high and our magnificent alpini, who under the admiring eyes of their German comrades had in short order also decided this new clash with the enemy, make every effort to obey the orders of their leaders.

Romanovko is reached at night and is occupied without resistance and the night is spent there. The 'Verona' battalion has been returned to subordination of the 6th Alpini.

Day 25

At dawn the usual formation resumes its movement towards Nikitovka. Luckily the area is full of houses in which the most varied and unbelievable foodstuffs are found. Nikitovka is occupied after sporadic resistance by partisans and regular troops.

The 'Verona' and 'Vestone' battalions, the 225th of the 'Val Chiese', a battery of the 'Bergamo' group and the German assault guns that make up the vanguard continue and then halt for safety and rest reasons at Arnautovo a few kilometers past Nikitovka where the rest of the column has halted.

Division headquarters, which had by now taken control of all of the troops in the area, issued orders for the following day:

> contemporaneous departure at 0600 of the vanguard (already pushed forward by a few hours) and the divisional column;
> attack against Nikolayevka (a key center on the road between the two locales which were known to be heavily garrisoned by the enemy) to be made by the vanguard supported by the rest of the divisional column, which was to have forced the movement, close the distance and held itself ready to take part in the action.

Day 26

During the night the vanguard as well as the remnants of the 'Val Chiese', which had taken positions at the entrance to Nikitovka, are attacked by partisans and regular Russian troops. After several hours during which there were losses on both sides, the enemy is forced back. The departure of the column is planned so that it is no longer split. But after having left Arnautovo, the column is attacked by large enemy forces that engage the 'Tirano' and the 'Val Camonica' group with the obvious aim of separating the bulk of the division from the vanguard.

The fight develops with alternating outcomes. In the culminating moment of the bitter battle, the enemy tries to flank the 'Tirano' by bringing in fresh troops which, buoyed by the success they feel is certain, advance while singing. But the regiment's alpini, with unequalled heroism and with an adroit maneuver attack the new forces, break the enemy action and overwhelm him, opening a gap sufficient to ensure the flow of the enormous mass of stragglers who, lacking weapons and any combat capability, followed the division, trusting their fate to it. From the fleeing enemy columns, from its dead, from the weapons destroyed and captured, it could be deduced that the Russians had made the attack with less than three battalions. The heroic sacrifice of many officers and of many alpini had also resolved this critical situation that threatened to break the column into two parts and compromise the outcome of the fighting at Nikolayevka.

Meanwhile, the battalions of the 6th Alpini got within sight of Nikolayevka and began their attack. The effectiveness of the men had been badly shaken by the hard fighting and by the particularly bad weather conditions that had left large voids in the ranks.

Ammunition was in short supply; nevertheless, surviving the violent reaction of automatic weapons, artillery and mortars, the men make it across the railway at the outskirts of town and at 1100 are inside the town, where the fighting is ferocious. But new heavy losses create a crisis situation. Even though the men are well armed, they are forced to withdraw past the railway line where they maintain contact with the enemy who they continue to fight. Around 1200 the bulk of the column begins to arrive.

Orders were then issued;

> That all of the artillery be deployed and sustain the resumption of the attack;
> That the 5th Alpini advance as soon as possible;
> That everyone without a specific assignment be formed into ad hoc units led by officers and be integrated into the battalions;
> That the attack be resumed upon the appropriate order.

But the defense was extremely effective; mortar and artillery fire continued to be violent, joined by air attacks by many aircraft which showed up over the battlefield. It is easy to imagine the results of such a concentration of fire against a mass consisting mainly of sleds, quadrupeds and vehicles driven by soldiers of various nationalities, speaking different languages and thus hard to control.

The attack launched with energy and pulled forward by the German tanks, which were led personally by the division commander, achieves an initial result: the railway line is crossed and the town is broken into. But the numerous and one can say tragic losses, especially among the officers, again put the brakes on the momentum of the men of the 6th Alpini. The masses that followed the to-and-fro of the battle had already moved ahead, but with this development, began a fearsome retrograde movement. However, at that moment, tired but not out of the fight, the men of the 5th Alpini arrived, excited by the success that had already been achieved by their comrades of the 6th, joined them and, in a brotherly competition, resumed the attack.

With this furious new impetus that has an epic air about it, because whoever is out of ammunition fights with hand grenades, he who no longer has grenades fights hand-to-hand, because the gunner leaves his piece which no longer has any ammunition to become an alpino amongst the alpini, because the mule handler leaves his mule to take the place of his fallen comrade and grabs a rifle, the enemy cannot hold out; those of them who are not killed flee, abandoning all manner of weapons on the field. The new encirclement is broken.

All of the column can descend upon Nikolayevka and stay there for the night. This is the day of the brightest heroism, the day in which even at a very high cost, the men earn the highest title of glory. More than 40 officers are killed or wounded (among these the commanders of the 5th Alpini and of the 2nd Mountain Artillery Regiment); the troop losses are incalculable. Alpini, gunners, engineers – all are marvelous – all are equal in throwing their life into the holocaust for the idea of glorifying Italian arms in the land of Russia in the presence of thousands and thousands of soldiers of the allied armies.

Small and medium caliber artillery, mortars of all types, countless automatic weapons lie inert as witness to the ferociousness of the fight, the great moral superiority of the Italian combatant. The breaking of the last encirclement at Nikolayevka by the 'Tridentina' alone, which had completed more than 200 kilometers of very tough marching, fighting all the time, lacking any resupplies and targeted by enemy aircraft, definitively opened the pocket to the rest of the column (about 40,000 men) who passively relied upon the 'Tridentina', trusting in the valor of the alpini in the certainty of being saved.

Day 27

In order to not give the enemy more time to bring in fresh forces and to not have to face the numerous partisans left on the outskirts of town and considering the serious shortage of ammunition, the division commander quickly reorganized the men and orders departure prior to dawn, putting the 5th Alpini in the vanguard, reinforced with the 'Bergamo' and 'Vicenza' groups, by the German assault guns (only one of which is still running) and by the Fischer Group which is down to two guns.

Leaving the town, it was greeted by automatic arms and antitank fire which caused losses. This last enemy resistance having been overcome by a quick action the road was definitively opened for the interminable column.

After a very tiring march of more than 40 kilometers, hit by air strikes that took many victims, the towns of Uspenska and Lutovinovo are reached. But the efforts expended have had a disastrous effect on the men's resistance. Men and mules fall while the column continues its weary calvary supported only by the vision of the far-off homeland and by the satisfaction of a huge job well done.

Day 28

In the morning, at 0600, the move resumes towards Novishol which, being occupied by the Russians, has to be attacked. However, because of the laughable availability of ammunition and the precarious physical condition of the troops, it is decided not to force the town and to detour to the left towards Olkovyi. The march continues in the new direction without any further action and ends in the Salonovka area.

This march is difficult beyond words. The thermometer has fallen to -35 to -45 below zero; those who froze increased in a shocking manner. The mules who were overcome by their loads fell by the dozen. A tragic dilemma was thus reached: save the guns or save the wounded and frostbitten? There was still a will to attempt the superhuman: guns and sleds overloaded with the wounded and frostbitten still plowed through the frozen steppe until, with the mules, the faithful companions of so many battles, reduced to just a few sparse numbers, the valorous gunners of the 2nd Regiment and the gunners of the 5th and 6th Alpini were forced to part with their guns, which were now however gloriously out of ammunition; it was a painful scene of men who are condemned by destiny to no longer be able to use their beloved instruments of war after having captured dozens and dozens from the more well-equipped enemy.

But the life of a hero serves the homeland better than does an old cannon.

29-31 January
The division continues its long and exhausting marches to Bessarab-Belshe Troizkoye-Shebkino. Shebkino represents a return to life for the invincible alpini who, even though they bear the signs of pain they have borne and of limitless suffering, they still form their depleted ranks around the flag that they have glorified with so much faith, tenacity, will, abnegation and sacrifice.

The huge ranks of the German and Hungarian allies who have returned to life because of the virtue of the 'Tridentina' now separate themselves from the division, but will bring to their homelands the admiring memory of the Italian soldier who in a foreign land for countless times challenged death so that the Italian flag would be respected always and everywhere. But the effort was great – it surpassed all human limits.

Meanwhile the ranks are reorganized and the survivors are counted. Beaten by the burdens he bore and by the sum of pain suffered, Colonel Paolo Signorini, commander of the 6th Alpini, dies. Perhaps destiny willed that this magnificent soldier, a splendid example of an athlete, would bear witness to the world with his sacrifice which was the frightful sum of the tribulations and sacrifices of the soldiers of the 'Tridentina' had borne not only to save the flags that were sacred to the country, not only to bring to safety thousands of comrades of the Italian and allied divisions, but most of all to slow the implacable enemy advance, to allow rebuilding a line and to create the indispensable premise for a recovery.

This is the recognition to which the alpini of the 'Tridentina' have a right, who reading about the new favorable operational cycle that is developing on the Eastern Front, justifiably think with pride that their dead, their wounded, their frostbitten, their suffering without measure all constituted a safe and most valid premise.

But another great credit is due to them: that of having been the object of the admiration of the world in one of the most difficult and dangerous wartime situations: the retreat.

It is nice to fight when one advances; it is easy to keep unit cohesion and order in the ranks when the sun of victory shines; the heart is sure and strong when the objective is past the enemy trenches and the enemy bends to our will; but when the tragic hour of retreat sounds and clouds all expectations, only soldiers of the purest steel can work miracles equal to those achieved by the 'Tridentina'.

To them was given the stimulating and fleeting satisfaction of large centers to conquer, not the names of cities with which to unite the memory of their deeds – but an obscure and great duty: to sacrifice themselves to contain and slow down the enemy's advance, inflicting the greatest number of losses.

THE COMMANDING GENERAL
Luigi Reverberi

THE CHIEF OF STAFF
Lt. Col. A. Ambrosiani

Source

Sito Ufficiale Alpini Battaglione <https://www.iltirano.org/>

Appendix VI

Cossack Volunteers in the Italian Armed Forces

In addition to the Croat Legion, formed with Croatian volunteers, other units formed with Russian volunteers, in particular the Cossacks, served alongside the Italian armed forces in Russia. Two units were formed with Cossack volunteers: the first to be formed was placed under command of Major Ranieri di Campello, a 'Savoia Cavalleria' officer, and subordinate to headquarters of Italian XXXV Army Corps beginning in July 1942. The second, led by Captain Stavro di Santarosa, was constituted as the 2nd Sotnia Volontaria Cosacca [2nd Cossack Volunteer Sotnia; the sotnia is roughly a company-size unit] at Millerovo on 25 September 1942 and was subordinate to the Italian II Corps headquarters. Building on the experience of German commands, which since 1941 had been busy recruiting volunteers for their units from among the masses of Russian prisoners, Major Ranieri di Campello, who belonged to the military intelligence service and who had been sent at his request to the Russian front, made contact with Cossack prisoners who had been captured by the Italians. Considering their legendary fame as horsemen on the steppe, he proposed to form a light cavalry unit with intelligence, reconnaissance and anti-partisan security duties. The cadre were formed by Cossack officers and NCOs who bore the rank that they had held in the Red Army; the uniform was the Soviet uniform with the insignia removed and with Italian rank stars added, and later, to avoid confusion, they wore the Italian uniform, with Russian rank insignia and a red-white-blue triangle on the right arm. However, blue trousers with a red stripe continued to be worn, and for the dress uniform with the overcoat (tscherkessa) and the silver dagger (kindjal). All volunteers used the shaska [a Cosssack sword] and armament was partly Russian and partly Italian.

The 2nd Cossack Volunteer Sotnia of II Corps, known also as the Cossack Irregular Band, was formed in September 1942, along the lines of the Banda Campello, led by Captain Stavro di Santarosa, working along with Lieutenant Copetzki, a Russian who held Italian citizenship, a reserve artillery officer who also acted as an interpreter, and by Second Lieutenant Piero Leonar, a Russian exile who had volunteered in the Regio Esercito as an adjutant. Santarosa earned the respect of the Cossacks to the point that he was 'enrolled' as an honorary Cossack. As headgear, the volunteers wore the kubanka (busby) with the cap – or crown – in colors that varied depending on the origin of the Cossacks of the Terek, the Kuban or the Don.

The more numerous Campello Group consisted of 360 men and consisted of three sotnias and a horse-mounted band. There were also plans, thanks to authorization by German headquarters, to recruit another two thousand Cossacks with which to form two regiments, one cavalry and one infantry.

The Cossack volunteers were used mostly for reconnaissance missions but there was no lack of sudden attacks against Soviet lines During one of these, Major Campello, who wore the tscherkessa over his Italian uniform, was wounded and saved by his Cossacks, who loaded him onto a sled, exposing themselves to intense Soviet fire. During the retreat from the Don front, the Cossack volunteers fought well; on 19 January 1943 at Rossosch, the Campello Group, after days of very hard fighting, was able to break through enemy lines and escape being surrounded.

Cossack volunteers being reviewed by General Gariboldi and Major Ranieri di Campello. The Cossacks have retained their Soviet-issue Model 1891 Mosin-Nagant rifles. (USSME)

As the retreat continued, partisan attacks intensified and this led to strong reaction by the Cossacks who showed themselves to be very efficient, operating mainly at night and also using their common language to strike the enemy. There were, however, some cases of desertion, especially following the German defeat on the Stalingrad front and some men showed themselves ready to return to the Soviet fold; one Cossack attempted to kill Ranieri di Campello at close range, but was prevented by Captain Vladimir Ostrovsky, who blocked his arm and made his weapon fall in the snow. These were however isolated cases; the Cossacks, because of their military traditions and because of the ferocious Stalinist repression which they suffered in the 1930s, proved to be less ready to desert than were other Russian volunteers.

'Savoia' Cossack Group

The two Cossack units were not joined together until April 1943 because of the heavy losses on the Eastern Front, officially constituting the 'Savoia' Cossack Group. At the end of the retreat, in April, on the eve of the return Italy, along with the remnants of the Campello group and of the 2nd Volunteer Sotnia, the 'Savoia' Cossack Volunteer Group, with its depot located with the 5th 'Lancieri di Novara'. It consisted of two Cossack sotnias (1 colonel, 9 officers, 24 NCOs, 266 Cossacks). The unit arrived in Italy in May 1943 and was billeted on the Jacur farm in Gazzo Veronese. The group was inspected by Gariboldi, who had words of praise for the Cossacks. At that time, the number of volunteers increased significantly, so much so that a third sotnia was formed. The unit was renamed the Cossack Irregular Band by a circular dated 22 July 1943. Plans called for an Italian headquarters, a Cossack headquarters and three sotnias, of which one was of Don Cossacks and two of Kuban Cossacks, each with three platoons. Manning was 13 officers, 23 NCOs and 243 Cossacks, in addition to 3 officers, 5 NCOs and 14 Italian soldiers, with 17 horses for officers, 238 for the troops and 24 draft horses for an equal number of two-wheeled carts, one truck, one van and two motorcycles. On 16 August, a new circular reduced the sotnias to two.

During the reorganization in Italy, the personnel of the Cossack Irregular Band were issued, in addition to the Model 1891 cavalry carbine, the Beretta MAB 38 submachine gun. Uniforms varied according to the ethnicity of the Cossacks. The Don Cossack dress uniform consisted of a black kubanka with a red crown and silver embroidery and of the tcherkessa, the traditional blue knee-length overcoat, with a white-grey cowl, shoulder straps and mock cartridge pouches, worn over a red shirt with traditional soft leather boots. The musicians were distinguished by their white kubanka. The Kuban Cossacks instead wore a Russian-style uniform, with a Russian visored hat with a red stripe and a cockade with the Russian colors, a grey-green jacket with closed collar and white insignia, red shoulder straps with Russian-style rank insignia, and the traditional blue trousers with red stripes characteristic of all of the Cossack units of the 19th Century, and Italian cavalry leg guards in lieu of boots. All personnel, even those who were dismounted, wore the traditional shaska on their side.

The unit was to have been employed against partisans in the Balkans and in Albania, a mission which the Cossacks had proven to be very capable of on the Eastern Front. On 8 September 1943 found the unit garrisoned at Maccacari, in the Verona area, about to be transferred to Albania. Faced with repeated and threatening demands by the Germans from Verona and Mantova between 9 and 12 September to surrender and disarm the Cossack unit, Santarosa tried to stall for time, refusing, however, to turn over any weapons. On the 13th, with telephone communications cut to the outside, with no hope of resupplying their food from the depot in Legnano which in the meantime had been occupied by the Germans and warned by a carbiniere that a German armoured unit was on the move from Ostilia to Maccacari to attack the barracks, Captain Stavro di Santarosa called an assembly of the Cossacks (rada) according to the Cosssack custom. Having heard their agreement, on the evening of 13 September Santarosa ordered the group's temporary disbandment and dispersion. According to the agreement, the group was to regroup several days later at Maccacari, as Santarosa felt that Italy's defection would necessarily lead to an immediate withdrawal of all German troops across the Alps. Because events evolved differently, Stavro di Santarosa reached his estate in Cormons (Gorizia province), which he left under the care of one of his Cossacks, while he himself moved to his house in Rome where, in early June 1944, he was arrested by the Germans. In the meantime, a large part of the Cossack group had moved to Camporosso in Val Canale in an anti-partisan role, and after having reached the German-controlled O.Z.A.K. (Operationszone Adriatisches Küstenland = Adriatic Coastal Operations Zone) they joined Krasnov's Cossack Army located there. Other Cossacks, however, having hidden their weapons, abandoned the group, some of them joining the Italian Social Republic while others joined the resistance movement.

L3 light tank: Gruppo Squadroni Carri L 'San Giorgio', 3rd Cavalry Division Principe Amadeo Duca d'Aosta, CSIR, Ukraine, October 1941. (Artwork by and © David Bocquelet)

L6/40 light tank: LXVII Battaglione Corazzato Bersaglieri, 3rd Cavalry Division Principe Amadeo Duca d'Aosta, ARMIR, Ukraine, September 1942. (Artwork by and © David Bocquelet)

L6 47/32 self-propelled gun: XIII Gruppo 'Cavalleggeri di Alessandria', 3rd Cavalry Division Principe Amadeo Duca d'Aosta, ARMIR, Ukraine, September 1942. (Artwork by and © David Bocquelet)

Bianchi Miles truck: 188o Autoreparto Pesante, 51o Autogruppo Pesante, CSIR, Ukraine, September 1941. (Artwork by and © David Bocquelet)

Spa 38R truck: 3a Sezione Trasporti, Divisione 'Ravenna', CSIR, Ukraine, July 1942. (Artwork by and © David Bocquelet)

TM40 artillery tractor: 178th Batttery, XXIV Gruppo, 9o Raggruppamento artiglieria d'armata, Ukraine, September 1942. (Artwork by and © David Bocquelet)

75/27 mod. 11 field gun: 2 Gruppo, 120 Reggimento artiglieria motorizzato, 3rd Cavalry Division Principe Amadeo Duca d'Aosta, ARMIR, Ukraine, March 1942. . (Artwork by and © David Bocquelet)

210/22 mod. 35 howitzer: 176th Battery, LXIII Gruppo, 9o Raggruppamento artiglieria d'armata, ARMIR, Ukraine, September 1942. (Artwork by and © David Bocquelet)

Appendix VII

Italian Weapons in Russia

When Italian forces set off to join the Germans in the fight against Bolshevik Russia, they were by and large woefully unprepared in terms of the weapons and equipment they had at hand; the few first-rate weapons they did have were habitually in short supply. The shortcomings of most of the weapons issued to Italian troops were further exacerbated by the harsh weather conditions that they would be subjected to during the Russian winters.

Rifles and carbines issued to Italian troops in Russia were all based on the 6.5mm Model 1891 bolt-action rifle which had served well in the First World War. Briefly, these weapons included the Model 1941 rifle which was essentially a slightly shorter version of the Model 1891, the Model 1891 cavalry carbine and several versions of the so-called "special troops" carbines, as well as the Model 38 fucile corto (short rifle). Although the 6.5x52mm cartridge was an adequate military round, by comparison to the German 7.92x57mm round and the Russian 7.62x54mm round it was somewhat underpowered.

With respect to sidearms normally carried by officers and NCOs, the most commonly issued weapon was the 9mm corto (.380 caliber) Beretta Model 34 pistol, which was legendary for its reliability under all circumstances. An oft-told apocryphal story relates to the Model 34; as the story goes, during a particularly bitterly cold winter night in Russia, an Italian officer went to sleep with his Beretta Model 34 by his side; when he woke up in the morning the Beretta was gone, and in its place was a German Luger, the exchange having been made by a German from a nearby unit who preferred the reliability of the Beretta to that of the Luger.

Machine guns issued to the Italians in Russia ran the gamut from almost totally unreliable to excellent weapons. At the lower end of the spectrum was the widely issued 6.5mm Breda Model 30 light machinegun, which suffered from a number of faults, including its closely machined tolerances which led to frequent jamming, and the fact that its cartridges were lubricated by an oil pump prior to chambering; the oil was a special viscosity Breda oil that attracted foreign matter in dry weather and was prone to freezing in the harsh Russian winter. The air-cooled 8mm Fiat Model1935 machine gun, normally issued at battalion level, was a somewhat more reliable gun. Rounding out the machine gun category was the 8mm Breda Model 37 heavy machine gun which was a very reliable weapon, performing well even under the extreme conditions encountered in Russia.

Because of the shortcomings of Italian small arms and machine guns the Italians availed themselves of captured Russian equipment whenever they could; there are numerous documented instances of Italians using the PPSh-41 submachine gun and the Degtyarev DP-27 light machine gun, among other weapons.

Another first-rate weapon fielded by the Italians was the 81mm Model 35 mortar. It was also a very reliable weapon that provided readily available fire support for the infantry regiment commander. In addition to the mortars at the regimental level, each of the infantry divisions in Russia also had a mortar battalion. This type of mortar served with the Italian army well into the 1960s.

By and large, Italian artillery assets in Russia were either obsolete or too light compared to the artillery assets fielded by the Soviets, although there were a few exceptions. With minor variations, each of the six Italian infantry divisions that served in Russia had two groups equipped with 75/18 howitzers and one group with 105/28 howitzers, as well as an 81mm mortar battalion, two antiaircraft batteries with the 20mm Breda mod. 35 or 39 gun, two 47/32 antitank batteries and a 75/39 antitank battery. Each infantry regiment also had an 81mm mortar company and a 65/17 support gun battery. Each of the three alpine divisions had an artillery regiment equipped with 75/13 mountain howitzers, two 20mm antiaircraft batteries, a 75/39 antitank battery and two 47/32 antitank batteries. The 3rd Cavalry Division had three 75/27 groups, two antitank companies and one 81mm mortar company.

Larger caliber guns were assigned to corps and army level units; 48 of the Škoda 149/13 howitzers were assigned to Russia, as well as three groups of the new 149/40 mod. 35 gun and three batteries of the 210/22 mod. 35 howitzer (a total of a dozen howitzers), which was the heaviest Italian artillery piece assigned to Russia. In terms of quality of equipment, the 20mm Breda Model 35, the 149/40 Model 35 and the 210/22 Model 35 were all excellent pieces, but, except for the Breda, were in woefully short supply.

Bolstering the Italian anti-tank capability was the 75/97/38 Pak 1897/38 gun supplied by the Germans, referred to in Italian as the 75/39; this gun was a quantum improvement in capability compared to the standard Italian 47/32 antitank gun which could do little against most Soviet armour.

In terms of armour assets fielded by the Italians in Russia, simply stated, they were totally inadequate for the task at hand. The only tracked vehicles sent to Russia were the laughably small L.3 light tanks, armed with nothing more than 8mm machine guns mounted in a casemate, the badly designed L6/40 light tank armed with a 20mm gun, and the L40 self-propelled gun, based on the L6/40 light tank, mounting a 47mm antitank gun. None of these vehicles came close to matching the armour fielded by the Soviets, and despite the bravery and dedication of the Italian crews, were basically useless in anything but small-scale actions in which they faced no opposing Soviet armour.

Essentially, all of the Italian armoured vehicles were assigned to the 3a Divisione Celere 'Principe Amedeo Duca d'Aosta' (3rd Cavalry Division 'Principe Amedeo Duca d'Aosta'). The III Light Tank Group, equipped with the L.3 light tank, was assigned to the division from July 1941 until the division's restructuring as a light mechanized division in March 1942, when the group was replaced by the LXVII Bersaglieri Battalion with an armoured car company with 24 AB-41 armoured cars and two companies of L6/40 light tanks (26 tanks per company, for a total of 52 light tanks). In addition, the division had the XIII Self-Propelled Group with about 20 47/32 SP guns. All told, only about 125 or so Italian armoured vehicles, including the AB-41 armoured cars, served in Russia. All of the Italian armoured vehicles sent to Russia were either destroyed or captured by the Soviets.

The Italians were acutely aware of the inferiority of their tanks and self-propelled guns in Russia. At one point they considered copying the Soviet T-34 tank, but nothing ever came of that proposal. In order to remedy the inadequate antitank capability, the Italians did in fact design and build a very potent self-propelled gun, the 90/53 gun mounted on a modified medium tank chassis, developed specifically for the Russian front. Although 30 of these systems were built in 1942, they came too late to serve in Russia, but rather were used to contest the Allied invasion of Sicily in August 1943.

Appendix VIII

Camouflage and Markings, Italian Armoured Vehicles in Russia

No unique markings or tactical signs were used on armoured vehicles on the Eastern Front; markings were regulation markings in use throughout the Regio Esercito, although the L6/40 light tanks of the LXVII Bersaglieri Battalion did bear tactical markings that were larger than usual and were positioned somewhat differently than normal. The same can be said with respect to the livery of the vehicles; no unique camouflage schemes were adopted, although the LXVII Bersaglieri Battalion did apply some field expedient measures. The L6/40 tanks of the LXVII Bersaglieri Battalion retained their standard sand yellow livery. To make up for the lack of a camouflage livery, during the summer months the Bersaglieri used what was immediately at hand and applied a somewhat rudimentary camouflage consisting of irregular patches of mud applied to the vehicle surface, which often managed to cover the vehicle markings. The circular white identification disc on the top of the turret was also present on the original livery, but, like the other markings, it was also partially obscured by the mud coating. During the harsh Russian winter, some of the L6/40 tanks also were given a hasty coat of whitewash or white paint, applied in a completely makeshift manner, but the coverage was somewhat uneven and because of the rather poor quality of the paint, the hasty application and the ravages of the weather itself the coating could not be relied upon to last long. The L3 tanks of the III Gruppo Squadroni 'San Giorgio' arrived in Russia with the colour scheme that they had when they left Italy, either solid green or small green splotches over a rust base. Likewise, the L6 self-propelled guns of the XIII Gruppo Squadroni 'Cavalleggeri di Alessandria' arrived in Russia with a mottled camouflage scheme (green splotches over a rust base); presumably, at least some of their crews applied the same type of mud or whitewash, depending on the season, as did the crews of the L6/40 light tanks of the LXVIII Bersaglieri Battalion.

The LXVII battalion used platoon and company markings that were larger than the regulation 20x12 cm dimensions, painted on the rear of the turret and covering the entire rear hatch. These makings differed from the regulation markings with respect to their position, as they were painted on the sides and rear of the turret, as well as on the rear of the hull; the presence of a fifth platoon called for the addition of a transversal bar on the rectangle; the position of the individual Arabic numeral, 10 cm in size, in red rather than in white or in the company's colour, was to the left of the lateral rectangles rather than above it; the colour and position of the battalion's roman numeral on the commander's tank was black, on the rear of the hull and on the turret sides. One detail seemingly peculiar to the L6 hulls in Russia (the L6/40 tank and the L6 self-propelled gun) was the rear license plate, which was divided into two sections due to the presence of the towing pintle. Seen from the rear, to the left was the Regio Esercito symbol and a red grenade, while to the right was a four-digit vehicle number. Based on observation, these numbers ran from 3812 to 4062. The glacis plate of the L6/40 bore the regulation Regio Esercito circular metal badge.

Appendix IX

Italian Uniforms in Russia

The basic uniform worn by Italian troops in Russia was the continental (or metropolitan) version; this uniform was based on the 1933 redesign of the combat uniform, resulting in the M33, M37 and ultimately the M40 uniform.

The tunic was an open collar with front lapels and was closed by three large evenly-spaced buttons. The tunic had two small breast pockets with scalloped flaps and two large-pleated pockets at the waist, also with scalloped flaps. The tunic was also fitted with shoulder straps, as it was with a cloth waist belt of the same material as the tunic itself. The tunic collar bore the soldier's branch or specialty insignia. Rank was displayed on the center of the tunic sleeve, between the shoulder and the elbow. Specialty insignia was worn on the left sleeve below the rank, and awards and service ribbons were normally sewn onto the tunic above the left breast pocket. A grey-green wool pullover shirt was worn under the tunic. The shirt had two pleated breast pockets with scalloped flaps. Soldiers of the Fascist Camicie Nere (Blackshirts) wore a black shirt instead of the grey-green shirt.

The grey-green uniform pants were a somewhat baggy breeches style, with two slash front pocket and a rear pocket. The pants were held up by a belt. Puttees, consisting of long grey-green wool strips, were worn with the pants. Alpini wore high wool socks in lieu of the puttees. Armoured vehicle crews routinely wore a one-piece coverall instead of pants and shirt.

Footwear consisted of an ankle boot with laces; the boots were hobnailed. The boots could be either brown or black, although brown was more likely to be encountered outside of metropolitan Italy. The alpine troops wore mountain boots.

The M40 overcoat was made of grey-green wool. It was a single-breasted coat with two large hip pockets. Armoured vehicle crews wore a ¾ length black leather coat.

Although headgear was standardized, there was quite a variety of headwear that could be encountered in Russia, ranging from the M35 side cap to the M33 steel helmet. Armoured vehicle crews used a padded leather helmet, bersaglieri wore their signature cockerel feathers applied to several types of headgear they wore, including the M33 helmet, the alpini wore a traditional alpine (Tyrolean) hat with a feather on it and Blackshirts could wear a black fez with a tassel.

Most rank insignia consisted of shoulder boards or tabs bearing various emblems and stars denoting rank for officers; NCO shoulder boards were quite simple, with rank denoted by braided stripes. Junior NCOs and other ranks wore chevrons on the upper sleeves of their jackets. Depending on the uniform, officer rank could also be displayed on the jacket cuff.

Based on their experience following the winter of 1941-1942, the Italians developed and produced several items of winter gear that were issued prior to the 1942-1943 winter season. These consisted of fleece-lined overcoats and gloves and copies of the Russian valenki, which were high felted wool boots. These items were not universally issued but tended to be issued to troops on guard duty or who would have to spend extended periods in exposed conditions. Notably, the Monte Cervino alpine battalion were also issued white camouflage smocks and pants which provided a significant degree of camouflage during winter operations.

Italian Fiat/Ansaldo L3/33 crew, summer 1941. (Colour artwork by Anderson Subtil © Helion & Company)

'Savoia' Cavalleria – Izbushensky, Russia, 1942.
(Colour artwork by Anderson Subtil © Helion & Company)

Gruppo Tattico M 'Leonessa', 1942. (Colour artwork by Anderson Subtil © Helion & Company)

Alpino 'Monte Cervino' 1942. (Colour artwork by Anderson Subtil © Helion & Company)

Capomanipolo HQ Company, Italian/Croatian Legion, 1941.
(Colour artwork by Anderson Subtil © Helion & Company)

Colonnello titolare 277° Rgt/156° Divisione Fanteria 'Vicenza', 1943.
(Colour artwork by Anderson Subtil © Helion & Company)

Alpino Divisione Alpina 'Tridentina', 1943. (Colour artwork by Anderson Subtil © Helion & Company)

Bersagliere 6° Reggimento Bersaglieiri – Ukraine, 1941.
(Colour artwork by Anderson Subtil © Helion & Company)

Bibliography

Primary Sources

Ufficio Storico dello Stato Maggiore dell'Esercito 1946, *L'8ª Armata italiana nella Seconda battaglia difensiva del Don (11 gennaio 1942- 31 gennaio 1943*

Ufficio Storico dello Stato Maggiore dell'Esercito 1948, *Le operazioni del C.S.I.R. e dell'Armir dal giugno 1941 all'ottobre 1942*

Ufficio Storico dello Stato Maggiore dell'Esercito, *L'Italia nella Relazione Ufficiale Sovietica sulla Seconda Guerra Mondiale*

Ufficio Storico dello Stato Maggiore dell'Esercito, *Le operazioni delle Unità italiane al Fronte russo*

Secondary Sources

Afiero, Massimiliano, *La Crociata contro il bolscevismo* (Marvia Edizioni, 2005).

Boschesi, B.P., *Le armi, i protagonisti, le battaglie, gli eroismi segreti della guerra di Mussolini 1940-1943*(Milano: Mondadori, 1984).

Barilli, Manlio, *Con gli alpini del 6o in tutte le guerre* (Udine: Edizioni Doretti,1966).

Carloni, Colonnello Mario, *La campagna di Russia* (Milano: Longanesi & C., 1956).

Catanoso, Carmelo and Uberti, Agostino, *La Divisione alpina Cuneense al fronte russo, 1942-1943* (Genoa: Stab. graf. Morino, 1982).

Cavallero, Ugo, *Diario 1940-1943* (Roma: Ciarrapico, 1984).

Cèpparo, Renato, *Fuori Uno! Sommerginili tascabili, MAS e mezzi d'assalto italiani nell'operazione Barbarossa* (Milano: Edizioni Cinehollywood, 1998).

Corradi, Egisto, *La ritirata di Russia* (Milano: Longanesi & C., 1965).

Corti, Eugenio, *Few Returned: Twenty-eight Days on the Russian Front, Winter 1942 – 1943* (Columbia and London: University of Missouri Press, 1977).

Fabei, Stefano, *Tagliamento. La legione delle camicie nere in Russia (1941-1943)*, (Editore In Edibus, 2014)

Fabei, Stefano, *La legione straniera di Mussolini* (Milano: Mursia, 2008).

Faldella, Emilio, *Storia delle truppe alpine 1872-1972* (Milano: Cavallotti Editori – Edizioni Landoni, Milano 1972)

Finazzer, Enrico and Riccio, Ralph, *Italian Artillery of WWII* (Sandomierz: Stratus s.c., 2015).

Glantz, David and House, Jonathan, *La grande guerra patriottica dell'Armata Rossa 1941-1945* (Gorizia: Libreria Editrice Goriziana, 2019).

Hamilton, Hope, *Sacrifice on the Steppe: The Italian Alpine Corps in the Stalingrad Campaign 1942-1943* (Haverford and Oxford: Casemate Publishers, 2011).

Lami, Lucio, *Isbuscenskij: L'ultima carica. Il Savoia Cavalleria nella campagna di Russia (1941-1942)* (Milano: Ugo Mursia & C., 1970).

Longo, Luigi Emilio, *I Reparti speciali italiani nella Seconda Guerra Mondiale 1940-1943*, (Milano: Ugo Mursia & C., 1991).

Madeja, W. Victor, *Italian Army Order of Battle: 1940-1944* (Allentown, Pennsylvania: Valor Publishing Co., 1990)

Malizia, Nicola, *Ali sulla steppa: la Regia Aereonautica nella campagna di Russia* (Roma: Edizioni dell'Ateneo, 1987).

Massignani, Alessandro, *Alpini e tedeschi sul Don* (Valdagno: Gino Rossato Editore, 1991)

Messe, Giovanni, *La guerra al fronte russo* (Milano: Rizzoli Editore, 1947).

Montanelli, Indro, and Cervi, Mario, *Storia d'Italia. Vol. 14: L'Italia della disfatta (10 giugno 1940-8 settembre 1943)* (Milano: Bur Biblioteca, Rizzoli, 2017).

Moro, Ermenegildo, *Selenyj Jar. Il quadrivio insanguinato: Il Battaglione Alpini L'Aquila nella campagna di Russia* (Milano: Mursia Editore, 1973).

Mosna, Ezio, *Storia delle truppe alpine d'Italia* (Trento: Tipografia Editrice – Trento, 1968).

Overy, Richard, *Russia in guerra* (Milano: Il Saggiatore, 2011).

Patricelli, Marco, *L'Italia delle sconfitte* (Bari: Editori Laterza, 2016).

Petacco, Arrigo, *L'armata scomparsa* (Milano: Arnaldo Mondadori Editore, 2014).

Rasero, Aldo, *Alpini della Julia: Storia della 'divisione miracolo'* (Milano: Ugo Mursia & C., 1972).

Rasero, Aldo, *L'eroica Cuneense: storia della divisione alpina martire* (Milano: Ugo Mursia & C., 1985).

Ricchezza, Antonio. *La storia illustrata di tutta la campagna di Russia: luglio 1941-maggio 1943. Volume III – La ritirata al sud. La ritirata al nord* (Milano: Longanesi & C., 1972).

Rochat, Giorgio, *Le guerre italiane 1935-1943* (Milano: Einaudi, 2008).

Romeo di Colloredo, P., *Croce di Ghiaccio. CSIR e ARMIR in Russia, 1941- 1943* (Zanica: Soldiershop Publishing, 2017).

Romeo di Colloredo Mels, P., *Le Camicie Nere sul fronte russo 1941- 1943* (Zanica: Soldiershop Publishing, 2017).

Salvatores, Umberto, *Bersaglieri sul Don* (Bologna: Tipografia Compositori, 1966).

Schlemmer, Thomas, *Invasori, non vittime – La campagna italiana di Russia 1941-1943*, (Bari: Editori Laterza, 2009).

Scotoni, G., *L'Armata Rossa e la disfatta italiana* (Milano: Editrice Panorama, 2007).

Valori, Aldo, *La campagna di Russia* (Grafica Nazionale Editrice, 1950).

Tallillo, Andrea, Tallillo, Antonio and Guglielmi, Daniele, *Carro L6. Carri leggeri, semoventi e derivati.* (Trento: Gruppo Modellistico Trentino, 2019).

Viazzi, L., *I diavoli bianchi. Gli alpini sciatori nella Seconda guerra mondiale. Storia del battaglione Monte Cervino* (Milano: Ugo Mursia, 2019).

Vicentini, Carlo, *Noi soli vivi* (Cavallotti, 2005).

Vitali, Giorgio, *Trotto, Galoppo…Caricat!: Storia del Raggruppamento Truppe a Cavallo, Russia 1942-1943.* (Milano: Ugo Mursia Editore, S.p.A., 1958).

Zizzo, R., *1942-1943. La tragedia dell'ARM.I.R. nella Campagna di Russia* (Foggia: Italia Editrice, 2008)

Electronic Sources

Comando Supremo: Italy in WW2 <https://comandosupremo.com/>

Sito Ufficiale Alpini Battaglione <https://www.iltirano.org/>

Regio Esercito <http://www.regioesercito.it/>

Lexikon der Wehrmacht <http://www.lexikon-der-wehrmacht.de/>

OKH: Oberkommando Heeres <http://www.okh.it/>

U.N.I.R.R.: Unione Nazionale Italiana Reduci di Russia <https://www.unirr.it/>